After more than three decades of research into cognitive behavioural therapy for anxiety disorders, there are now scientifically-based protocols for treating them. This book pulls them together in a way that is accessible to therapists, sufferers and their families. As many people have more than one type of anxiety problem, the book first describes the principles of cognitive behavioural therapy that cut across specific forms of anxiety. It also contains a comprehensive set of chapters on the treatment of the full range of anxiety disorders from international experts. It will be an invaluable resource to those concerned with the treatment of people suffering from anxiety, as well as to those with anxiety who want to learn how they can help themselves.

Lord Richard Layard
Programme Director at the Centre for Economic Performance at the London School of Economics

Everyone suffering from various forms of anxiety and fear as well as therapists trying to help people with these difficulties will find this beautifully written manual extraordinarily valuable. For in it one will see what is common about different types of anxiety disorders from social anxiety to obsessions, as well as the essential differences, along with all of the important strategies for overcoming and mastering these thorny problems. This manual should be prescribed to everyone attempting to grapple with anxiety and its disorders.

David H. Barlow Ph.D, ABPP
Professor of Psychology and Psychiatry
Founder and Director Emeritus, Center for Anxiety and Related Disorders at Boston University

Nicole M. Alberts is a PhD student in clinical psychology at the University of Regina, Canada. Her research and clinical interests include health anxiety as well as the assessment and treatment of mood and anxiety disorders and their associations with health conditions.

Lee Brosan is a Consultant Clinical Psychologist in the Cambridgeshire and Peterborough Foundation Trust and Trust Lead for the Development of Psychological Therapies. She is a Clinical Associate at the MRC Cognitive and Brain Science Unit in Cambridge, and a founder member of the Cambridge Clinical Research Centre for Affective Disorders (C2:AD). She has been qualified as a cognitive therapist for nearly twenty years.

Gillian Butler is a Consultant Clinical Psychologist working with Oxford Cognitive Therapy Centre and Oxford Health NHS Foundation Trust. Through ten years of clinical research with the University of Oxford in the 1980s she helped to develop CBT for social phobia, and to evaluate its effectiveness. One of her interests is in writing about current practices in CBT, so as to help people resolve problems such as the social anxiety that can otherwise interfere with their lives.

David M. Clark is Professor of Experimental Psychology and Fellow of Magdalen College, University of Oxford. He is a Fellow of the British Academy (London), a Fellow of the Academy of Medical Sciences (London), an Honorary Fellow of the British Psychological Society, and Distinguished Founding Fellow of the Academy of Cognitive Therapy (USA). Among other awards and honours, he has received the following during his career: the May Davidson Award (British Psychological Society); the American Psychological Association Distinguished Contribution to Applications of Psychology Award; the Academy of Cognitive Therapy's Research Award; an Honorary Doctorate of Science from the London School of Economics (LSE), and has been voted a World Leader in Anxiety Disorders Research by members of the Anxiety Disorders of America Association (1998).

Peter Cooper is Co-director of the Winnicott Research Unit and Research Director of the Berkshire Child Anxiety Clinic. He holds a research chair in the School of Psychology and Clinical Language Sciences at the University of Reading. His principal current research interests concern elucidating the impact of early environmental factors on child socio-emotional development and evaluating intervention programmes to mitigate this impact; and developing and evaluating interventions to (i) improve clinical outcomes in anxious children and children with certain congenital abnormalities, and (ii) facilitate optimal child socio-emotional and cognitive development in the developing world.

Anke Ehlers is a Wellcome Trust Principal Research Fellow and Professor of Experimental Psychopathology at the Department of Experimental Psychology, University of Oxford. She is Co-director of the Centre for Anxiety Disorders and Trauma, Maudsley Hospital, London, and the Oxford Centre for Anxiety Disorders and Trauma. She is a Fellow of the British Academy and the German Academy of Sciences Leopoldina. Her main research interests are the etiology and treatment of anxiety disorders, in particular post-traumatic stress disorder (PTSD), panic disorder, and social phobia. She co-chaired the NICE Post-traumatic Stress Disorder Guideline (2005) Development Group.

Mark Freeston is Head of Research and Development at the Newcastle Cognitive and Behavioural Therapies Centre and Professor of Clinical Psychology at Newcastle University. He divides his time between NHS duties, where he directed the Newcastle Diploma in Cognitive Therapy for ten years, and the University of Newcastle, where he teaches research methods. He has published extensively on intrusive thoughts, OCD, worry and their treatment, leads an active research programme, and provides workshops on their treatment in the UK and elsewhere.

Nick Grey is a Consultant Clinical Psychologist and Joint Clinical Director of the Centre for Anxiety Disorders and Trauma (CADAT), South London & Maudsley NHS Foundation Trust. He helps develop and disseminate cognitive therapy treatments for people with anxiety disorders and post-traumatic stress disorder (PTSD).

Heather Hadjistavropoulos is a Professor of Psychology and Director of Clinical Training at the University of Regina, Canada. She founded the Psychology Training Clinic and the Online Therapy Unit at the University of Regina, and offers training to students and community providers in the assessment and treatment of anxiety and mood disorders. Her research aims to improve: anxiety and depression in medical and nonmedical populations; quality of health care; and training in clinical psychology.

Shannon L. Jones is in the final year of her training as a PhD student in clinical psychology at the University of Regina, Canada. Her research interests focus primarily on anxiety disorders and anxiety-related conditions, health psychology, and online cognitive-behaviour therapy. Clinically, Shannon's interests are in the assessment and treatment of adults with anxiety and mood disorders and in clinical health psychology settings, including psychosocial oncology.

Freda McManus is a Consultant Clinical Psychologist. She is currently Acting Director of the Oxford Cognitive Therapy Centre, and a Clinical Research Fellow in the University of Oxford's Department of Psychiatry. She has worked clinically for twenty years and has a range of experience in developing and evaluating CBT interventions for anxiety disorders as part of research teams at the University of Oxford and at the Institute of Psychiatry, King's College London. She has published widely in both clinical and academic texts, in the areas of CBT for anxiety disorders, and on training healthcare professionals to carry out CBT interventions.

Kevin Meares is a Consultant Clinical Psychologist and an accredited Cognitive Behavioural Therapist. He works for the Northumberland, Tyne and Wear NHS Foundation Trust at the North East Traumatic Stress Centre. He has been a therapist for more than fifteen years. He is an experienced supervisor and trainer, regularly leading CBT workshops on GAD and PTSD. In 2008 he co-authored the self-help book *Overcoming Worry* with Professor Mark Freeston.

Lars-Göran Öst is Professor of Clinical Psychology at Stockholm University, Sweden, and also has a part-time position as Professor at the University of Bergen, Norway. He has published more than 200 articles, book chapters and books, and runs his own private practice. His main research interests include: phobias; panic disorder; generalized anxiety disorder; obsessive-compulsive disorder; anxiety disorder in children; therapy outcome studies; therapist behaviours; therapist–patient relationship; working alliance; etiology of anxiety disorders; field efficacy; implementation, and schizophrenia.

Adam S. Radomsky is an Associate Professor in the Psychology Department at Concordia University in Montreal, Canada, and was the Founding President of the Canadian Association of Cognitive and Behavioural Therapies. His research on the roles of cognition in understanding and treating OCD and other anxiety disorders is funded by the Canadian Institutes of Health Research and has garnered several national and international awards. Dr Radomsky maintains a small private practice in Montreal, and is actively engaged in the training of new CBT therapists.

Roz Shafran is Professor of Clinical Psychology at the University of Reading and founder of the Charlie Waller Institute of Evidence-based Psychological Treatment. She is a former Wellcome Trust Career Development Fellow at the University of Oxford. Her clinical research interests include cognitive behavioural theories and treatments for eating disorders, obsessive compulsive disorder and perfectionism across the age range. More recently, her work has addressed the dissemination and implementation of evidence-based psychological therapies. She has numerous research papers, book chapters and conference presentations in these areas. She is the scientific co-chair of the British Association of Behavioural and Cognitive Psychotherapies and associate editor of *Behaviour Research and Therapy*. She recently received an award for Distinguished Contributions to Professional Psychology from the British Psychological Society and the Marsh Award for Mental Health work.

Jennifer Wild is a Consultant Clinical Psychologist and Senior Research Fellow in Clinical Psychology at the University of Oxford. She is an international expert in the treatment of post-traumatic stress and anxiety disorders. She treats victims of major traumatic events, such as the 2011 Oslo shootings, the 2004 Indian Ocean tsunami in Thailand and the 2012 *Costa Concordia* disaster. Jennifer is currently leading a programme of research with the London Ambulance Service, the world's largest emergency service, to develop a programme to reduce psychological stress after trauma. She frequently appears in the news and writes articles for TV, radio and the press about psychological issues and PTSD.

The Complete CBT Guide for
Anxiety

Roz Shafran, Lee Brosan and
Peter Cooper

ROBINSON

London

Constable & Robinson Ltd
55–56 Russell Square
London WC1B 4HP
www.constablerobinson.com

First published in the UK by Robinson,
an imprint of Constable & Robinson Ltd, 2013

A copy of the British Library Cataloguing in
Publication data is available from the British Library

Important Note
This book is not intended as a substitute for medical advice or treatment. Any person
with a condition requiring medical attention should consult a qualified medical
practitioner or suitable therapist.

Although we have tried to trace and contact copyright holders before publication,
this has not been possible in all cases. If notified, the publisher will be pleased to
correct any errors or omissions at the earliest opportunity.

ISBN 978-1-84901-896-8 (paperback)
ISBN 978-1-78033-132-4 (ebook)

Printed and bound in the UK

1 3 5 7 9 10 8 6 4 2

Dedication

We dedicate this book to our families for all their support,
particularly to David, Matthew, Anna and Rachel Gittleson,
Tina and Michael Shafran, and Angus Mackintosh.

Contents

PART 3:
Tackling other problems and maintaining progress

Acknowledgements

We would like to acknowledge all the friends, colleagues and patients who taught us about the science, principles and practice of cognitive behavioural therapy.

Introduction

Why we wrote this book

I want a self-help book that addresses all my different worries and is based on scientific evidence; I want to be able to use it by myself, but also for it to be useful for my husband and children, who have suffered with me and who want to help.

Ana, 54

I'm so confused. I feel anxious so much of the time, and I can't work out what's wrong with me. My friend said she thought I had social anxiety, but my GP said it was generalized anxiety disorder. How can I get help if I don't even know what's wrong with me? I feel like I've got bits of everything.

Tom, 23

There are lots of books on overcoming anxiety, and many of them are based on cognitive behavioural therapy. So, why write another? The reason is that the other books either tend to talk about anxiety *in general*, or else they talk about overcoming a very *specific form* of anxiety such as social anxiety or panic disorder. In this book we provide a general account of anxiety and the means to overcome it, as well as specific guidance on strategies for overcoming particular forms of anxiety.

We are committed to the idea that all therapies need strong scientific support to back up their ideas about treatment. We can have interesting ideas and theories about which treatments are best, but unless we have good evidence to show that they work, we are really just making it up!

In research carried out on anxiety, all the strong scientific support for treatments comes from studies into *specific forms* of the disorder, not anxiety *in general*. We can apply the same general principles of cognitive behavioural therapy to any psychological problem, but this is not quite the same as having tailor-made CBT approaches for specific anxiety problems. Only the tailor-made approach has real evidence to support it.

Even with a tailor-made approach, there is a further problem: people usually have more than one anxiety problem at a time. According to one large study, 29 per cent of people have problems with anxiety at some point of their lives – this is more than one in four of us (Kessler et al, 2005). In addition, if we *do* have problems with anxiety, 40–80 per cent of us will have more than one type. This means that we need to tackle each problem with the 'disorder-specific' approach that has been shown to work. There is a great deal of similarity and overlap between these individual approaches, but there are also key differences in the way that they fit the approach to the problem. Unified or 'transdiagnostic' approaches to the treatment of emotional problems are currently being developed (e.g. by David Barlow and colleagues) which offer the potential to address multiple anxiety problems simultaneously. Such approaches are relatively new, however, and not yet sufficiently developed to form a self-help programme.

What's the answer? We decided that what was needed was a self-help book which does two things. Firstly, it should explain the ideas and the techniques that are common to the CBT treatment of all forms of anxiety disorder and, secondly, it should describe the tailor-made treatments for the different disorders in separate chapters. In this way, the similarities between the different approaches would be described for people with more than one anxiety problem at the same time as describing the specific treatments that have been found to work for the particular problem.

We also felt that almost all the existing books are written either for someone with the problem, or for therapists. Although there is a great deal of overlap in their content, they are often pitched to different readerships, written as separate books using slightly different language.

We wanted to produce a book that could be used both by people who are experiencing anxiety problems and those who are supporting their efforts to recover – friends, family members and therapists. In this way, people could be sure that they were all talking the same language and sharing a common understanding, rather than reading separate books that might explain problems in slightly different ways.

In addition, because we are committed only to treatments with a sound evidence base, we wanted the people who have actually developed and researched the specific CBT approaches for the specific anxiety problems to write the chapters in this book, and we were very pleased that everyone we asked agreed to this! This means the chapters on specific anxiety problems are written by international experts, and the treatments are in fact those that are recommended by the National Institute of Health and Clinical Excellence (www.nice.org.uk), who provide treatment guidelines to health professionals.

We have given a brief treatment programme for each disorder, and each chapter should give you all the basics you need, but for readers who would like more detail we have also included recommendations for further reading. You will only have to read and follow the specific chapters that are relevant to you, so you'll be able to skip many of them.

Is this book for you?

Almost everyone has experienced anxiety at some time in their lives, and to do so is not only natural, but probably quite sensible, too. In some sense the feeling of anxiety is like a signal to us that we need to take action. If we are walking alone down a dark street and start to feel anxious, we might think, 'This is getting spooky – I think I'll nip into the pub and call a cab', so we will be doing something to get ourselves somewhere safe. If we have an exam coming up, we are likely to start feeling anxious. We might think, 'It's no use; I can't pretend it's not happening – I've got to revise or I'll totally mess up.' Once again, anxiety can guide us to behave in a way that is in our best interests. Not only will anxiety help to guide what we should be doing, but sometimes it will help to make us better at it, too. It can make us stronger or faster if we need to respond physically, for example if we are in physical danger and need to run away. The text box on 'Fight or Flight' on pages 5–6 outlines our body's natural response to anxiety.

However, no doubt you know all too well that anxiety can also become unhelpful. It can become unhelpful in two different ways. First, anxiety does not help if we become anxious in situations where there is really no danger or threat. Examples of this are being frightened that a house spider will jump out of the bath at us (spiders won't do this), or being scared that people are laughing at us when they are not, or thinking that we're dying of a heart attack when we are not. In these examples people feel anxious because they think that something bad is going to happen, even when it is not.

The second way in which anxiety becomes unhelpful is when there is some kind of real threat to you, but the amount of anxiety you feel is out of proportion to the reality of the situation. As in the example earlier, it is natural to feel anxious if we have an exam coming up, but for some people the anxiety can become so overwhelming that instead of motivating us to revise, it completely interferes with our ability to concentrate, or we get so frightened at the thought of failing that we avoid even thinking about the exam. For another example, many people don't like being in crowds, but if we are so frightened of getting caught in a crowd that we can't leave the home, then anxiety is clearly having a serious impact on our life.

Whichever way anxiety is unhelpful to us, the reason that it does not help is that instead of protecting us, it imprisons us. It stops us from doing what we would like to do, and living our life the way we wish. If you are reading this book, then you will almost certainly have experienced this for yourself. If you recognize that this has been happening, the book is for you!

The aim of this book

The aim of this book is to help you overcome your anxiety so that you can go freely about your daily life doing what you wish without being unduly scared. We hope that the first part of the book – the common ideas and techniques of CBT – will help you understand more about anxiety and cognitive behavioural therapy. Given that the different CBT treatments for anxiety problems all have a common structure and style, we hope we are being efficient by describing these common features so that they don't have to be repeated in the second part of this book. Part 2 provides you with an understanding of what keeps different forms of anxiety going, and will give you the tools to change so that your anxiety comes down to acceptable levels. The goal is not to live an anxiety-free life – for one thing, nobody ever does; and for another, anxiety can be useful in that it prepares us for real danger – but to live your life with acceptable levels of anxiety in a rich and full way.

How to use this book

Getting help: We know from studies that many people get most from self-help books if they have help and support from a therapist or therapy assistant as they work through them. If you do not have a therapist, then you may want to try to get a friend or family member to help you with the book, to read it along with you and support you as you try to make changes. For this reason we have added 'Tips for supporters' throughout the text. These come from our experience of supervising therapists, and from the feedback we've received from family members of the people we have treated. Don't worry if you don't have support; just try to be as objective as possible as you read through the book, and try to be your own therapist – just apply the tips to yourself.

Making a commitment: If you want to make real changes in your life then it will not be enough to simply *read* the book. You will need to really commit yourself to doing the tasks and exercises in the specific chapters. Otherwise it is rather like exercise – *reading* about going jogging doesn't make us any fitter!

Understanding common factors: The good news is that you do not have to read the whole book, though it would be sensible to read Part 1 on common ideas and techniques before moving on to the chapters that are relevant to your particular problem in Part 2.

Identifying your problem: It may be that you don't know which chapters are relevant for you, or think all of them could apply. Each chapter opens with some information about the nature of the specific problem being considered, which should help you decide how relevant it is to you. Don't try to decide if that's the only one for you – just see if the problems they are describing would be good for you to try to tackle. You might find that you need to work through more than one chapter in Part 2. If so, then you should find that the skills you've learned from the first one make it easier to work through the next one.

If more than one chapter is relevant to you, there are two ways to decide which chapter to start with. The first is to start with the problems that are causing you the most difficulties in your life – perhaps you feel that if this was sorted out, your day might be a lot easier for you. Alternatively, you could start with something that you think might be reasonably easy to tackle – that way you will start to see changes quickly and hopefully your confidence will grow. If you have a supporter working with you, you can discuss together where to start, but there's no golden rule – as long as you start somewhere then you will have begun to overcome your problems.

Anxiety and medication

Although this book is about self-help through CBT, you may be wondering whether medication would be able to help you. If you would like to know more about this, then your General Practitioner (GP) will be able to advise. The medications that are most useful for anxiety can be obtained by prescription from your GP, but not bought over the counter from the pharmacist.

Medication can be useful on its own, but also in conjunction with CBT. Taking medication may make it easier for you to use this book, or to benefit from further help from a therapist, so you don't need to think of it as an *either* CBT *or* medication decision.

We have included below links to the guidance on anxiety disorders that is produced by NICE – the National Institute for Health and Clinical Excellence. NICE reviews all the available evidence about treatments for physical and mental health conditions, and produces guidance about which treatments should be offered. This covers both psychological and drug treatments – you will see that CBT features heavily. The numbers at the end of the address relate to the most recent version of the guidance for that disorder.

In relation to the anxiety disorders covered in this book, NICE has produced guidance for those shown below. In each case we give the disorder and the web link to the guidance. At the time of writing, NICE had not yet produced guidance for social anxiety (due out in May 2013) or for health anxiety or specific phobias, but if you would like to explore the use of medication for these problems then your GP will be able to assist you.

For generalized anxiety disorder and panic disorder:
www.nice.org.uk/CG113
For obsessive compulsive disorder:
www.nice.org.uk/CG31
For post-traumatic stress disorder:
www.nice.org.uk/CG26

Finally, we have included a chapter on post-traumatic stress disorder (PTSD), the anxiety that overwhelms people when they have been through a highly traumatic event. While research has shown that self-help works for other forms of anxiety, to date it does not support the use of a self-help book without a therapist for people who have PTSD. The chapter on PTSD is therefore not designed to be used as a self-help manual but to provide you with information on effective cognitive behavioural therapy for this problem and how to access it.

Key messages

- You will get out of this book what you put in. If you work hard at the exercises and follow the suggestions, you are likely to get more benefit than if you skim-read it on the way to work and decide to do the exercises later.

- Try to be open minded to thinking about your anxiety with a new perspective and living your life in a different way. Changing your beliefs and behaviour is hard, but if you can begin to do this, then you will have started to overcome your problems with anxiety.

- If something is unclear to both you and the person helping you, use your judgement as to whether it is fundamental to what you are trying to achieve, or whether it can be ignored.

- Keep your eyes on the prize: the big picture of recovery and what it will mean for you.

Tips for supporters

- It is difficult to change. Be 'empathic but firm' when helping someone. That is, show them that you really do understand how difficult it is for them to confront their anxieties and deal with them differently, but don't let the difficulties stand in the way of making changes.

- Make sure that the person you are supporting is ready to commit themselves to change, and you are committed to helping them. People tend to have a 'right time' to take on challanges like this – a kind of window of opportunity when they are in the right frame of mind. You can help to motivate your 'supportee' by pointing out all the benefits of change to them, but, most importantly, you can help them decide whether this is the right time to change.

Part 1

Common features of cognitive behavioural therapy for different anxiety problems

Introduction to Part 1: What is anxiety?

I wake up in the morning worrying; I go to sleep at night worrying. I feel like my head is going to explode!   Pieter, 18

I know people think I'm being stupid but I can't bear anything to do with spiders. I can't let the children play outside in case they come home with a spider on them, and I have to check all the bedrooms before we go to bed to make sure there's nothing there. Just thinking about spiders makes me break out into a sweat.   Mary, 37

I know everyone gets worried about talking in meetings, but I get so anxious that I can't even go to them. I'm sure everyone will think I'm stupid and pathetic if I talk, but I keep making such feeble excuses that they probably think that anyway now.   Kai, 28

I keep getting stomach aches, and every time they start I think, 'That's it, I know I've got cancer.' I spend my whole time feeling my stomach to see if I can feel lumps growing. My doctor says there's nothing wrong, but I just don't believe her.   Jane, 43

Feeling anxious is undoubtedly a fact of life, and there are few of us who could say that we have never experienced any problems with it. Many of us feel nervous before job interviews, or get butterflies in our stomach at the top of tall buildings or steep cliffs. Sometimes anxiety can be 'normal' in the sense that it fits the occasion, but it can also be 'abnormal' – that is, the anxiety starts to take over our thinking processes and our lives, and makes it difficult for us to function.

If you think about the last time you were anxious it is likely that you experienced a number of different thoughts and feelings. You might have felt your heart beating fast, your breathing speeding up, your palms becoming sweaty. You might have noticed that you were thinking, 'Oh no – something terrible is going to happen. I must get out.' You might have had a great sense of fear, and a strong desire to get out of the situation.

The two stories below describe two people who experience very different kinds of anxiety. We will come back to them throughout Part 1 of this book.

Nicky: Nicky is a 19-year-old woman from a sporty family, all of whom are physically fit, and Nicky is very athletic. She is the youngest child and the only girl. Her older brothers have always teased her about being less strong than them. No one in their family is ever ill, and they are proud of how fit they are. The family was having a barbecue in the summer when a chicken bone got lodged in Nicky's throat and she nearly suffocated. She remembers the horrible feeling of not being able to breathe. It became so serious that her friend had to do the Heimlich manoeuvre on her to dislodge the bone. Since then she has become frightened about eating in case it happens again. She has to check everything that she is going to eat very carefully to make sure there are no bones or lumps that could catch in her throat. She has also started to get out of breath for no reason – she just starts feeling breathless out of the blue. When this happens she can feel her heart pounding and she breaks out into a sweat. She becomes terrified that she'll die and becomes overwhelmed with anxiety. She also has nightmares about the barbecue experience and wakes up in a cold sweat. Her brothers are now teasing her a lot more – they don't realize how serious it is – and she has to leave the room if she thinks they're going to start talking about her fears.

Stefan: Stefan is a 31-year-old builder and decorator from the Czech Republic who has a wife and two children in his home country. He came to England because he could not find work at home. He comes over for a few weeks at a time. He works ten–twelve hours a day, and spends very little money, so that he can take most of what he earns back to his family. He is pleasant, speaks English well, and works hard, so people are happy to recommend him to their friends, but the change in the exchange rate and the economic downturn mean that the jobs are drying up. Meantime, his wife is now pregnant again. He is worried that he won't be able to support his family and they'll have to leave their home. He is tense and can't sleep well at night, because he is worrying about what the future holds. He has always been confident about his skills, but now thinks everything he does is full of mistakes, and is afraid people will stop recommending him. He misses his young children, and feels sad and guilty that he is away from home so much. He is starting to feel low and struggles to keep going at work; he gets irritable and snappy when things go wrong.

The function of anxiety

Almost everyone has experienced anxiety at some time in their lives, and to do so is not only natural, but also sensible. The box below explains why.

Fight or flight

To understand why we're designed to feel anxious from time to time, we need to go back a few hundred thousand years! When humans were evolving they lived in tough environments, and had some tough competitors – including each other – for food and shelter. Most of the situations that were dangerous involved physical threat – the sabre-toothed tiger stalking people as food, the younger man about to take over the prime position in the tribe – so humans developed a response known as the 'fight-or-flight' response. This means that the moment that we sense danger our bodies act quickly to prepare us to tackle it. Adrenalin and other hormones are released that result in physiological changes – for example, our heart beats faster in order to pump more oxygen around our bodies. These changes mean that we are primed to be as strong and as quick as we can be, so that we can fight our enemy, or get out of the situation fast. We undergo some psychological changes, too – we become intensely aware of things around us that might be dangerous and we react quickly. This is sensible as well – if a sabre-toothed tiger is about to spring it probably isn't sensible to think, 'Hmm . . . I wonder if he'll attack me – how's he looking? What do you think?' It's more sensible to get out and think later.

There is another aspect of our evolutionary response to anxiety that gets talked about less, and that is the 'freeze' response. As many people will know, particularly if you have watched *Jurassic Park*, the vision of predator animals is attuned to movement. Their vision is less accurate for stationary objects. If you are in a situation when fighting or running away isn't going to be much help, your body freezes – much like a rabbit caught in car headlights – so that you stay absolutely still and can't be seen.

The problem with the fight-or-flight response is that many of the situations that we now face don't require a physical response. When you sit down to revise for an exam feeling nervous, it's really not that much help if your body is in full swing for action. The racing heart and increased strength in your muscles aren't needed in that situation and can make you feel more tense. Freezing is not much use either, particularly if you find that your mind freezes as well and you can't even think.

So anxiety is in fact a useful development for us – it makes us react to dangerous situations quickly, and it gears our bodies up to make sure that we are as strong and fast as possible. In modern life, however, this primitive survival mechanism can be less useful than in times past, and makes life more difficult.

A word about 'danger' and 'threat'

Throughout the book we talk about danger and threat, so it might be helpful to explain what we mean. As the fight-or-flight description explains, 'danger' at its simplest means immediate physical danger – like the danger of being attacked. Danger also has a wider meaning – you might be in 'danger' of losing your job, or of people laughing at you if you stammer. Any situation in which you might come to harm is threatening, even if the harm is social or psychological rather than physical, could be described as dangerous.

This is similar to 'threat', which describes any situation in which you might come to harm. In theory 'threat' refers to situations in which there is a possibility rather than a certainty of harm, but in practice 'danger' and 'threat' are often used interchangeably.

Helpful versus unhelpful anxiety

It would be odd if we never experienced any anxiety at all, but anxiety can become a problem in two ways. Firstly, you may find that you become anxious when there is no real danger – but to you it seems as though there is. Secondly, you may find that you become anxious in the sort of situation where most people would feel a bit nervous, but that your anxiety is more marked and excessive. Table 1.1 below shows five important differences between helpful and unhelpful anxiety (adapted from a book by Clark and Beck, published in 2010).

It may be more useful to think about unhelpful anxiety as being on a continuum or a scale – that is, anxiety could be a mild problem, or a moderate one, or a severe one. At the point where you are feeling anxious and distressed a lot of the time, and anxiety is dominating your life, dictating what you can and can't do, then we would say that you have developed an anxiety disorder.

Table 1.1: Helpful and unhelpful anxiety

	Helpful	**Unhelpful**
How you interpret things	You see the danger in situations where there is something to be concerned about, but are pretty realistic about what this is	You confuse non-dangerous situations with dangerous ones
How well you function	Even if you feel anxious, your anxiety doesn't stop you from doing what you want to do	Your anxiety interferes with your daily life, socially or at work
How long anxiety lasts	Your anxiety wears off once the danger has passed	Your anxiety persists much longer than would be expected under normal conditions – it doesn't wear off even though the danger has passed
False alarms	You don't get anxious unless you are in a threatening situation, i.e. there are no 'false alarms'	False alarms are common; you get anxious even when there is nothing to be scared about
Hyper-sensitivity	You feel anxious to a level justified by the situation	You get anxious very easily, and to a quite exaggerated extent

Adapted from *Cognitive Therapy of Anxiety Disorders: Science and Practice*, D.A. Clark and A.T. Beck, (2010). Copyright Guilford Press, New York. Adapted with permission of The Guilford Press.

Different kinds of anxiety disorder

So far we have spoken about anxiety as if it is just one kind of problem, but there are many different types of anxiety disorder. There are two commonly used systems of classifying disorders, the *American Diagnostic and Statistical Manual of Mental Disorders*, or *DSM-IV* as it is known, and the one used by the World Health Organization, the *International Classification of Diseases* or *ICD*. These classificatory systems are shortly due to change and *DSM-V* will soon be published by the American Psychiatric Association. Only a trained mental-health professional can diagnose you as having a particular mental-health disorder. However, there are questionnaires and checklists published by various bodies, including the American Psychiatric Association and the World Health Organization that may help you assess yourself.

These two systems aren't identical, but they do overlap considerably. The main anxiety disorders are the ones listed in Table 1.2 below, which also gives a brief description of each of them. We have included health anxiety although it is not formally classified as an anxiety disorder. These are the anxiety disorders covered in this book, and each of the chapters that follow this introduction contains an in-depth description of a specific problem.

Table 1.2: Symptoms of specific anxiety disorders

Disorder	Fundamental feature (adapted from *DSM–IV*)
Specific phobia	A specific phobia is diagnosed when people are frightened of one particular object or situation. Common phobias include flying, heights, dogs or spiders, but there are less common ones, too, like a fear of buttons or wigs. The person suffering from a phobia is likely to become anxious if you go anywhere near these situations. See Chapter 6.
Panic disorder	Panic disorder is diagnosed when people experience frequent periods of intense fear and anxiety when there is no real danger. These periods of intense fear are accompanied by marked physical symptoms, and by thoughts that you will die or lose control. See Chapter 7.

Generalized anxiety disorder (GAD) and worry	GAD is diagnosed if people feel anxious most of the time, for long periods of time, about a number of different things. Sufferers of GAD could also be restless or tired or irritable and find it hard to concentrate. See Chapter 8.
Social phobia	Social phobia, or social anxiety, is diagnosed if people become excessively anxious in situations where there are others who the sufferer believes are judging them. Sufferers might be terrified of embarrassing them-selves, or of other people thinking that they are lacking in some way, or just not liking them. See Chapter 9.
Health anxiety	The essential feature of health anxiety (also known as hypochondriasis) is the fear of having a serious disease, or of contracting one. This fear continues even when doctors have done the appropriate tests and reassured the sufferer that they have not got the disease. People are likely to see the smallest physical symptom (e.g. having a headache) as evidence of something seriously wrong (such as having a brain tumour). See Chapter 10.
Obsessive compulsive disorder (OCD)	OCD is diagnosed where people have thoughts, impulses or images that make them anxious (the obsession), and then have to carry out complicated or particular actions and behaviour (the compulsions) to prevent harm or make themselves feel better. For the diagnosis to be made, sufferers would be carrying out compulsions for more than an hour a day, and would feel very distressed by what they are thinking and/or doing. See Chapter 11.
Post-traumatic stress disorder (PTSD)	PTSD can occur if people experience an event where they thought they (or someone close to them) would die or be seriously hurt. In PTSD, memories of the event come back with no warning as 'flashbacks', and make the sufferer extremely anxious. They are likely to make strong efforts to keep away from any reminders. They might also feel that they have to watch out for danger all the time, and that everything else in their life has faded into insignificance. See Chapter 12.

Table 1.2 above describes the different symptoms of these specific anxiety problems. It is also important, however, to remember that anxiety disorders have a lot of symptoms in common. These common symptoms are shown in Table 1.3 below.

Table 1.3: Symptoms characteristic of most anxiety disorders

- *Avoidance*: Commonly, anxiety makes you want to run away from the situations or objects that make you anxious – or avoid the situation in the first place.
- *Intrusive thoughts/images/memories*: Thoughts come into your mind about your problems and symptoms – these thoughts are upsetting and make you experience symptoms of anxiety.
- *Bodily arousal*: Your whole body gets agitated. Common symptoms include your heart racing, breathing getting difficult, sweating, butterflies in the stomach, tingling or pins and needles in your hands and feet.
- *Over-vigilance to danger/threat*: Without even realizing it, you are constantly on the look-out for things that might be harmful to you.
- *Overestimation of danger/threat*: When you are having problems with anxiety, the way that you interpret your experiences becomes distorted. You experience situations as threatening even when they are not, and your ideas about the level of things get out of proportion to the danger that is really there. Together, over-vigilance and overestimation of danger mean that you are constantly on the look-out for danger, and that if you see anything that has a hint of threat about it, you assume the worst and assume that the danger is real. As a result the world comes to seem like a very dangerous place.
- *Compensatory safety-seeking behaviour*: In order to try to make yourself feel safe you start taking steps to make you feel better. Sometimes these can help in the short term but they often backfire and make you feel worse in the long term.
- *Low mood*: Anxiety and low mood go together a lot of the time. This can be because you get worn out and feel defeated by your anxiety problems, or because low mood had started to drain your confidence even before the anxiety starts.
- *Worrying*: If you are anxious, you will probably have lots of anxious thoughts that go round in your head even if you are not in a particularly difficult situation. You will spend a lot of time thinking 'what if' and going over various past, present and future scenarios.

Nicky's story

Eventually Nicky's anxiety got so bad that she decided to seek help. After she spoke to her GP she was assigned to a psychological well-being practitioner (PWP) to assist with her self-help. When Nicky was told about the symptoms of different anxiety disorders she immediately recognized that she was having panic attacks. She had episodes when she felt intensely frightened and was convinced she was going to choke, and these had started to happen out of the blue, even if she wasn't eating anything. She also realized that she had some mild symptoms of OCD – she spent a long time checking her food to make sure that it was OK before she could eat anything at all. She also had some symptoms of PTSD – at the barbecue she had seriously thought that she would die, and she was still having nightmares about it, and couldn't stand it when her brothers reminded her about the event.

Stefan's story

When he went home Stefan talked to his wife, Magda, about how he had been feeling. She was really sympathetic and they decided that he should start trying to do something about it. When he looked up his symptoms he thought that he probably had generalized anxiety disorder, or GAD. He was worrying about a lot of different things – his work, his finances, his family – and had many of the symptoms, particularly being tense and anxious and finding it hard to sleep. He decided that he would try to tackle this himself with Magda's help.

What anxiety disorder do you have?

In some ways, what you label your anxiety disorder may not seem important but because the different treatments for the anxiety disorders have been developed for specific forms of anxiety disorder, it is important to identify your anxiety problem correctly. Table 1.2 may not provide enough information, in which case use the flow chart on the following pages to help (adapted from www.iapt.nhs.uk – http://www.iapt.nhs.uk/silo/files/the-iapt-data-handbook-appendices-v2.pdf (Appendix C, page 20).

Having identified the exact nature of your anxiety problem, you will know what anxiety disorder(s) you may have and which chapters in this book you should read. Rather than simply jumping to them straight away, we suggest you read through Part 1 first, which gives you information about how cognitive behavioural therapy is structured and how to get the most from the different chapters that follow.

Does it make sense to classify anxiety disorders?

We have seen that anxiety disorders have shared symptoms, and a lot of people have more than one type of anxiety problem. Because of these common factors, it is not surprising that the treatments for the different anxiety disorders have a lot in common – often they are trying to tackle the same problem. You will see later on that the methods outlined in Part 1 are designed to help address these common symptoms. People with panic disorder often worry excessively about real things (as in people with generalized anxiety disorder). People with obsessive compulsive disorder also worry a great deal, have panic attacks, and often are socially anxious as well. It is this overlap in symptoms that partially explains why cognitive behavioural therapy for the different anxiety disorders has so many things in common – the treatment is trying to change similar problems. But it is by concentrating on the 'pure' forms of the disorders – that is, when people only have *one* problem – that researchers have been able to understand them, and develop effective treatments.

Figure 1.1: Questions to help identify your anxiety problem

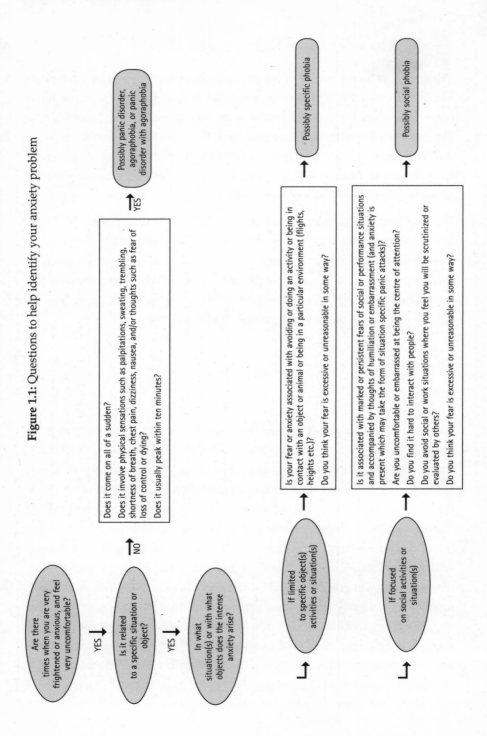

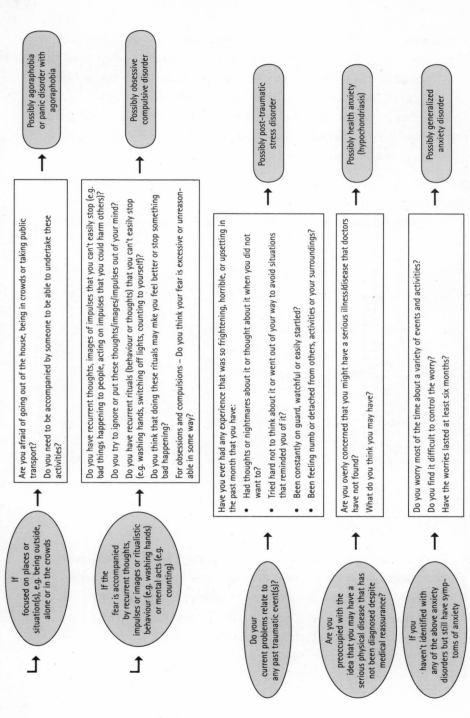

Figure reproduced with kind permission from the Department of Health, www.iapt.nhs.uk. *IAPT Handbook* (2010)

The answer to whether it makes sense to classify the disorders is both Yes and No. Yes, because the classification tells us something about the key features of that particular problem, what sustains it and how best to treat it, and No because the disorders have so many features that overlap. Despite this confusion, it remains the convention to classify anxiety into this or that type of disorder, and for the purposes of this book this is a convention to which we will adhere.

We hope you have now been able to think about what form of anxiety disorder is most relevant to you, and we will show you how to overcome it, using ideas from both Part 1 and the individual self-help programmes in Part 2.

Key messages

- Some anxiety is helpful but if it interferes with life then it becomes problematic.

- There are different types of anxiety disorder – many people have more than one type.

- The different anxiety disorders have much in common (as well as some aspects that are distinctive).

Tip for supporters

If you want to help the person you are supporting to find out more information about the different disorders, look at the individual chapters and also look up the different problems directly by finding the criteria used by *ICD-10* or *DSM-IV* on the internet. You could help them to find this guidance rather than letting them seek it on their own so that they don't feel overwhelmed.

1 How CBT works

Everything seems to be cognitive therapy these days!

Asif, 30

Cognitive behavioural therapy (CBT) has developed enormously over the past thirty years. It has been adapted in a lot of different ways to address different problems, so there are a lot of different versions of it. This is good in fact, since it means that CBT is developing and improving all the time!

In order to explain CBT as it applies to anxiety, we are going to look at a number of key ideas. We have called them the 'key principles' of cognitive behavioural therapy for anxiety, since they are the bedrock of all the treatments that are outlined in this book.

In this chapter we will briefly describe the five key principles, and we will look at the first of these in detail. In the chapters that follow we will go through the remaining four.

Key Principle 1: CBT is semi structured, personalized, and time-limited. It is *scientific* both because it has been shown to work in research trials and because it shows you how to assume a 'scientific' stance and examine ideas and evidence as rationally as possible.

Key Principle 2: The reason you feel anxious is that you are seeing situations, events or people as more dangerous and threatening than they really are.

Key Principle 3: Thoughts, feelings, physical symptoms and behaviour are closely linked to each other: making changes to one of these will bring about change in the others, too.

Key Principle 4: You need to understand what factors are causing your anxiety currently to persist.

Key Principle 5: In order to reduce your feelings of anxiety you need to change the factors that keep your anxiety going.

The structure and style of cognitive behavioural therapy

How do you imagine therapy? Many people still imagine that therapy involves them lying down on a couch and saying whatever comes into their mind (possibly something to do with their childhood and feelings towards their parents). This is not cognitive behavioural therapy. You may have had some experience of psychotherapy where a warm, empathic therapist is silent, and just lets you talk about whatever you would like. This is not cognitive behavioural therapy either. In CBT, the therapy often takes place around a table (or on chairs with a low coffee table between you). The therapist explains something about the therapy, and asks you what problems you are having and what you would like to be different. What the therapist does, which is very different from earlier forms of therapy, is to *structure* what happens in the therapy sessions. Rather than just talking about whatever comes into your mind, you and the therapist will concentrate on the aspects that are most helpful and important for you. As therapies have developed, we have realized that structure is one of the most important things that make them helpful. Structure refers to how the therapy progresses from session to session – from beginning to end – and also what happens within each session.

You may be reading this book and using it to help yourself without a therapist or anyone else involved. Even so, following the same practice of structuring how you do the exercises will make a big difference to how well you do.

Structuring therapy from beginning to end

What this means is that therapy has a clear beginning, middle and end.

In the beginning stages, the aim is to understand your problems. This means learning about the role of thinking in your anxiety problems (see Chapter 2), and then looking at the 'maintenance factors' – the vicious cycles that keep anxiety going (see Chapter 3). The beginning sessions also involve thinking about what changes you'd like to make – the changes are often described as your 'goals'.

Once you have set the scene for working with your problems, therapy moves on to the next stage – the middle sessions. The aim of these sessions is to think about what strategies will help you to start implementing these changes, and see how you get on.

The final sessions focus on how to keep those changes going even when therapy has ended, and on how to prevent problems returning.

Structuring therapy within a session

The first session or two will have a slightly different structure. In these sessions, the structure is geared towards the following aims:

1. Getting a good grasp of the problem, including all the aspects that are problematic.

2. Starting to work out the 'formulation' – the map of the problems that fits them together and explains how/why they keep going.

3. Defining goals for therapy.

4. Working out the best way to monitor the problem and keep track of progress.

Following this introductory phase, each individual therapy session has a clear beginning, middle and end. Each session begins with making a plan (or 'agenda') for the session and reviewing progress since the last session. The middle part of the session involves discussion about the problem, sometimes adding to or changing the formulation, and deciding on how to take things forward. Sometimes the middle part of the session will involve the therapist doing 'behavioural experiments' with you (see p. 62). The last part of the session usually involves summarizing what has been discussed and clarifying what the 'homework' will be.

It is important to realize that the structure is flexible – hence we talk about it as being 'semi structured'. If something important comes up, then it needs to be addressed, regardless of the original plan. Throughout therapy the basic structure is constantly adapted to fit what is important to you.

CBT is based on the principles outlined above, but it also has techniques – specific tasks and suggestions for how to tackle problems. Using the techniques and learning how to apply the principles are both important. Learning how to apply the principles means that there is a lot of flexibility in how therapy is conducted, which is good, since no two people are the same and no two CBT sessions are the same.

Style of therapy

Normally when we talk about the 'style' of CBT we mean the techniques the therapist uses during the sessions. Even if you are using this book on your own, it is helpful to consider the style with which you want to conduct your sessions with yourself and how to proceed. 'Firm but empathic' is our favourite style. Some people might also describe this as 'tough love'! You are not harsh or self-critical, but nor do you let yourself get away with things that you know in your heart you were really able to tackle or perhaps that you could tackle another day with some additional support. Self-criticism rarely helps. A recent development by Paul Gilbert, and many others, talks about trying to have compassion for yourself and your circumstances. We think this is a helpful attitude.

If you do have a supporter helping you overcome your problems with anxiety, your supporter should also be firm but empathic. Working together with your supporter should be a collaborative exercise – that is, together you can bring different expertise and experience to bear on your problem. Overcoming your difficulties is a joint venture between the two of you. Whether or not you have a supporter, the style of therapy reflects that you have a specific task ahead of you – understanding what is keeping your anxiety going and then making changes to reduce it. Keep your focus on the prize at all times. The prize is freedom from anxiety.

Therapy is time limited

At the time that CBT was being developed there was a strong tradition in psychotherapy of open-ended therapy, sometimes going on for years. CBT, on the other hand, is time limited, and for most anxiety problems this means that it tends to last for somewhere between ten and twenty sessions. If the problem is mild, then it can sometimes take even fewer sessions – maybe only five or six. Therapy is also time limited in the sense that each therapy session lasts around fifty minutes.

Therapy gives you tools for life

Although the therapy itself is time limited, its effects last for much longer than the therapy itself. One of the advantages of CBT is that it gives you skills for life – it teaches you a new way of thinking and coping with your problems that you can use when times get tough. This is why the techniques are often called a 'toolkit'. People tend to keep the benefits they make during CBT. This is not to say that there aren't times when the anxiety does return, and some periods are certainly more stressful than others. It does mean, however, that people are able to spot when their anxiety is getting worse, bring out the CBT 'toolkit' they learned to use before, and then stop the anxiety from becoming as big a problem as it was previously.

Therapy is scientific

The concept of 'science' in CBT is critical. Cognitive behavioural therapies are scientific in two ways. Firstly, a lot of research has been carried out on what makes us anxious, and why anxiety can be so persistent. These ideas have been tested in research studies, and the treatment has been tested with thoroughly scientific methods.

The second way in which CBT is scientific is that you have to learn to be a scientist yourself – you have to put on a white coat (though not literally!) and learn to examine the problem as objectively as possible. Although some people might laugh at the idea of themselves as scientists, you do need to learn to ask yourself: 'What *evidence* do I have for my way of thinking? How can I gather evidence to assess the validity of this belief? How can I gather evidence to see if another belief might fit the situation better?' Once you have the evidence, you then need to be able to assess it and decide whether there is a better explanation for that situation than your anxious one. Being able to be such a scientist will help your heart and head become allies in the fight against anxiety.

If you absolutely hate the idea of science, then think about it in another way: doing CBT is also a bit like being a lawyer. In a court of law the jury is asked to decide between two versions of events. So the lawyer's job is to find the evidence that backs up their point of view, and persuade the jury that this is the truth. In a sense, tackling your anxiety is a bit like this – like the lawyer trying to gather evidence to show the jury the true situation; you are trying to gather evidence to establish the most accurate account of events.

Structuring therapy for yourself

Given the structure of CBT is so important, we will spend some time describing how to do this – whichever specific chapters you read, the principles of structure will be the same.

How many sessions?

The self-help programmes described in Part 2 of this book are mostly designed to be completed over four to five months or about twenty sessions. You should see some changes in your anxiety after around six sessions of working through a specific chapter. However, if your anxiety shows no sign of improving after six sessions of using the chapter, then it would be sensible to think about what to do next. If you have a supporter who is not a professional helper, then you and they could think about whether it is time to seek professional help. It is important not to be discouraged if you think you're not making progress. Self-help isn't for everyone, and there are a lot of other options that your family doctor can discuss with you.

Many chapters in Part 2 contain information on how to keep track of your progress; measuring your progress weekly will help you gauge the extent to which your anxiety is improving.

How often should I have sessions?

Having decided which chapter in Part 2 seems most appropriate to how you are feeling, we would suggest that you plan to have sessions twice a week for the first three weeks. This may seem like a lot to ask, but it will help you to kick-start the process. Once your therapy plan is up and running, then once a week would be fine.

What is a session anyway?

A 'session' should last around fifty minutes or so and is the time that you set aside to focus on the exercises in the book, go through what you have done since your last session and think about what to do next. If you have a supporter, it would be good to do the session with them, if you can. Sessions should be planned in advance, and kept like any other appointment, even though it may only be with yourself. It's a good idea to find a quiet place where you will not be disturbed for an hour. If that sounds too difficult, then plan for shorter sessions. Use a notebook or laptop to help plan how you can use the book to help yourself, and to make notes as you go along. This is what happens in face-to-face therapy and the same principles apply when using this book.

If you have a supporter, then we usually say that it is not a good idea to start the self-help programme if either of you will be going on holiday soon, as breaks will interrupt the momentum of change. This is the same for you on your own – if necessary, it is better to delay starting to work through this book until your children are back at school, work is a bit easier, or your partner can help take care of some responsibilities, so that you can really commit yourself to change when you start.

Beginning therapy – the first few sessions

Your first couple of sessions will have a slightly different structure to the remainder of the sessions, since they are aimed at helping you to get a good understanding of your problem, and to set goals, before starting to use the techniques and strategies described. We will describe the process of understanding your problems later in this book.

Goal setting

Many self-help books talk about goal setting and there is a useful acronym to consider: goals should be 'SMART' – Specific, Measurable, Achievable, Realistic and Time limited. This is to stop oneself setting unrealistic goals such as 'I want to be the best at everything I do'. This is not an achievable goal for any therapy. In the same way, setting yourself the goal of 'I never want to be anxious again' is neither helpful nor realistic. We do know, however, that many people overcome their anxiety disorders after both face-to-face CBT, and following specific self-help programmes with or without the help of a therapist or a supporter. A reasonable goal to set yourself therefore might be:

> By the end of twenty sessions of treatment/self-help, I want to have normal levels of anxiety and be able to get on with my life. That means I'll be able to take the children to school, shop in the supermarket without feeling panicky, and go out with my husband without feeling anxious. I could also start to look for a part-time job.

This sort of goal is challenging but realistic if you work hard and focus on the task in hand. If you stick to the sessions you have planned, set yourself an agenda for each session, do the homework, and assess your progress every step of the way, you are likely to achieve your goal. You will know if you have achieved your goals by measuring your anxiety levels before and after completing the self-help programme.

Stefan's goals

To start with, Stefan found it really hard to say what his goals were. In the ideal world, he would have liked to have somehow earned enough money to be able to go back to the Czech Republic and not to need to work away from home. He knew, however, that he needed a more realistic plan as well. After a while he was able to write down the following goals:

1. Regain confidence in the quality of my work – stop looking for and exaggerating tiny flaws in everything I do.
2. Stop assuming that no one will recommend me any more, and go back to actively asking people if they know anyone who needs work done.
3. Be able to sleep at night.
4. Be less tense and tired in the day.
5. Be more of a support to Magda.

Carrying on with therapy – the middle sessions

You can either start each of the middle sessions with setting the agenda or with reviewing your progress so far – the order does not much matter as long as you do both. See the Appendix for an example of a session plan.

Setting the agenda for your sessions

'Agenda' is a good word as it implies business – and CBT is about getting down to the task in hand, focusing on it, and achieving change.

When setting your agenda, there will be some regular items such as:

1. Reviewing progress (0–5 minutes) refers to whether your symptoms are getting better, and whether you are closer to your goals.

2. Reviewing homework (0–5 minutes) refers to looking at what therapy strategies and techniques you used in your homework, and whether these worked.

3. Moving forward (most of the session) is the point where you would use the book to get new information and think about the next stage of your self-help programme.

4. Homework (0–5 minutes) means setting yourself precise tasks to carry out before your next session, so that you know exactly how and when you will implement the strategies.

5. Summarizing (0–5 minutes) means making sure that you know what you are doing and why.

1. Review your progress

When reviewing your progress it is helpful if you can use clear measures of how you are doing. This will enable you to compare how you are now with how you were at the previous session, or when you started your therapy. Using questionnaires is one way of doing this – you can add up scores and compare them with your previous scores. Sometimes progress can be measured by looking at what you have been able to do, and comparing this with what you could do before your therapy started. Several of the specific chapters in Part 2 include questionnaires and forms that you can use to measure progress.

2. Review your homework from the previous week

Reviewing the work you have done between sessions is important but it is likely that you will be critical of both your efforts and your achievements. We say this based on our experience of hundreds of people who suffer from anxiety who turn up to therapy having done fabulous work and then apologize for their efforts! While it is true that you can always do more, the point is not to do your homework perfectly, or necessarily to do huge amounts; the point is to do what you can between sessions to facilitate your learning and change the beliefs and behaviours that are keeping your anxiety going. Anything you can do towards this goal is a real achievement and if you can recognize it as such, it will help boost your confidence and self-esteem, and that in turn will motivate you to continue making changes. If you have done any homework that is consistent with your goal of changing, then please pat yourself on the back and acknowledge it.

When you are reviewing your homework, keep one thought uppermost in your mind: *What did I learn from this?* Did you learn anything about what is keeping your problem going? Did you learn anything about the validity of your thoughts and beliefs? Did you find out something new about yourself or how your emotions work? If you ask yourself these questions, even if the homework went badly, it can still be useful as a way of understanding things better.

The next questions to ask yourself are: *How can I build on this? What do I have to think about next? What do I have to plan next?* Make sure that the answers to these questions are put on your session notes either under the item to do with homework for this week, or else somewhere within your main agenda item.

3. Moving forward

Exactly what you cover here will differ according to the type of anxiety problem you have, what kind of person you are, and the stage of the self-help programme you are at. CBT is a bit like Lego – you need to build on good foundations and add new layers slowly and carefully. Moving forward could involve a test to see if an alternative new belief, which you might have learned in the previous session, applies in a different situation or under different circumstances. It may involve another attempt to change thinking patterns and view situations more objectively but in more challenging circumstances than before. It may be about doing something you have not done for a long time and that you know would improve the quality of your life if only you could do it. Whatever the specific item, it is about moving forward slowly but surely.

4. Homework

There are certain ways to approach homework that make it more likely that you will actually do it. Firstly, if possible, it is better to do it straight away while it is uppermost in your mind. Secondly, it is better to do it when you are feeling strong and fresh, rather than after a bad day when you feel tired, hungry and irritable. It can also be a good idea to ask someone to help you with it in case you get stuck. Lastly, it is generally a good idea not to do too much in any one go because you may end up feeling overwhelmed. Of course you may be good at making time to do homework, but in any case it is important to do a reasonable amount of work between sessions so that you can build on your learning in lots of different situations.

5. Summarizing

It is important to summarize what you have covered at the end of each session, to think about what you have learned and what you are going to do next so that you have clear in your mind what will be the focus of your work between this session and the next one.

Stefan's agenda

Stefan found that he liked the idea of structuring his therapy in a focused way. After he'd worked out his problem and goals, his agenda for his next 'session' was as follows:

1. Review my progress. I've been using a measure called the Intolerance of Uncertainty scale. My score has come down a bit this week, so I think that just deciding to tackle the problem is starting to have an effect. I do feel a bit more hopeful.

2. Review homework. My homework was to look up information about anxiety and see if I could make sense of my thoughts and feelings. It was really helpful to find that my symptoms do all fit the GAD description – makes me feel less of an outcast.

3. Moving forward – OK, now I have to make a plan! I'm going to work on trying to stop picking faults with myself all the time – it just makes me feel worse.

    The chapter on generalized anxiety disorder says that I'm worrying because I find uncertainty so difficult, and I can't tell the difference between 'real' worries and 'hypothetical' worries. I think this is really helpful – a lot of what I'm worrying about is what I'm imagining could happen, but I can see that my imagination is really running away with me – these aren't things that are happening now.

4. Homework

    Every time I start worrying, I'm going to ask myself whether this is a real worry or a hypothetical one. I am then going to tackle the real one and NOT worry about the hypothetical one. I'll write it down to help think about it, and talk to Magda too.

---

5.   Summarizing

I've learned that I have generalized anxiety disorder, and that everything I am feeling is pretty understandable. I've read about worry, and the difference between real and hypothetical worry, and I'm going to work on this.

Next session: I'm going to have my next session in five days time when I've had a chance to notice whether this is making any difference or not.

Key messages

- CBT has a clear structure and style. The structure involves setting an agenda for your therapy session, reviewing any homework you've done since your last session, working your way through this session's agenda and then summarizing the session and agreeing homework to do before the next session.

- Try to use this structure for your own sessions as you work through this self-help book, whether or not you are doing it with the help of a supporter.

- The style of therapy should be 'firm but empathic'.

- CBT has a 'scientific' attitude towards obtaining information.

Tips for supporters

- Try to help keep the person you are supporting on track but don't be bossy.

- You are supporting them in their effort to make change, but you should not try to force change.

- If they feel a lot worse, again think about whether this might be to do with events in their lives, rather than being a 'failure' of therapy.

- Remember that starting to tackle problems can sometimes make people more anxious to start with, particularly if they have been avoiding thinking about the problem. Don't be discouraged, and don't let them become discouraged either.

2 The importance of your interpretations

Nobody else I know feels the way I do. I am so lonely. I wish I knew why I am this way.

Fiona, 37

> **Key Principle 2:** The reason you feel anxious is that you are seeing situations, events or people as more dangerous and threatening than they really are.

All the different CBT treatments for anxiety disorders are based on the view that a major problem is that *you believe* that you are in a situation which is dangerous and threatening to you. In other words, the problem is the way you are *interpreting* the situation. We know that when you are suffering from anxiety this is a very hard concept to take on board, and it may sound as if we are not taking seriously how distressed you are, but this idea is central to CBT so let's look at what it actually means.

What do we mean by 'interpretation'?

Cognitive behavioural therapy talks a lot about 'interpretation', so it is worth trying to clarify what we mean by this. When we say 'interpretation' we do not mean that you are consciously or deliberately weighing up situations – well, not usually anyway – but all of us need to make sense of the world around us, and so we are constantly evaluating situations without even being aware that we are doing it. What we *are* aware of are the thoughts (sometimes) and feelings (usually) that result from our evaluation. We all have shortcuts in the way that we do this. Unfortunately, in anxiety, the shortcuts are usually along the lines of 'if in doubt, treat this situation as dangerous'. This is what we mean when we say that you see situations as dangerous and threatening even when they are not. Some cognitive therapists refer to interpretations as 'appraisals', or 'personal meanings' or 'personal significance'. For most purposes these different terms – interpretations, appraisals, explanations, personal significance and personal meaning – all refer to the same thing, *the meaning of the situation to you*, created by your way of evaluating the situation. It is because the anxious interpretations so often distort the reality of the situation and don't follow the facts that we often refer to them as '*mis*interpretations'.

We thank Professor Paul Salkovskis for his very clear way of explaining this using the 'dog mess' joke:

Four people go outside and step in dog mess. The first, who is depressed, thinks, 'There you go, I'm useless, I can't do anything right and I may as well go back to bed'. This person feels sad and low. The second, who is anxious, thinks, 'Oh no, I've stepped in dog mess, I will need to change. What if I am late for work? What if I am fired?' This person feels highly anxious. The third, who has problems with anger, thinks, 'If I find the b**?!d that let his dog s*!t on my doorstep I will beat him up so badly that he'll never walk another b**?!y dog again'. This person feels angry. However, the fourth, who has had cognitive behavioural therapy, thinks, 'Well at least I remembered to put on my shoes'. This person feels pleased.

The point of this joke is to illustrate that all these people had the same unpleasant situation of stepping in dog mess, but it was their *interpretation* of the situation that led to their particular emotional reactions. This is a fundamental principle of CBT – it is not *the event* that causes you to feel anxious but *your interpretation* of the event.

Let's look at another example that illustrates this further. Imagine that you are lying in bed one evening. Your partner is away for the night so you are alone in the house. Suddenly you hear a rattle at the back door. You might think, 'Oh no, someone is breaking in; they are going to kill me and take everything.' Or you might think, 'Oh bother, the stupid catflap is stuck and the cat can't get in.' Or you might think, 'Oh good, perhaps my lovely partner has come back early.' Furthermore, these different explanations, or interpretations, would result in very different feelings. In the first case you would feel frightened, in the second probably rather irritated, and in the third very pleased. So, the same situation – a rattle at the back door – can be interpreted in different ways, and as a result will produce different emotional reactions.

As a final real-life example, we would like to share a true story with you. One of us (Roz) was crossing the road with her three-year-old daughter, who suddenly became hysterical and started crying in pain. She showed her mother her hand, which was red, and the child assumed it was blood. She was anxious, crying and seemingly in pain. Once safely on the other side of the road, she and her mother examined her hand and saw that it was not blood, but red ink. The crying immediately stopped, the anxiety stopped and the pain disappeared. The child had been given an alternative explanation for the redness of her hand, one that was plausible, in keeping with reality and significantly less threatening.

But what if there really is something dangerous going on?

This is not to say that you will never find yourself in situations where there really is a problem, or where there really is some threat to you. At the time of writing this book we are in the middle of an economic downturn, so many people's jobs are at risk. You may have real problems with your health that need a doctor's help, for example. If this is the case, then the issue is that you have a problem with your job, or your health. You may well feel anxious, but if it is appropriate to the situation, then the way to move forward is to tackle the problem itself. If the problem gets better, so will your anxiety. With an anxiety problem, however, the situation is more complicated. Your anxiety may be out of all proportion to the problem, and your interpretations of the situation magnify it and make it difficult to tackle the problem. Even if you can tackle it, the anxiety may carry on long after the problem has been solved.

Different interpretations in different disorders

All the cognitive behavioural treatments are based on the view that you are interpreting events as more threatening than they really are, but the content of interpretations differs from disorder to disorder. There is usually a particular kind of situation that is likely to provoke anxiety, and a typical way of interpreting it that is central to that particular disorder. In panic disorder for example, the threat comes from your body sensations, such as feeling your heart beat faster than usual. Although the sensation is 'normal' or 'natural' or 'harmless' (your heart is beating faster because you have just walked up a steep flight of stairs or are anxious), you interpret it to mean that you are about to have a heart attack, or die, or lose control. As a result you start to feel intensely anxious. In social anxiety, the threat comes from a fear of being judged in a negative way – for instance, that other people may see you as boring or stupid. If you are socially anxious you might interpret something that is completely innocuous – someone yawning because they are tired, for example – as evidence that they do think you are boring and stupid.

In both of these examples, the situation was benign – that is, there was no real threat to you, but because you are anxious, you believed that the situation was threatening, and became more anxious as a result.

We often use the term 'misinterpretations' for times when your understanding, or interpretation, of what is going on is due to your anxiety rather than the objective threat of the situation.

A list of the typical misinterpretations for each anxiety disorder is shown in Table 2.1.

al misinterpretations in different anxiety disorders

	Situation	Typical misinterpretation
Panic disorder	Body sensations	These sensations indicate immediate catastrophe (death, madness, another panic attack)
OCD	Unwanted intrusive thoughts	These thoughts mean I am mad, bad or dangerous
PTSD	Symptoms of PTSD	These symptoms mean I am mad; I will never recover from the trauma
Generalized anxiety disorder	Worrying	Worrying is a sign that I am a kind and caring person; by worrying about something, I can prevent something bad from happening
Social phobia	Social event	I am socially incompetent; everyone is going to judge me negatively; I will become anxious and humiliated
Specific phobia	Encounter with a feared object	I am in danger
Health anxiety	A mole or spot	This is a sign that my health is at serious risk; I could have a fatal and undetected disease

Misinterpretation or the truth?

You may be thinking, what if there is real danger? As we said earlier, you could be in a situation where your interpretation was in keeping with the reality of the situation, and so the anxiety was well founded. If this is so, we would not be talking about an anxiety problem, but about a real-life problem that needs to be addressed. It is when your view of situations, and your consequent anxiety, is out of proportion that we talk about 'misinterpretation'.

If you can accept that your way of thinking is a fundamental part of the problem, and that your interpretation of events is not 'the truth' but a misinterpretation, then you have made a vital step in beginning to change your anxiety. There may be a part of you that accepts this may be the case (maybe your head) but another part of you (perhaps your heart) that does not accept that the problem is one related to how you think. Many people with anxiety problems struggle with this at first, but if you truly can accept that there is no real danger, just your misinterpretation, then you are beginning to make the change necessary to recover from your anxiety disorder. The goal of CBT is to help you reach the conclusion that the problem is one of your thinking and behaviour, rather than that you are, for example, dying from heart palpitations (panic disorder), your thoughts mean you're bad (OCD), or people will judge you negatively (social phobia).

The first step in helping your head and heart reach this conclusion that applies to all anxiety problems is distinguishing between whether the problem is a real one (you *really* have a fatal disease) or one of worry (you are *worried* you have a fatal disease). This has been described by Professor Paul Salkovskis as 'Theory A vs Theory B' (Salkovskis, 1996). Theory A (your current theory) is that you are vulnerable to dying (panic disorder), you're bad for having these thoughts (OCD) or that you're boring (social phobia). Theory B (an alternative theory) is that *you are worried* that you are vulnerable to dying, that you're bad for having these thoughts, or that you're boring. In other words, Theory A is 'the truth' whereas Theory B is that you are *worrying* about these situations. If you can accept that the problem is your worry, then it follows that we have to understand what is keeping your worry going and what is at the heart of why you are misinterpreting harmless events in this way.

Why do we misinterpret? Cognitive biases and cognitive errors

We know that when people become anxious – for whatever reason – the way they process information changes. When you feel anxious your brain starts to see everything through 'anxious lenses' without you even realizing that it's doing it. It is because you are seeing situations in an anxiety-related, threatening way, you feel even more anxious.

Cognitive biases

When you are anxious, you tend to process information differently and in rather biased ways. We have already spoken about the way in which you *interpret* events and situations around you in a very anxious way. Another significant factor is that you may find your attention is *biased*. You become attuned to the possibility there may be some danger or threat nearby, so you start to keep a close look-out for potential sources of harm. We sometimes call this bias of attention being 'hypervigilant' for danger. For example, imagine that you have been beaten up once and are scared of being attacked again. You are walking down the street with your friend who is not at all anxious about being attacked. You will find that you notice events that your friend does not – someone down a side road who looks a bit suspicious, or a car slowing down by you on the kerb.

Both these biased ways of thinking – your interpretations and your attention – occur automatically, and an important part of the role of CBT is to help make you aware of them so you can think in a more balanced way.

Cognitive errors

The box below outlines a number of common cognitive errors as described by Aaron T. Beck in the 1970s and others such as Judy Beck. The error that is most important in anxiety is 'catastrophizing', and we will come back to this often in Part 1 and the rest of this book.

Cognitive errors

Catastrophizing
You blow events out of proportion, so that you think that a small mistake or problem will have devastating consequences, completely out of proportion to the reality of the situation.

Overgeneralizing
You make too much of situations. For example, if you make a mistake with a small part of a report at work you might think that it means you are rubbish at your job. If you overcook the rice, you would think it means you're a terrible cook!

Black and white thinking
You tend to see things as either *completely* good or *completely* bad. It means that if something isn't absolutely brilliant then it must be absolutely awful. The fact that situations normally aren't brilliant means that you spend most of your time thinking that they're awful.

Mind reading
This is a problem in all sorts of anxiety problems, but particularly in social anxiety. You think that you know what other people are thinking about you, and you normally think it's bad! You then react as if your mind reading were the truth, when in fact it's just what *you* think someone is thinking.

Fortune telling

You imagine what *could happen* in the future, and then respond emotionally as if these actually *are going to happen*. For instance, if you are frightened of spiders and tell yourself that there could be one in your bed that night you will be anxious, even though it hasn't happened.

Discounting the positive

You find ways of dismissing things that don't fit with your anxious view. You tend to ignore evidence that doesn't fit, or come up with arguments to say it doesn't count. For example, if you are socially anxious and someone starts chatting to you during your coffee break at work, you might think, 'They're only doing it because they feel sorry for me', rather than thinking it's because they want to. Discounting the positive means that it's easier to hang on to your anxious interpretations.

Filtering

You see only the bad and ignore the good. You see your problems and weaknesses, but disregard your strengths and your accomplishments.

Labelling

You tend to apply simple, and often personal, labels to explain events that happen. For instance, if you weren't given a promotion at work you might tell yourself it was because you're a 'loser' or you're 'pathetic', rather than thinking it was because the person who was promoted had five years' more experience than you. You might tell yourself that other people are mean or that the world is a bad place. These labels then make you feel more inadequate and anxious.

Stefan's misinterpretations

Stefan was putting up a shelf in a client's house when he realised that the wood that he'd used had a lot of knots. He thought, 'Oh no, that looks dreadful; my employers are so perfectionist they're going to be really furious. They'll sack me, and won't recommend me to their friends, and I'll never get more work. We'll lose the house; we'll end up homeless.' This was clearly a catastrophic misinterpretation. As a result of this misinterpretation he understandably felt anxious, and found it hard to concentrate on what he was doing for the rest of the day. Later in the evening when he spoke to Magda, she said, 'I think you've blown it all out of proportion! I thought that you told me that your employers liked ethnic wood; they'll love the knots. Anyway, even if they don't you could always change it. We're not going to lose the house because of one shelf!' Magda helped Stefan to see the difference between real and hypothetical worry about the knots. The real worry was that his employer might not like them. The hypothetical worry was that he'd be fired.

Nicky's misinterpretations

Nicky was out for a meal with friends when she realized that they were about to serve her chicken. (Remember that she had nearly suffocated when a chicken bone got stuck in her throat at the family barbecue.) She thought, 'Oh no, I can't eat chicken. What if it has bones in it? What if I choke again?' She started to feel very frightened, and then she noticed that she couldn't breathe properly, and she started to feel like she was suffocating. She thought, 'I can't breathe, I'm suffocating, I'm going to die.' Not surprisingly, she felt extremely anxious. Like Stefan, she was showing very clear catastrophizing – in other words she was expecting the absolute worst – thinking that changes in her breathing meant that she was going to suffocate and die. In fact, it is common for people to experience difficulties in their breathing when they get a bit anxious, and so a more accurate interpretation might be: 'Oh, I'm breathing too fast. I had better try to slow my breathing down and then it'll feel better.'

Key messages

- CBT for the different anxiety disorders is based on the view that the problem is *your interpretation of events,* and not the event itself.

- Think about adopting a different perspective. For example, instead of seeing the problem as being that you are really at risk of dying from a heart attack, or that people think you are stupid, try to consider the problem as your being WORRIED about those events.

Tips for supporters

- Do all you can to try to help the person you are supporting see that it is reasonable to consider that the problem is their way of thinking. Help them to see that it therefore follows that what they have to do is to examine this and, ultimately, to change it.

- If you know them well, try to find examples of misinterpretation in their lives – perhaps when they might have misinterpreted something and then seen it in a different way later. Try using questions like 'What would you say to a friend who thought like that?'

3 Vicious versus virtuous cycles

I often think of the song by Queen, 'I want to break free'. I do want to break free but I don't know how.

Aryan, 30

Key Principle 3: Thoughts, feelings, physical symptoms and behaviour are closely linked to each other: making changes to one of these will bring about change in the others, too.

We have mentioned different symptoms of anxiety. When we look at them we can see that they fit into four different groups, or categories. CBT often starts by looking at all the different symptoms of anxiety you are experiencing and placing them into these four categories. The categories are:

- physical symptoms (what your body does when you get anxious);

- cognitive symptoms (how you think);

- emotional symptoms (how you feel); and

- behavioural symptoms (what you actually do).

Remember Nicky and Stefan from Chapter 2? Their symptoms can be summarized using these categories.

	Nicky's symptoms	Stefan's symptoms
Physical symptoms	Breathless, heart pounding, palpitations, sweating	Difficulty sleeping, low energy, irritability
Cognitive symptoms (thoughts)	'I'll choke; I'll die'	'I won't be able to manage; we'll lose our home'
Emotional symptoms (feelings)	Terrified	Worried, tense
Behavioural symptoms	Checks everything she eats; avoids eating chicken	Able to do less; snappy at other people

How do thoughts, feelings, physical symptoms and behaviour create vicious cycles?

We will talk a lot more about thoughts in the next section, but for now will just say that thoughts are a crucial part of anxiety – even if you are barely aware of them. In anxiety, thoughts are often the result of a rapid weighing-up of a situation and coming to the conclusion that there is a danger. If you think there is danger, you will feel anxious. Thoughts will also trigger a reaction in your body, which means that you will start to experience strong *physical symptoms,* too – your heart may race; you might start to sweat and get butterflies in your stomach. If you feel this way, it makes sense that you would want to do something to make yourself safe. That may mean leaving a situation (or avoiding it in the first place may be even more appealing); making sure there is no danger, for example by repeatedly checking the doors are locked, or that you are not in danger of having a heart attack; or if you feel you need to stay in a situation, doing things that make you feel safer, for example, slowing down if you feel anxious when you are driving. However, the things that you do, your *behaviour*, will also influence your thoughts, feelings and physical symptoms, making the anxiety worse and worse.

Let's look at Nicky's story to see how this works.

As we saw, Nicky was sitting down to a meal with friends when she realized that she was being served chicken. Her immediate thought was, 'Oh no, I might choke again' (*cognitive symptoms*). As a result – and understandably – she started to feel extremely frightened (*emotional symptoms*). Her body started to react: her heart started racing, and she started hyperventilating – breathing very fast but feeling like she couldn't get enough air in (*physical symptoms*). Unsurprisingly, her thoughts got even worse – she thought, 'It is happening. I'm going to suffocate, I'm going to die' (*cognitive symptoms*). As result she felt even more terrified (*emotional symptoms*) and her body started to react even more strongly; she found it more and more difficult to breathe (*physical symptoms*). She was in the grip of a full-blown panic attack. She rushed out of the room into the garden to try to get more air into her lungs (*behavioural symptoms*). Eventually she started to calm down, but she was absolutely clear that she would never go out to eat again unless she knew exactly what she was going to get, and that she would never go anywhere where there might be a chance she might be given chicken (*behavioural symptoms*).

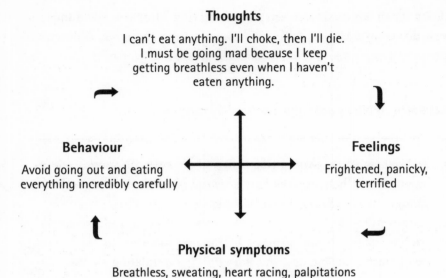

Thoughts

I can't eat anything. I'll choke, then I'll die.
I must be going mad because I keep
getting breathless even when I haven't
eaten anything.

Behaviour

Avoid going out and eating
everything incredibly carefully

Feelings

Frightened, panicky,
terrified

Physical symptoms

Breathless, sweating, heart racing, palpitations

Figure 3.1: The vicious cycle of anxiety applied to Nicky

We can see how Nicky's thoughts about the dangers of eating out had become so frightening that the next time this arose she was bound to feel even more worried from the outset, and much more likely to make catastrophic misinterpretations. She started to avoid eating out, and checked all her food very thoroughly; she never had the opportunity to learn that eating out could be safe and enjoyable.

The importance of the links

There are two important aspects to notice that come into all of the cognitive behavioural treatments for anxiety disorders.

Firstly, it is important to understand the specific cycles and connections that are operating for you. This is the reason why every evidence-based cognitive behavioural treatment for anxiety disorders described in this book starts with trying to understand your own specific cycles and connections. It uses the framework typical for that type of problem, but puts your own symptoms of anxiety into the framework. You will find that the cycles for the different anxiety disorders often overlap and are likely to include the following:

- Interpreting situations as dangerous when they're really perfectly safe (see p. 35 above).

- Being hypervigilant to threat and danger (see p. 38).

- Avoidance of difficult situations and difficult emotions (see p. 67).

- Adopting counter-productive strategies: short-term solutions that may seem to help you in the immediate moment, but actually make the problems worse in the long term.

The second area of importance to understand is that the strong connections between your thoughts, feelings and behaviour mean that *if you make a change in one area, it will influence the others*. If you can change your way of thinking, that will change your feelings and your behaviour. If you can change your behaviour, it will change your feelings and your thoughts. Instead of getting caught in a vicious cycle, you can start to turn the links between symptoms into a *virtuous* cycle, so that the problem diminishes.

In Nicky's case, for example, as her therapy progressed she learned how to recognize when she was catastrophizing and misinterpreting. She learned how to think in a more realistic way, and could say to herself, 'Don't be daft. You're not choking, you're just breathing too hard.' As a result she started to feel much more in control of her anxiety, and could start to eat a bit more confidently and check the food in front of her less frequently.

Key messages

- Thoughts, feelings, physical symptoms and behaviour are inter-connected.

- As a result, vicious cycles of anxiety develop, particularly when we misinterpret situations as threatening.

- A change in any one of these areas will lead to changes in the others.

- Consequently, vicious (negative) cycles can be turned into virtuous (positive) ones when we change how we think or act.

Tips for supporters

- In general, feelings can be described in one or more simple terms, such as 'scared' or 'upset', whereas thoughts tend to be longer and more complicated: 'If I go to the supermarket I'm going to lose control and have a panic attack and make an idiot of myself.'

- Try not to get too hung up on whether something is a thought or feeling – it is important to understand that all four categories are linked, and that it's the connections between them that can make anxiety worse or better.

- Help the person you are supporting to spot the connections and see if you can get an example from their own experience that shows how the vicious cycle works.

4 Why your anxiety persists

I have suffered from anxiety ever since I can remember. I ask myself, 'Why me? What did I do to deserve this?'

Lorraine, 49

> **Key Principle 4**: You need to understand what factors are causing your anxiety to persist.

The development of anxiety

When people have a problem, particularly a serious one like anxiety, which causes great distress and interference in their lives, they naturally want to understand why they have it. In order to help with this we will talk a little about the development of anxiety before we go on to talk about why it persists.

With any kind of psychological problem, it is helpful to think about three levels of cause.

Firstly, we can talk about *'predisposing factors'*. These are the things that might make you vulnerable to anxiety. There are two main types of predisposing factor: physical and environmental (sometimes known as nature and nurture). There seems to be some evidence that anxiety is inherited, and that some people have genes that make them vulnerable to anxiety. Anxiety does run in families, though of course this may be as much to do with the effect of growing up in that family as of the genes themselves. Being brought up in a difficult or insecure environment can make you more vulnerable to developing anxiety problems as you grow up. This may be partly because difficult early experiences lead you to develop an underlying 'mind set' of beliefs that make you prone to anxiety. Examples of such underlying beliefs may be 'the world is dangerous; people will attack me if they think I'm weak'.

Secondly, we can talk about *'precipitating factors'*. These are the triggers in your life that set the anxiety off. It might be that you were bullied at school or work, or you had a serious illness, or you had financial problems and lost your home. These life events may have a more severe effect if you are already vulnerable to anxiety. They are often called 'critical incidents' as they have played a critical role in the development of your anxiety. Critical incidents can spark off underlying beliefs and lead you to interpret things in an anxiety-related way.

Thirdly, we talk about *maintaining factors*. These are the factors that keep your anxiety going and which are the basis of the vicious cycles in Chapter 3.

To summarise these three factors, some of us may be more vulnerable to develop anxiety problems because of our genetics or our upbringing, but we can all get anxious if life gets difficult enough. Difficulties may be a single particular trigger, like Nicky's experience of choking, or they may be ongoing problems, like Stefan's pressure of work and finances. Once we get to this point, we start to interpret things in an anxious way, and we fall into the vicious cycles that keep anxiety going.

It can be very helpful for you to think about what was happening when you got anxious so that you can learn to cope with these difficult situations in a different way. Strange as it may seem, though, it is not actually necessary to know what caused your particular anxiety problem in order to treat it successfully. If you think about it, you do not need to know the cause of a broken leg in order to fix it; neither do you need to know the cause of your child's tears in order to be able to comfort them. Aspirin works for headaches even if you don't know why you've got one. Regardless of why your anxiety problem started, it is the maintaining factors that keep it going. If we can change the maintaining factors, which are essentially the vicious cycles of anxiety described above, we can change anxiety, too.

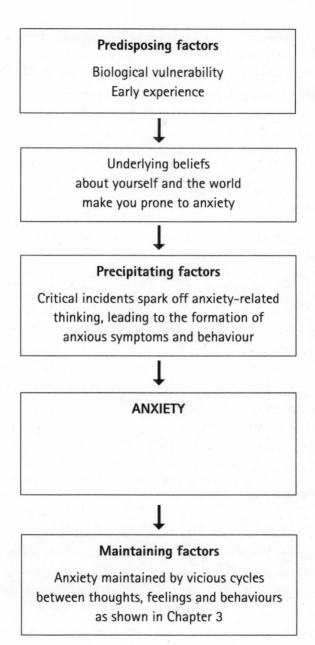

Figure 4.1: Why your anxiety persists

Anxiety persists because of vicious cycles

The CBT approaches described in this book are remarkably successful. Why? Because they focus on what is keeping your anxiety going NOW. Regardless of the earlier cause, research has repeatedly shown that working with the factors that keep anxiety going will help you to recover. Understanding the whole picture does undoubtedly help you to feel more at ease with yourself, but it does not help you overcome the problem. CBT is unique in this respect – it works with what is keeping anxiety disorder going.

In Nicky's case, understanding how her anxiety problems had started was helpful, but it was not enough to produce change. Sadly, almost no one says, 'Oh, I get it – that's why my anxiety developed and now I feel completely better.' For Nicky, the maintaining factors can be seen in the vicious cycles (see p. 46). By understanding how the vicious cycles made her anxiety persist, she and her supporter could start to make a plan for change.

Key messages

- Many people want to understand why they have the problems that they have. Sometimes it is easy to track the development of a particular person's anxiety, but sometimes it is not obvious.

- It is important not to get hung up on the development, because this is not essential to recovering from anxiety.

- Treatment is about changing the factors that maintain anxiety – the vicious cycles – that keep it going.

Tips for supporters

- If the person you are supporting wants to think about how their anxiety developed then help them by open and honest discussion.

- But don't get side-tracked for too long discussing how their anxiety started, and help them not to be concerned if they can't make sense of it at once.

- Try to keep the focus on the 'here and now' and on discovering how the vicious cycles maintain their anxiety.

5 Making changes

It's so frustrating. I know what I do is irrational but I can't help the way I think.

George, 27

Key Principle 5: In order to reduce your feelings of anxiety you need to change the factors that keep your anxiety going.

As we have seen, it is the vicious cycles that keep anxiety going. What this means is that in order to help change these into virtuous cycles we need to make changes. Unfortunately, although it may feel that this is easier said than done, it is a necessary step in recovering from all anxiety disorders.

Once you have worked out what factors are keeping your problem going, you need to work out how to change them. There are a number of ways to do this and they can be broken down into five separate steps. What these steps have in common is that they are all based on the idea that the reason you feel anxious is the way that you are interpreting events or situations. **All the different ways of trying to make changes are just ways of helping you to get the information you need to test your interpretations of events, and learn to interpret them in a different way.** In the different treatments described in Part 2 of the book, you will find that Steps 1 and 2 come first but Steps 3, 4 and 5 can be done in any order and are often carried out at the same time as each other.

Step 1. Monitoring

You will see in the self-help programmes in Part 2 that they almost all involve you keeping records and monitoring some aspects of your anxiety. While it may at first seem strange to spend time 'analysing' your anxiety, there are three important reasons for you to monitor it:

1. Self-monitoring in real-time as you go about your daily life will give you an understanding of what is keeping your anxiety going.

2. Self-monitoring is an important first step to change. It helps you gain some distance from your thoughts, step back and view them objectively, and then take some time to think about them and evaluate them rather than automatically assuming that whatever you are thinking is 'the truth'. Being able to view your thoughts objectively rather than assuming that they are reflecting the truth is important because it helps change your behaviour.

3. Getting your thoughts down helps stop them go round and round in your head. People with anxiety disorders spend a lot of time thinking, thinking, thinking, thinking (this is often called 'ruminating'). Being able to interrupt that incessant thinking, by getting some of it down, can be really helpful.

Preparing for monitoring

It may seem obvious, but you need paper to monitor. Some people buy a 'therapy' notebook so they can keep everything together. You will also need a pen, and a ruler will be useful, too. Or you could use an iPad or other tablet. Whichever you use, you should be able to carry it around with you so that you can write things down *as you go, in real time.*

Worksheet 5.1 is an example of a typical record sheet that you are likely to use when working on a particular anxiety problem, and you will see variations on this in the different chapters in Part 2. Nicky's completed record sheet shows what kind of information to insert.

Nicky's worksheet

Situation	Thoughts	Feelings	Behaviour	Context/comments
Sitting at home – phone rings	Oh, I bet it's Gordon (my brother) phoning to see if he can come round. He'll just tease me though; he thinks I'm an absolute idiot	Anxious Ashamed Angry (with Gordon for not understanding and me for being like this)	Don't answer the phone	I know this is stupid, it could have been anyone on the phone, but I just can't face talking to Gordon if he's going to take the mickey
Going to work	I can't do this; something will go wrong and I'll have another panic attack – everyone will know I've lost it	Terrified!	Make myself go, but don't really have the energy to do a good job, so I think people will think I'm no good any more	I've got to do something to get out of this, or I'll go absolutely crazy! I hope this self-help programme is going to help!

See my Mum – she says, 'Come on, let's eat a bit of chicken together. It'll be OK'	I can't do it; she knows I can't. I'll choke; there's no one here strong enough to help if I need it	Really, really scared	Mum persuaded me, so ate one small bit of chicken!	Hmm . . . OK, I didn't choke! Maybe there is no need to panic quite as much!
Wake up at night in a panic – remembering the feeling that I thought that I'd die	I can't stand this; it's so terrible. I'll never be able to put this behind me	Absolutely terrified	Got up and made tea. Couldn't go back to sleep for hours	I did eventually go back to sleep. When I woke up the next morning I tried to tell myself that it was OK – I will get over it

Worksheet 5.1. A standard record sheet

Situation	Thoughts	Feelings	Behaviour	Context/comments

Difficulties monitoring and how to overcome them

What if I'm dyslexic or I can't write very well?

If you have learning difficulties such as dyslexia, you may be put off self-monitoring. Please don't be. There is more than one way to self-monitor. For example, you can draw pictures, use Dictaphones, or you can invent something that you think will have the same effect – it doesn't matter. It is not important if you make spelling mistakes, or only write one word. What is important is that you get down what is going through your mind so that you can view your thoughts objectively.

I'm worried that writing things down will make me feel worse

It is true that writing things down initially makes some people feel worse. This can happen for a variety of reasons. Sometimes, writing things down makes people feel bad because they realize the extent to which their anxious thought is dominating their life. Sometimes it makes people feel foolish because rationally they know that their fear is excessive, but they still remain fearful. Sometimes people feel ashamed. For every person who feels this way, there is another who finds writing things down a real relief, and the beginning of change. They feel less confused. Even if it does make you feel worse, bear in mind that the feeling is likely to pass. Remember how bad your anxiety makes you feel – monitoring is a necessary first step to change.

Writing things down will make bad things more likely to happen

Some people think that writing things down will make bad outcomes more likely. Even when people *without* anxiety disorders are asked to write down that something bad will happen to their loved ones, the majority refuse to do so because of the fear that it could somehow cause the bad thing to happen. If you hold this belief very strongly, then you can do some behavioural experiments to address the belief before you start self-monitoring (see p. 62.) In the meantime, try writing down what you can, and perhaps use symbols or make up a code if you don't want to write something in particular.

What if someone sees my monitoring sheets?

It is important to keep your monitoring sheets in a safe place. If those around you are curious, especially those close to you, make an agreement that you will tell them about what is going on when you are ready, but make it clear that you would like them to give you the space at the start. Some people complete their monitoring sheets in the bathroom or somewhere else private so they can monitor in real-time without anyone asking difficult questions.

It is too difficult to monitor in real-time. Can I do it at the end of the day?

In reality, it can sometimes be too difficult to monitor in real-time without anyone noticing and there will be times when it has to be done a bit later, and occasionally at the end of the day. This is not a problem, as long as you follow the principle that what you are trying to do is work out your thoughts, feelings and behaviour *at the time* of feeling anxious. If there is too long a gap between the situation that made you feel anxious and your recording it, you will forget the immediate thoughts and intensity of emotions that characterized it. Your thoughts in retrospect are interesting, but writing things down too long after the event will also prevent you from having the opportunity to change when the anxious situation is actually taking place.

I can't face re-reading what I have written

It is no surprise that re-reading what you have written will at times be difficult and emotional. After all, anxiety disorders are emotional problems. However, it is important to do this at the start of your next session either alone, if you are using this self-book without any support, or with your supporter or therapist. Reviewing your monitoring sheets will provide you with important information about what is keeping your problem going and how to make changes.

Step 2: Fact-finding

CBT involves you receiving correct factual information. Fact-finding or 'psychoeducation' can be enormously helpful (and we hope that this book is a good start) because it provides a more balanced, unbiased perspective on what you are feeling, and helps to make sense of your problems. It should give you information about the facts rather than the feelings of the situation. It will help most if the information feels personally relevant to you.

Many of the self-help programmes in Part 2 contain some psychoeducation or factual information. Typical examples of psychoeducation for each of the anxiety disorders is given in Table 5.1.

Table 5.1 Psychoeducation for anxiety disorders

Disorder	Examples of psychoeducation
Panic disorder	The body has a fight-or-flight response and the body's reactions during an anxiety attack are appropriate ways of dealing with a real danger
OCD	Everyone has unwanted intrusive thoughts – the difference between people with OCD and others is not the content of their intrusive thoughts but their frequency, intensity and persistence

PTSD	There is no relationship between PTSD symptoms and insanity
Generalized anxiety disorder	There is no connection between worry about an event and that event occurring or not; worrying about an event does not prepare you better if the worst occurs
Social phobia	You are likely to be significantly overestimating how much other people notice you blush/shake/ stutter
Specific phobia	Spiders cannot look at you in a particular way
Health anxiety	You cannot catch HIV from a toilet seat

Step 3: Behavioural experiments

Across the anxiety disorders, behavioural experiments are used to try to gather personally relevant information to help change misinterpretations into more realistic interpretations.

What is a behavioural experiment?

A behavioural experiment is a way of gathering information to help you test out which is true – your anxious interpretation of events, or a more balanced one. It is also a way in which you can see how the way that you behave affects your anxiety. Importantly, it provides information that is relevant to *you*, and it helps what you rationally know to be true in your head to also reach your heart. When cognitive therapy was first developed, behavioural experiments were emphasized as an important way to obtain new evidence to help people change their way of thinking. Nearly forty years later, their importance is still undiminished and all the treatments for anxiety use such experiments.

Different types of experiment

There are different types of behavioural experiments, and the chapters on specific disorders will set out those that are relevant for that particular problem. We will just give a couple of examples here for illustrative purposes.

For example, one form of behavioural experiment is to carry out a survey. In OCD people may think they are bad because they have unpleasant 'intrusive' thoughts, for instance about harming people (see Chapter 11). Almost everyone has such thoughts, but the best way for someone with OCD to believe this is to find out for themselves. So the person with OCD may be asked to do a survey – to ask other people, particularly people they like and respect, whether they have unwanted intrusive thoughts about harming people. They will find out that a lot of people do have such thoughts – even good people. So the behavioural experiment – the survey – has shown them that it is normal to have such thoughts, and having them does not mean that they are 'bad'.

For another example, in panic disorder a person may fear that changes in their breathing mean that they are going to have a heart attack and die. This thought is so frightening that it makes their physical sensations worse, and the belief gets even stronger. It's hard to believe that it's your thoughts that are causing such drastic sensations! In a behavioural experiment, a therapist might try to produce a panic-like state by asking someone to breathe very heavily. This will produce normal physical changes in breathing, but the person who panics will start to interpret them by thinking they're having a heart attack and become terrified. The therapist can help the person to see that it's their *interpretation* of the symptoms which causes the anxiety – after all, it's unbelievably unlikely that you'd suffer a heart attack just at the moment the therapist asked you to breathe a bit more heavily. See Chapter 7, p. 173 for a detailed description of this process.

You can use Worksheet 5.2 to work out how to carry out a behavioural experiment. It is included here because some of the chapters in Part 2 refer to experiments and it may be useful to have such a worksheet to help you. The same worksheet can be used whether you are testing a belief related to panic disorder, OCD or any other type of anxiety problem. If you want to modify the worksheet to fit your individual problems better, you can do so.

Behavioural experiments and predictions

Before looking at the worksheet however, let's talk a bit about 'predictions'. In anxiety, when we have an anxious thought we are essentially *predicting* what is going to happen. If you are worried that your children might have an accident while they are away you are in some sense *predicting* that they will have one. If you are socially anxious and worry about going to a social event, you are *predicting* that people won't talk to you, or that they'll laugh at you. Whenever we worry there is a hidden prediction, which it can be very helpful to identify. Worksheet 5.2 asks you not just to say what your belief or worry is, but what the prediction that follows from it is. In this sense the behavioural experiment is very useful – you are going to see if your prediction comes true or not, just like a scientist testing a theory.

Worksheet 5.2. Behavioural experiment sheet

1) Thought/Belief to be tested and strength of conviction (0–100%):

2) Ideas for experiment to test the thought/belief. Circle the best one:

3) Specific predictions about what will happen and how you will record the outcome:

4) Anticipated problems and potential solutions:

5) Describe the experiment you carried out:

6) Describe what happened:

7) Re-rate your conviction in the original thought/belief (0–100%):

8) Revised thought/belief/behaviour that can be tested:

Example: Stefan's behavioural experiment worksheet

1) Thought/Belief to be tested and strength of conviction (0–100%):

(Remember that Stefan had got very upset that a shelf he put up was knotted and damaged and he felt he should have noticed beforehand.)

If I show Trevor and Nancy (my employers) the shelf they'll be furious and they'll fire me (100%).

2) Ideas for experiment to test the thought/belief. Circle the best one:

I could tell Trevor and Nancy about someone else putting up a knotted shelf and see their reaction (easier than actually showing them but it's not a direct test).

Show them the shelf and see what happens.

3) Specific predictions about what will happen and how you will record the outcome:

I think they will be very disappointed, and ask me to take it down and replace it. I think they will say they'd like to get someone else in to 'help' and that they'll tell me that their friend Mike has found someone else to do his decorating.

I will write down the outcome in my appointments book as I always carry that with me.

4) Anticipated problems and potential solutions:

I think the main problem is just that I don't want to do it – I want to avoid it, so I'll bottle out of it. But I know that if I do that, then I won't be gathering evidence about whether or not what I am frightened of actually happens.

5) Describe the experiment you carried out:

When Nancy came home I said I was worried about the shelf and wanted to show her to see what she thought of it.

6) Describe what happened:

She looked at the shelf and said, 'What? What's not right?' I had to point it out to her and she looked at me as though I was mad. She said, 'It's a shelf. It's fine. When are you going to get on to the bathroom? Mike keeps nagging me to let you finish here as he wants you.'

> ### 7) Re-rate your conviction in the original thought/belief (0-100%):
>
> *Well, I don't know about Trevor's reaction. He is more picky than Nancy but she did think it wasn't a big deal (and made that very obvious) so I guess it's down to 50%. It would be zero if Trevor had the same reaction as Nancy.*
>
> ### 8) Revised thought/belief/behaviour that can be tested:
>
> *I care more about my work being perfect than other people and they don't notice the flaws in the way that I do.*

Behavioural experiments and avoidance

Experiments can also be used to help people reduce their avoidance behaviour, since avoidance in many cases keeps the anxiety disorder going. Reducing avoidance is an important part of therapy for a number of reasons. Firstly, we know that although when you avoid things you might get an immediate sense of relief, your anxiety usually *gets worse in the long term*. It is as if by choosing to avoid a situation you are giving yourself the message: 'You were right to avoid that, it would have been awful.' Avoidance means that you never get the chance to check whether the bad things you are afraid of might happen – or not. Avoidance also means that your life becomes restricted – you avoid more and more and don't live your life in the way that you'd like to. At some point you might also start to avoid your own emotions (for example by getting drunk). One of the reasons that avoidance keeps anxiety going is that it can prevent you from obtaining the information that might change how you interpret events. In many cases, avoidance is a real problem in its own right because it is so restrictive. Many people with anxiety disorders are unable to have friends round to their houses, cannot walk freely about town, cannot shop to buy objects that they wish to buy and essentially become prisoners. Why? Because they're avoiding situations that make them anxious. Reducing avoidance is part of treatment and so behavioural experiments that help the person with anxiety to find out what happens if they stop avoiding certain situations are used in the treatment of all anxiety problems. For some anxiety problems, such as specific phobias, 'exposure' is used; this exposes the anxious person to a feared situation so that they can get used to it; 'hierarchies' are built in which they start by getting used to a situation that provokes some anxiety, but is manageable, and they slowly build up towards putting themself in situations that at the start of treatment would have been unthinkable for them to endure.

Behavioural experiments to reduce other counter-productive behaviour

There are some other behaviours that might also be considered unhelpful or counter-productive if you are anxious. For example, if you have social phobia, avoiding eye contact is highly likely to be counter-productive as someone who doesn't make eye contact is often perceived as odd or unfriendly. A behavioural experiment targeting this counter-productive behaviour would set out to discover what happened (in terms of emotions, behaviour and the situation) when eye-contact was *not* avoided.

One of the most common fears among those with an anxiety problem is the fear that the anxiety problem is so severe that it will make the person 'go mad'. This commonly links to beliefs about losing control, or that having the anxiety disorder is a sign of madness. To challenge such beliefs, a common behavioural experiment would be to plan for the person to become very anxious, as anxious as humanly possible, and see if they become 'mad'. A discussion would immediately follow as to what 'madness' might look like – babbling, incoherence, loss of movement might all be part of the person's idea of going mad. In reality, what happens when a person becomes very anxious is that . . . they become very anxious! They do not babble, lose movement or become incoherent. So, doing a behavioural experiment like this provides the anxious person with important and valuable information that high levels of anxiety do not cause madness. Such an experiment would then be repeated in a range of situations so that more and more evidence is gathered that anxiety does not cause madness, which helps to reassure the person that the results of the first behavioural experiment were not a one-off. As you are reading this, you may be feeling more reassured, having been given the information that anxiety does not cause madness but you might still be a bit afraid that you may be an exception to this rule. Many of the chapters that follow include information on behavioural experiments and you will need to conduct such experiments in order to gather personally relevant information about your beliefs and interpretations of events.

Step 4: Changing habits of anxious attention

Attention to threat

We briefly discussed the importance of cognitive biases earlier (p. 38). If something is important to you, you are more likely to pay close attention to it. This is natural and usually helpful. It is why our loved ones absorb so much of our attention, and why we notice (sometimes) if our friends appear sad or disheartened. It is because people with anxiety disorders are so preoccupied with the possibility of something bad happening, they pay much closer attention to possible threats than other people. Sadly, this has an unfortunate consequence, since paying attention to threat means that you see more and more potential threats and become more and more anxious.

The nature of a specific threat and the type of object or situation that capture attention will vary depending on the anxiety problem. Some examples of specific threats are shown in Table 5.2. This table is the same as Table 2.1 but with additional columns showing how paying attention to the perceived threat can make things worse.

Table 5.2: Examples of specific threats

Disorder	Situation	Typical mis-interpretation	Attention	Consequences
Panic disorder	Body sensations	These sensations signal immediate catastrophe (death, madness, another panic attack)	More attention is paid to body sensations	Normal fluctuations in body sensations are observed and interpreted as threatening
OCD	Unwanted intrusive thoughts	These thoughts mean I am mad, bad, dangerous	More attention is paid to thoughts	Person believes even more that they must be going mad or are bad/ dangerous as they have no explanation for why they have such thoughts
PTSD	Symptoms of PTSD	These symptoms mean I am mad; I will never recover from the trauma	More attention is paid to symptoms of PTSD	The belief that the person will never recover is reinforced
Generalized anxiety disorder	Worrying	Worrying is a sign that I am a kind, caring person; if you worry about it, it won't happen	More attention is paid to potentially worrying situations	Worrying is increased

Social phobia	Social event	I am socially incompetent; everyone is going to judge me negatively; I will become anxious and humiliated	More attention is paid to one's social performance	There is less noticing of others in social situations which can lead to a worse social performance
Specific phobia	Encounter with a feared object or animal	I am in danger	Notice feared objects or animals more	Fear increases and can spread to similar objects or animals
Health anxiety	Some bodily abnormality	This is a sign my health is at serious risk; I could have a fatal and undetected disease	Notice more bodily lumps, bumps and freckles	Increases the worry that these are signs that something is wrong with health

When you have an anxiety problem, your attention to specific threats becomes part of the problem and traps you in a vicious cycle, and your belief that threat and danger is all around you is reinforced.

Reducing your attention to perceived threats

Almost all the different CBT approaches to anxiety include ways of helping people to stop paying attention to threat. In panic disorder, for example, another behavioural experiment might be conducted that asks someone with panic disorder to focus on their bodily sensations and to then switch to focusing their attention on something interesting in the external environment. What tends to happen is that the anxious person will notice their bodily sensations more when they focus their attention on them than when they do not. This helps the person come to understand that their problem is not that there is something wrong with their body and that they are vulnerable to something terrible happening but rather that their focus of attention is the problem.

In some cases, psychoeducation is also used to help people understand that part of the problem is their increased attention to threat. To use an analogy, if you buy a particular car, you are likely to suddenly notice that lots of other people have the same car. You might even think that the number of cars has increased but accept that it is more likely that in fact you are just noticing the cars more. There are a number of specific exercises that can be done to help shift the focus of attention away from a perceived threat. The kind of exercise that you do will depend on the nature of the anxiety problem, and many of the chapters on the specific disorders will give examples.

Do you remember that Nicky's brothers had started to tease her, and that she was worried that people would think she was pathetic? In social anxiety, it is common to focus our attention on ourselves. Every time Nicky saw her brothers she would be very aware of how she was coming across. She would notice that her voice was trembly, and that she felt flushed. The more she paid attention to these signs, the more anxious she got, and the more pathetic she felt she was being. With help from her supporter, Nicky realized that this was making the situation worse. Together they decided that what Nicky should do was to concentrate her attention on other people, not herself. So when she met other people she made herself think about what they were saying and doing. Although her attention automatically went to how she was feeling, she decided that she would say 'switch' (short for switch attention) and try to go back to thinking about them. With her brothers she made this easier by getting herself to count how many spots they had, or whether they needed a shave!

Step 5: Changing your patterns of anxious interpretations

We have talked about how people pay attention to threat. What people are doing is scanning the environment to see if there is anything threatening in it. Then if there is anything that is at all uncertain, the sufferer interprets it as dangerous rather than as neutral. This means that the combination of increased attention and the interpretation leads them to think of a great many things as scary. A fundamental lesson of cognitive therapy is that *thoughts are not facts.* This cannot be overstated. All the techniques we talk about below show that our thoughts are just that: they are thoughts about the situation, not facts about it.

In thinking about anxiety, we often talk about the probability of danger – is this situation threatening or not, and if so, how bad a threat is it? There is an 'anxiety formula' that helps to show these and other relevant factors that determine how anxious you might get. The tendency to misinterpret things in an anxious way is relevant to all these four factors.

1. The 'Anxiety Formula'

$$\text{ANXIETY} = \frac{\text{PROBABILITY OF HARM} \times \text{SERIOUSNESS OF HARM}}{\text{RESCUE} + \text{COPING}}$$

This formula described by Salkovskis (1996) suggests that the amount of anxiety we feel will depend on two things:

- How likely you think it is that something bad will happen (probability of harm); multiplied by

- How bad it will be (seriousness of harm).

If we think that something is very likely to happen, and that it will be very bad, we are likely to feel very anxious indeed. Even if this is so, then there are situations, people or coping mechanisms that can make it better:

- Is there anyone around who would help us, and prevent the harm (rescue)? and

- Are there things that we ourselves can do to cope (coping)?

When we are anxious, we tend to overestimate the **probability** of harm (i.e. think it is very likely something bad will happen), overestimate the **seriousness** of harm (i.e. think it will be very bad) and underestimate our ability to cope or be rescued (i.e. there's nothing that will help). As a result our anxiety levels get very high.

For example, it may be that we are overestimating the risk of going mad by having a panic attack (the risk is zero), or catching AIDS from a cash-point (the risk is zero) or a traumatic event occurring again (in this case, the risk may not be zero but is unlikely to be as high as we are estimating).

It is therefore important to make *realistic* estimates of the probability of harm, and the seriousness of harm (or danger) and of our ability to cope with such challenges. A common goal of the treatments for anxiety problems is to help people make more realistic estimates in each of these areas through fact-finding, experiments and by helping people step back and examine how realistic their thoughts and estimates are when looked at objectively.

Nicky's 'anxiety formula'

When Nicky was worrying about eating chicken, her 'anxiety formula' was as follows:

- Probability of harm: I'll eat some chicken and I'll choke – at the moment I think this is 100% likely.

- Seriousness of harm: If I do choke, then I'll suffocate and die – I think I believe this almost 100%, too, even though I didn't last time.

- Rescue: No one will be able to help me – I know it's stupid to believe this, since lots of people were there to help me last time, but I still do!

- Coping: I won't be able to cope – I think I believe this pretty strongly, too – I've been such a wimp in the past.

- Overall anxiety: Very high.

As a result of looking at each of the parts of the anxiety formula separately, Nicky could understand why she was feeling so anxious. She could also see that there were at least two items that she could think about differently. She knew that she hadn't suffocated and died when she had eaten chicken in the past, and she also knew that other people were willing to help her if needed. As a result, she was able to see that maybe the situation was not quite as bad as she had been thinking.

The anxiety formula and help

It is also important to emphasise the factors that refer to our ability to cope, and the help that is around us. When we are anxious we not only overestimate the probability and seriousness of threat; we also *underestimate* our ability to cope, and the possibility that other people will be around to help and support us. This book intends to give you ways to help you cope better, but it is also possible that you are already coping much better than you think. It might help you to think about times when you have coped with difficult situations, and remind yourself of the ways in which you did it. If you are working with a supporter who knows you well, ask them if they can remember times when you have coped. Make a note of these times and the qualities you displayed so that you can look at them and remind yourself of them when you feel you cannot cope.

It might also be worth keeping a record of what happens in your daily life – many of us do cope with difficult and complicated situations without even realizing that we're doing it. Try to tune in to your positive coping qualities and make them feel like a real part of you.

Some people with anxiety might rely too much on other people because they doubt their ability to cope alone. If you identify as someone who tends to do this, then it would be better for you to work on your faith in your own abilities. Others ignore that other people are willing to help. If this is you, then think about who is around who could help or 'rescue' you in difficult times. This might be friends or family, but it could also be more official sources of help, like the Citizens Advice Bureau (CAB), or self-help organizations such as those listed in the Appendices at the end of the book.

2. Catastrophizing

In Chapter 3 we talked about how we make a number of 'cognitive errors' in our thinking when we are anxious. A particularly important one is 'catastrophizing'. An example of catastrophizing might involve being afraid that we will be struck by lightning if there is a thunderstorm while we are out walking. (In fact, the chances of being struck by lightning are one in 500,000, and the chance of being *killed* by lightning is one in 10 million.)

You probably know all too well about 'catastrophizing'. If we are catastrophizing, we have a tendency to interpret situations as disastrous, and to expect the worst outcome rather than the most likely one.

If you find that you are catastrophizing, one way to tackle it is by using the anxiety formula on p. 73. When we catastrophize, we are saying that something bad will definitely happen, and it will be awful; that no one will help and that we can't cope by ourselves; that what happens will be disastrous.

By looking at each element of the formula separately, you can scrutinize each step of this prediction and arrive at a more balanced prediction of what is likely to happen.

3. Aversion to risk taking

Sometimes working out the probability this way is helpful to put our fears into perspective and therefore reduce our anxiety. Sometimes though, people respond by saying, 'I can't take the risk of the catastrophe occurring, even if it is 1 in 50 million and there is more chance of winning the lottery' (which is 1 in 14 million in the UK).

The problem of aversion to risk taking needs to be addressed. By 'aversion to risk taking' we mean that you might find it so frightening to take risks that you just cannot face it. Even though you might realize that it would be better in the long run to do something, you cannot bring yourself to do it. So you need to learn to take risks!

There are different ways of addressing the aversion to taking risks. The best is to do a 'risk taking' behavioural experiment that involves a small risk to see if this turns out as bad as predicted.

Think about risks that you take every day. There is a 1 in 43,500 chance of dying in a workplace accident, a 1 in 2,300,000 chance of dying falling off a ladder, a 1 in 2,000,000 chance of dying after falling out of bed, and a 1 in 8,000 chance of being killed in a road accident. Nevertheless, we do still go to work, climb a ladder to change a lightbulb, go to bed, and travel in cars. Why? The reason is that the quality of our life if we avoided all risks would be extremely poor. We decide to take the risks because otherwise we would become housebound (and anyway, there are dangers in the home, too).

It is impossible to guarantee 100 per cent that you and your loved ones will always be safe. However, it is easy to guarantee that you will continue to have a problem with anxiety if you live your entire life trying to reduce all risks in order to protect yourself and loved ones from harm. You may want to consider that the best way to protect your children is to overcome your anxiety problem so that you and they together can make informed decisions about risk and harm, in order to protect yourselves properly as you all go about your daily lives.

4. Tackling anxious interpretations directly

Remember that we said earlier that thoughts are not facts. They are our interpretations of events, not the only way to see things. One way we can learn to tackle anxious interpretations is to subject them to a process of looking for evidence for and against them. Do you remember the idea of a scientist looking for evidence? When you are trying to think whether your anxious interpretations are real or not, try to work through the following questions:

- What exactly is my negative thought?

- What is the evidence in favour of this interpretation?

- What is the evidence against it?

- What would I say to a friend who said they were thinking something like that? Would I agree or would I be able to put a different view forward?

- What would a friend say to me if I asked them how they saw it?

- What is the alternative view?

- If I were a scientist, which theory would convince me more? The theory that it *is* true or the theory *I am worried* it is true?

- If I were in a court of law, would I have convinced the jury that the anxious view is the right one?

Using these questions, use worksheet 5.3 to write out your thoughts, and an alternative view when you have questioned them.

Worksheet 5.3. Taking a new perspective

Situation	Feelings	Thoughts	Alternative view after working through questions above	Feelings now
Where I am, what I'm doing	E.g. frightened, scared etc. How bad is it (0–10)?	Exactly what is going through my mind?	What is a different way of thinking about the situation?	E.g. frightened, scared. Re-rate how bad it is (0–10).

Remember in Chapter 3 we described Stefan's worry about the shelf that he'd put up in his client's house? Here is how Stefan filled in the form.

Stefan's new perspective worksheet

Situation	Feelings	Thoughts	Alternative view after working through questions above	Feelings now
Where I am, what I'm doing.	E.g. frightened, scared etc. How bad is it (0–10)?	Exactly what is going through my mind?	What is a different way of thinking about the situation?	E.g. frightened, scared. Re-rate how bad it is (0–10).
Sitting up at night worrying about the shelf I put up today.	Very frightened, nervous, stressed. I feel sick with anxiety. 9	Trevor and Nancy (my employers) will hate it, it looks so awful. They'll ask me to leave and I won't get any more work. I'm so stupid now, I can't do anything right.	Well, Magda (my wife) told me that I'm mind-reading – I don't know what they think. I could just ask them! Even if they don't like that shelf, it doesn't mean they don't like anything that I've done – in fact I know they do like it because they've said so. They're not going to sack me because of one shelf. Anyway, I am a good craftsman even if I don't feel like one at this minute and I can always change it.	A bit better – maybe 4. I'm going to bed!

5. Working with images

Sometimes the way that we think is not in words, but in pictures or images. It might be that you are worried that your partner or child will be involved in a terrible accident on the way home. You might not say to yourself, 'They'll have a crash' – you might just see a picture in your mind of a smashed car and a shattered body. These images can cause us terrible distress and anxiety, and can be even more distressing than words or thoughts.

For instance, when Stefan was worrying about losing his job and his home he had a very strong picture of himself and his wife walking through the rain carrying their crying children – a truly upsetting image. When Nicky was worrying about choking she had an image of herself lying on the ground gasping for breath with her face turning from red to blue.

Some of the treatments described in the second half of this book involve trying to reduce these troublesome images. The most well developed of these treatments involving changing images are for post-traumatic stress disorder (PTSD) and social anxiety, but they also have a role to play in many of the other disorders.

The first step is to be aware of what the image means to you. For instance, one of the authors was talking to a friend about their marriage difficulties. The friend said that when she thought she and her husband might split up she had an image of herself sitting alone in a dressing gown in a dark room, with the curtains still pulled, and mess and dirt everywhere. She realized that the meaning of the image was that she would go to pieces if they split up, and would have no friends and be completely alone and unable to function. As soon as she realized this, then she was able to say to herself, 'OK, even if the worst comes to the worst I will be able to cope. I'll be sad, but my life will carry on, and I'll still go to work and have friends and interests. I won't look like this.' It is therefore important to be aware of your own images, and the meaning you place on them, so you don't go along with the meaning without realizing you are doing it. Once you have put the meaning into words, you can use the questions on p. 78 to help you to think differently.

Key messages

There are five steps to starting to make changes:

- Monitoring anxious thoughts, feelings and behaviour.

- Information gathering.

- Carrying out behavioural experiments.

- Changing your attention to threat.

- Changing the way you interpret things by using:

  ° the anxiety formula;

  ° dealing with catastrophizing;

  ° dealing with risk taking;

  ° tackling anxious interpretations directly;

  ° identifying anxious images.

Being able to distinguish between thoughts and facts is of fundamental importance, and will come into all the chapters in Part 2 of this book.

A range of methods is available to obtain the personally relevant information you need to change how you interpret events.

Experiment with the methods and see which works best for you.

Tips for supporters

- Make sure that you understand the difference between thoughts and interpretations and facts.

- Encourage the person you're supporting to work through techniques in a detailed and thorough way.

- Let them know that at first it is very difficult to think of different ways to view the situation – this is where you come in! As time goes on the process will become easier, and they should be able to think of more and more for themselves.

Closing comments

We have now reached the end of Part 1.

We have outlined the key principles of CBT, which have guided all the specific interventions that will be discussed in Part 2. We introduced some case studies to demonstrate how some of these common principles work in practice and discussed some common treatment techniques. You should now have more of an idea of the type of anxiety problem you've been experiencing and which chapter(s) will be the most helpful to work through Part 2.

In Part 3 we will come back to common issues in anxiety. We talk about some of the other things, such as your mood and your relationships that play an important part in anxiety. We show what happened to Nicky and Stefan, and how they managed to overcome their anxiety and plan for the future.

Part 2

CBT for
specific anxiety disorders

6 Specific phobias

Roz Shafran and Lars–Göran Öst

Overview

Most people know the meaning of the word 'phobia' – an intense fear that is excessive for the situation, which causes avoidance and interferes with your daily life. If you think you might have a phobia or you know that you definitely have this problem, then working your way through this chapter should help you to better understand why you have your phobia, what keeps it going, and how to overcome it.

After many years of treating people with specific phobias, starting in the mid 1970s, Lars wondered what would happen if he used a session that was long enough to get rid of all someone's anxiety in one extended session of three hours rather than weekly for an hour. The first evaluation of the treatment for twenty patients found that 65 per cent were completely recovered and another 25 per cent much improved, and that 90 per cent showed a good long-term outcome. Other research has subsequently produced the same findings. The treatment that you will read about here is based on the extended treatment session that shows such good outcomes. It therefore has an extremely good chance of helping you get over your phobia so that you can go on to lead a fulfilled and unrestricted life.

What is a specific phobia?

People with a specific phobia have a marked and persistent fear that is excessive or unreasonable. This fear is brought on by the presence or anticipation of a specific object or situation (e.g. flying, heights, animals, having an injection, seeing blood). When confronted by the object/situation, an immediate anxiety response is provoked that can be like a panic attack (see Chapter 7). In children, anxiety may be expressed by crying, tantrums, freezing or clinging. If you have this fear, you will recognize that when you are in a calm situation, away from the object or feared place, you can see that the fear is excessive or unreasonable, but it is hard to appreciate this at the time. People with phobias tend to avoid the objects and situations of which they have a phobia, or they endure them with intense anxiety or distress. For it to be the kind of phobia that warrants a treatment programme like the one described in this chapter, the avoidance, anxious anticipation, or distress felt in the feared situation(s) interferes significantly with your normal routine, work, studying or socializing, and you will be upset about having the phobia. You will probably have had this phobia for many months or years.

Surriane's story

Surriane was a 26-year-old woman who had a lifelong fear of spiders. She could not recall a specific incident that triggered this fear, but she did remember hating Halloween and all the cobwebs and spiders that were around at that time. She also recalled seeing an enormous spider in the bath when she was about eight that she described as 'menacing'. Her brother and parents didn't like spiders but they were not petrified of them in the way that she was. She recalled with great detail that she begged her mother to kill the spider but her mother refused, put it in a glass, and took it outside. She didn't see her mother do this but began to worry soon after that, in fact, the spider had jumped out of the jar and was lurking somewhere in the house. Since then she always looks out for spiders when she goes to a new place, shakes out her duvet cover, sheets and pillowcases, and only showers rather than bathes in case a spider comes up the plughole into the bath, even though rationally she knows this to be an impossibility if the plug is in place. She came for treatment because she was embarrassed by her fear of spiders with her new partner, and because she was refusing to let him watch the TV channel with *I'm a Celebrity . . . Get Me Out*

---

of Here! on it in case there was an trailer for it that had a spider crawling across the screen.

Do you have a phobia?

The questions below are taken from the national 'Improving Access to Psychological Therapies' assessment measures – www.iapt.nhs.uk. These are measures widely used by the UK National Health Service in their treatment of anxiety and depression.

All three questions are marked on a scale 0–8 depending on how much you avoid the situation described. Choose a number from the scale below, then record the number in the box opposite the situation. 0 = Would not avoid it, 2 = Slightly avoid it, 4 = Definitely avoid it, 6 = Markedly avoid it, 8 = Always avoid it. In-between answers (1, 3, 5, 7 are allowed).	
1. Social situations because of a fear of being embarrassed or making a fool of myself	
2. Certain situations because of a fear of having a panic attack or other distressing symptoms (such as loss of bladder control, vomiting or dizziness)	
3. Certain situations because of a fear of particular objects or activities (such as animals, heights, seeing blood, being in confined spaces, driving or flying)	

Reproduced with kind permission from Department of Health, *IAPT Data Handbook, 2010*, www.iapt.nhs.uk/silo/files/iapt-data-handbook-appendices-v2.pdf (p. 24).

If you scored 4 or above on question 1, then Chapter 9 on social phobia is probably best for you; if you scored above 4 on question 2, then look at Chapter 7 on panic disorder. If you scored 4 or above on the third question, then the programme described in this chapter is appropriate for you. A longer, more detailed measure to assess the severity of your phobia is given at the end of the chapter. If you have decided that you do indeed have a phobia that needs treatment, you need to try to understand what is keeping your phobia going. Why is it so persistent?

Step 1: Understanding what keeps your phobia going

In Part 1, we talked about how cognitive behaviour therapy focuses on what is keeping the problem going. Indeed, all effective cognitive behavioural treatments are based on a model that specifies how the disorder in question is maintained once it has started. In each chapter in Part 2 of this book you will see such models. People with specific phobias see particular objects/situations as potentially harmful and, unsurprisingly, this leads them to avoid the objects or situations. When you fail to avoid your feared object (such as a snake, spider, injection), then you're likely to have thoughts of something terrible happening, such as being attacked by the spider, fainting, going crazy and losing control, being sick, and so on. You are also likely to have feelings in your body that are associated with your thoughts of danger, consistent with the fight-or-flight response (see pp. 5–6). Your heart may race, you may get butterflies in your stomach, you may feel sick, your throat may tighten, and you may feel dizzy. These feelings in your body and your thoughts can affect each other, with some people thinking that the feelings in their body show that the thing they are worried about (going crazy, being attacked, fainting etc.) will come true. The result of this is that the feelings in your body and your thoughts about danger escalate even further.

It is understandable, given the thoughts of danger and the strong physical sensations, that you'd try to leave the situation causing the problem.

This is a natural reaction. If you are unable to leave the situation, then you're likely to try to do something in order to reduce the danger and prevent the disaster from occurring. Such 'safety behaviour' is described in Part 1 and occurs with all anxiety disorders.

After leaving the situation or using 'safety behaviour', the short-term good news is that the dangerous event doesn't occur (e.g., the spider doesn't attack you; you don't go crazy) and the strong feelings in your body begin to fade away. The longer-term bad news is that you do not learn that there is little (if any) danger in the situation: you continue to have your phobia. After leaving the situation, when your anxiety has faded, you are likely to conclude that it was *only* by escaping or carrying out the safety behaviour that you *prevented the danger* from occurring. Your original belief about the dangerousness of the object/ situation is confirmed and the phobia remains unchanged. In cognitive behaviour therapy you will be helped to find out that this conclusion is incorrect and the reason that the dangerous event did not occur is that there was in fact minimal danger – or even no danger – in the first place.

Our understanding about what keeps phobias going can be summed up as follows:

> Everyone has some fears about particular situations, but if you have a phobia you will almost certainly think that your feared object/situation is more dangerous than it really is. You will feel anxiety because of this perceived danger. By leaving the situation or engaging in certain behaviours to prevent the danger from occurring, your original belief about the danger of the particular feared object/situation remains unchanged and you continue to have a phobia.

Figure 6.1 illustrates this.

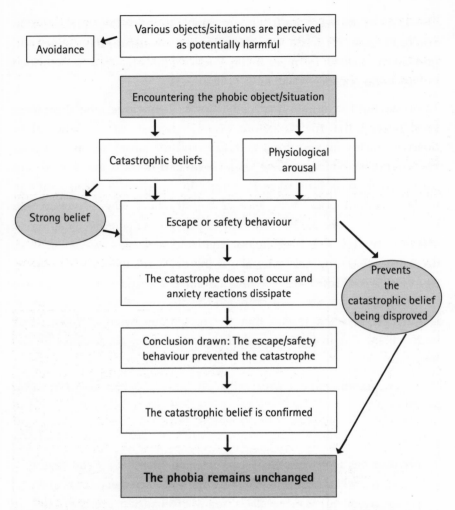

Figure 6.1: How specific phobias are maintained. Reproduced with kind permission from *Intensive One-Session Treatment of Specific Phobias*, T. Davis, T. Ollendick and L-G. Öst (eds), New York, Springer 2012, (Chapter 4).

The figure above indicates that you should focus your effort to change on obtaining new information that can correct the false beliefs about danger and about what would happen if you came face to face with the object of your phobia. By facing your fear situation and staying in the situation until anxiety fades, your belief in the dangerousness of the object/situation will diminish. This is because you are getting new information that the object or situation is much less dangerous than you first thought. When you do not avoid the phobic object/situation, have no anxiety symptoms in your body, and no longer believe that the object/situation is dangerous, then you have recovered.

Helping you change

What needs to happen for you to change

Simply knowing that avoidance keeps your phobia going and that you need to reduce avoidance is not enough to get better.

You need to find out what kinds of beliefs about danger you have about the phobic object or situation you fear. This is illustrated below in a conversation between Surriane and her therapist.

Spiderphobia

Therapist: Imagine that you walk into a room and you see a spider, about 1 inch in size, on the wall. What thoughts run through your mind then?

Surriane: I have to run out of the room and call for help.

T: OK, now imagine that you can't leave the room, for some reason.

S: I'd cry loudly so that someone could come and rescue me.

T: Imagine that you're alone in the house, and there's nobody who can hear you.

S: I'd panic and then freeze and just stare at the spider.

T: What will happen then?

S: I don't know. I can't think about it. I feel panicky just talking about this.

T: Please bear with me and continue to imagine that you're in this room with the spider, and you can't leave. What do you fear will happen?

S: I don't know because I've always been able to run or get help.

T: I fully understand that this is unpleasant to think about, but close your eyes and imagine that you're in the same room as the spider. What's the worst that you fantasize will happen?

S: The spider will crawl up on my body, and I won't be able to brush it off because I'm petrified by fear.

T: What will happen then?

S: It will crawl underneath my clothes and that would be the end.

T: How do you mean, the end?

S: I would die.

T: How would you die?

S: I would get a heart attack from the strong panic and die; because the heart can't stand the palpitations.

S: OK, let me summarize what we have arrived at with this thought experiment. The worst consequence that you believe may happen if you encounter a spider is that you would die because of a heart attack. Is that correct?

S: Yes, I suppose so, but I've never dared to think it through like this before.

T: Now I want you to rate, on a scale from 0–100 per cent, how strongly you would believe that this would happen if you were in that situation, if you encountered a spider in a room and could not leave the room, that you would die of a heart attack.

S: I'm not sure, but I guess it is high, about 90 per cent.

T: And when you sit here and think rationally about it?

S: It is lower, say 40 per cent.

Another example is given below for Pete, 48, who suffered from claustrophobia.

Claustrophobia

Therapist: What do you think will *happen* if you go in a lift?

Pete: The lift could get stuck between two floors.

T: What would happen with you then?

P: I'd have a really bad panic attack.

T: What would happen then?

P: After a while the lift would run out of air.

T: What would happen then?

P: I would suffocate to death and definitely embarrass myself in front of anyone else in the lift.

T: OK. Imagine the situation that you are in a lift and it gets stuck. How certain (0–100 per cent) would you be *when in the situation* that it will lead to you suffocating or embarrassing yourself?

P: Completely certain.

T: 100 per cent?

P: No, say 99 per cent then.

T: And now *when you are sitting here* talking rationally to me?

P: 95 per cent for dying; 100 per cent for embarrassing myself completely.

Working out your beliefs and assessing their strength

Ask yourself the following questions to work out your own beliefs.

1. What do you think will happen if you confront your phobic object/ situation and cannot leave?

2. And then what do you think would happen?

3. What is the worst thing that would happen?

4. Imagine you are in the situation where you confront your phobic object/situation and cannot leave. How certain would you be *when in the situation* that it will lead to the worst thing happening?

5. And now, when you are sitting here reading this book, how certain are you that it would lead to the worst thing happening?

Working out your safety behaviour

Once you have worked out your belief about the danger, ask yourself: 'When I am in contact with the object/situation I fear and have this belief, do I do anything to prevent the danger from happening?' Maybe you cannot remember using any safety behaviours, but when you start to make changes and face your fear it will usually be obvious what you do. When you identify your safety behaviours you will need to let them go in order to see whether the danger occurs or not. This is easier said than done, but is necessary in order to change your belief, and some of the information about behaviour experiments in Part 1 should help you to find the courage to do this.

Key message

To help yourself change you need to work out what specific beliefs about danger are keeping your problem going, along with whether you are using safety behaviour that may be keeping those beliefs strong.

Tips for supporters

- Help the person you are supporting think of times when they had a specific belief about some danger but then found out that their belief was not correct and the situation was less 'dangerous' than they first thought. For example, a time when they were convinced they had upset someone and they hadn't; a time when they had done some work and thought it wasn't very good but it was – anything will do! Discuss together how they found out their belief was wrong, and what would have happened if they had not had the opportunity to test it.

- It can also be valuable to 'normalize' your friend's phobic behaviour by saying something like: 'Since you believe so strongly in the danger it is logical to want to avoid or escape the phobic situation. But this prevents you from obtaining new information that can correct your false belief, and your phobia remains unchanged!'

- It may even help to tell your friend that if you believed, for example, that there is a 90 per cent chance that you would get run over by a car and die when crossing a busy street at a pedestrian crossing while the WALK sign is lit, it would be rational to avoid this. Instead you would walk a long distance to find a bridge across or a tunnel underneath the street.

Treatment overview

Figure 6.1 on p. 92 illustrated that escape, avoidance and other safety behaviour keep your belief going.

The aim of the treatment is for you to face your fears of the particular objects / situations in *a controlled way,* thus enabling you to realize that the consequences you fear do not actually occur. The treatment in this chapter should be completed *in a single three-hour session* and should be seen as a *start*: you must continue to face your phobic situations in everyday life after you have gone through the treatment described in this chapter. A phobia of twenty–thirty years' duration will not completely vanish after only one three-hour session. However, the single, extended session will enable you to continue on your own with facing your fears: by following a voluntary 'keeping it up' programme that we will describe at the end so that, within a few months, any remaining phobic symptoms and responses will disappear.

Starting treatment

Discovering what is keeping your phobia going

Having asked yourself the questions on pp. 95–6 to work out your own beliefs and any safety behaviour you might be using, fill in the diagram in Figure 6.2 (p. 99) to get a picture of what is keeping your phobia going. If you find this difficult, find a supporter to help you.

Obtaining the information about anxiety that you need

A picture of what happens when you encounter a phobic object/situation is shown in Figure 6.3. This shows two important things. Firstly, that when you encounter the phobic object/situation, your anxiety level will increase rapidly because you fear you are in danger. Once you leave the situation your anxiety quickly fades. Secondly, it shows that you are likely to think that your anxiety will increase catastrophically and may itself lead to danger; whereas an alternative prediction (and one we would make) is that your anxiety will level out and then gradually decrease *while you continue to face your fears*. It is important to be clear about what 100 on the y-axis means: it is the highest degree of anxiety that you have ever experienced in the phobic situation before the treatment starts. It is worth replotting your anxiety at the end of treatment so you can see the changes you have made and if the level of anxiety you experience in those particular situations has come down at all.

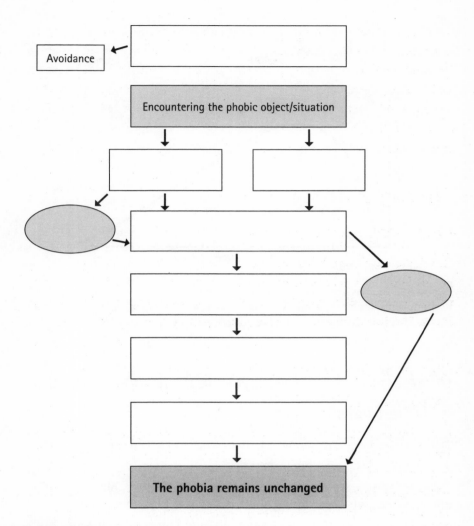

Avoidance

Encountering the phobic object/situation

The phobia remains unchanged

Figure 6.2: Discovering what maintains your phobia

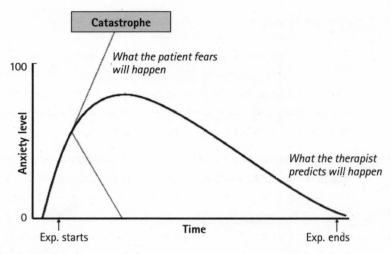

Figure 6.3: The anxiety curve
Reproduced with kind permission from *Intensive One-Session Treatment of Specific Phobias*, T. Davis, T. Ollendick and L-G. Öst, New York, Springer, 2012 (Chapter 4).

Differences between facing your fears during treatment and in natural situations

There are important differences between natural encounters with phobic objects/situations and being exposed to your fears during treatment. First, in natural situations the exposure is unplanned, ungraded, and uncontrolled, whereas during the treatment it is planned, graded and controlled. Second, in natural situations the exposure is usually brief, whereas in treatment it is prolonged (up to three hours). This time difference means that there is ample opportunity to test the two predictions about what will happen to you and your anxiety, and find out which one is correct. Finally, in natural situations you are often alone, whereas when you are doing the treatment, even in a self-help format, it is a good idea to have a supporter available to help you deal with your phobic reactions. A supporter can provide the encouragement you need to keep going with the treatment, even if you feel anxious.

Tips for supporters

- At the beginning of treatment, emphasize how you are there to support your friend and that you will do your utmost to help them in carrying out the treatment, and achieving a good result. Acknowledge that this kind of therapy is hard work and emphasize that you will both fulfil your part in the team-work.

- Many people fear that some kind of 'shock treatment' may be used, e.g. that you might suddenly take out a spider and throw it in your friend's lap. It is important to inform them that you will never do anything unplanned, but that, instead, you will work together with your friend to decide what will happen, you will demonstrate it, and finally will get their permission to do it. Although you will work together to find the right number of steps in the exposure, it is always the person with the phobia who has the final word on whether he/she will carry it out.

Troubleshooting some of your concerns

Another fear that you may have is that you will be subjected to such a high level of anxiety over such a long time (three hours) that you will not be able to cope with it, mentally or physically. You may believe, for example, that you will suffer a heart attack and die from anxiety. Here it is important that you think back on the most anxiety-arousing situation you have ever experienced in relation to your phobia (call this 100%). You can be assured that even if this session exposes you to much more contact with your feared object than you ever have experienced in natural situations, you will not 'break your personal record' of anxiety in the phobic situation. This is because the planned, gradual and controlled way the exposure is carried out means that your anxiety will never be higher than you have experienced in unexpected natural encounters. This information is comforting, because it means you have survived your most anxiety-arousing situation. Many people believe that a high level of anxiety is necessary to help you overcome your fear. This is not the case. You can become fear-free even if your anxiety does not rise above 40–50 out of 100, as long as you have not been engaging in avoidance and you have obtained new knowledge to help you correct your erroneous beliefs about the phobic object.

The one-session treatment

When this treatment is used for people with animal phobia, it consists of a combination of facing your fear in real-life and in demonstrations from a supporter, whereas other specific phobias do not require such demonstrations. If you do not have a supporter, you can still make significant progress on your own.

Facing your fear. The purpose of exposure is to help you change your beliefs about the danger relating to the phobic object/situation or resultant anxiety that you have learned from the cognitive-behavioural model on p. 92, Figure 6.1. The exposure is set up as a series of behavioural experiments (see pp. 63–9) to evaluate your beliefs about danger; such behavioural experiments are highly specific and not simply 'facing your fear' in the general sense. Carrying out a specific exposure (behavioural experiment) can help you to achieve your goal of changing your beliefs about the danger you believe you face in a much shorter timeframe than traditional exposure programmes. The general principles for these behavioural experiments are as follows:

- You make a commitment to remain in the exposure situation until your anxiety fades away (it will, we promise – but you have to find out for yourself!).

- You agree to try to approach your feared object/situation as much as possible, and remain in contact with it until your anxiety has decreased.

- You will not leave the 'therapy session' (i.e., working your way through this chapter) until the level of your anxiety has been reduced by at least 50 per cent, and preferably completely vanished.

> ## Tip for supporters
>
> It may be helpful to demonstrate how to behave with the phobic object/situation. At this step it is important to get the person you are supporting to continuously watch what is happening, and not close their eyes or look away. After doing this for a while, you should help them to come closer to the object/situation, e.g. by first holding their hand, then their arm, and then gradually reducing your physical assistance. It may be that you have to reduce and increase the physical help a number of times before they are ready to proceed to the next step of interacting with the feared object on his/her own.

Spider phobia

The treatment for a spider phobia is described below, but should *not* be considered as the only way of doing the treatment, but instead as how it can be done. You will need to have some flexibility regarding the specific content of your own treatment and the description that follows is just an illustration of the principles of the therapy. As you will see, it helps if you have a supporter to help you overcome your phobia. Ideally you would have a supporter who is not afraid of spiders and who would be able to stay calm themselves during the treatment.

Getting prepared

Ask your supporter to prepare for the treatment by catching three or four spiders in increasing sizes, from 0.5 to 3 cm and placing each in a separate glass jar with a lid on it. Have ready a glass and a postcard. The spiders should be the kind that you will encounter in natural situations where you live.

The first step

During the entire treatment you should keep the spider you are working with in a large plastic bowl (50 X 30 X 15 cm) to keep it from falling on to the floor.

The first step is for you to try to catch the smallest spider with a glass and a piece of paper (e.g. a postcard) and throw it out of the house, which is the goal for natural – in other words, non-therapy – situations. What are you thinking right now? 'AAAAHHH! I CAN'T DO THAT!'? Trust us: you can and you will. The 90 per cent of people who went on to make significant improvements all thought the same thing. So, ready to start?

You can be at the opposite end of the room to your supporter if you like, but you should be able to see what they do. Your supporter should put the glass upside down over the spider in the bowl,

and slide the postcard under it. The postcard functions as a 'lid' and by putting one's fingers under the postcard the glass can be turned upright and the postcard removed carefully in case the spider has spun a thread on the card. After you have watched your supporter do this from a distance, try approaching and watch your supporter doing it again. Then it is your turn to do the same thing, catching the spider with the glass and the postcard. After you have done this three or four times, you should hold the glass in the palm of your dominant hand and close to your body. Figure 6.4 illustrates this process. At this point you will carry out a brief role play to help you to look closely at the spider. The role play consists of you describing what you are looking at in the glass as if you were describing it to a blind person. For example, 'The spider has eight legs, two eyes, and it is dark brown.' Try not to use any judgemental words like 'disgusting'. This exercise usually leads to a marked reduction in anxiety over time.

Figure 6.4: Illustration of treatment of spider phobia

The second step

The next step involves touching the spider. Before starting this step you should ask yourself what you believe will happen if you put your hand in the bowl. Almost 100 per cent of people say that the spider will crawl up on their hands, up their arm and underneath their clothes. This prediction can be tested by your supporter putting his/her hand in the bowl, then touching the spider from behind with their finger. What will happen, much to your surprise we are sure, is that the spider usually runs away. By repeating this ten times you will realize that the spider gets tired quickly and runs gradually shorter distances. The same procedure is then repeated from the left side, from the right side, and from the spider's head. You will soon realise that the spider does not crawl up on your supporter's finger. Next, it is your turn to touch the spider in the same way, which usually involves your supporter helping you. By doing this for long enough, your assumption that the spider will react differently towards you for some reason (perhaps because it 'senses' your fear), will change.

The third step

The third step involves letting the spider walk on your hands. If you are just reading the first two steps, rather than actually doing them, you may think that this is impossible. However, if you have actually done the first two steps, you will be able to realize this is an achievable goal. Honest! Your supporter should first of all take the spider on his/her hands, letting it walk from one hand to the other. Then you, with your supporter's help, should put your index finger on your supporter's hand so that the spider can walk across your finger and back on to your supporter's hand. This is repeated a number of times, until the spider is gradually allowed to walk on all your fingers, on the whole hand, and across to your other hand. Gradually your supporter withdraws their physical support, letting you manage on your own, just following their guidance. During this step the goal is to have the spider walk up to your elbow (on both arms), allowing you to realize that you can move your hands faster than the spider can run and that you can prevent it from crawling underneath your clothes.

Throughout this three-hour session you are learning that you can have indirect control over the spider by gradually being more accurate in predicting what the spider is going to do. You will learn that the spider isn't going to turn 180 degrees and suddenly run in the opposite direction. Basically, it will crawl in the direction that its head is pointing.

The fourth step

If you are skim reading and read this before you have started, it will seem extreme. Don't let this put you off now – once you have made a start these steps will seem much less extreme and more manageable. And remember that this is your therapy and you are in control. If you decide you don't want to go this far then it is up to you.

The fourth step involves having the spider walk on your body. You can start putting it on your trousers (at knee level) and 'guide' it as it crawls up towards your waist. When this has been done a number of times, and your anxiety has been reduced, the spider can be put on your shirt at waist level and have it crawl up to your neck. Naturally, this has to be repeated until you notice a marked reduction in your anxiety. As with the other other steps, it is best if your supporter does this first.

The above four steps should then be repeated with another two or three spiders of gradually increasing size, the largest being about 3 cm (including legs). When you have accomplished this, we would encourage you to have the two largest spiders walking on your hands simultaneously. This step is, of course, more difficult, but by being relaxed in your arms and hands you should be able to control the spiders.

'Over-learning'

If you are really enthusiastic and the above session has gone extremely well, you may want to go through 'over-learning', which probably is not necessary in order to obtain a good result. This means first having the largest spider put in your hair, while your supporter is standing behind you to watch the spider and prevent it from crawling underneath the neckband of your shirt. You may think, 'You must be joking!' but by the time you have done the previous steps, this will seem more manageable. During this step you should indicate exactly where you think the spider is by pointing with your index finger. It is common for people to be wrong because they cannot really feel the spider. The final step is to have the spider put on your cheek. You should hold one hand over your neckband to prevent the spider from falling inside your shirt while your supporter cautiously puts the spider on your cheek. Your supporter needs to make sure the spider does not crawl on your ear, eye, nose or mouth. It is fine, though, for the spider to walk a bit on the cheek.

Whether you decide to use the 'over-learning' approach or not, the final goal is for you to be able to handle spiders with low or no anxiety and to no longer believe that the spider poses any danger.

What if you don't have a supporter?

We do not know how well this technique works if you are alone. Practically, there are a number of problems. How do you get the spiders in the jars in the first place and how do you read the written guidance at the same time as you are trying to implement the treatment? It is for this reason that we would encourage you to try to find a supporter who can help. It may be that if you contact your GP or share this book with your practice nurse or therapist, then he/she will be able to act as the supporter and prepare the spiders. Alternatively, you could see if there is a local self-help charity such as NoPanic in the UK (www.nopanic. org.uk) who would be able to help. We would strongly encourage you to try to find someone. If you absolutely cannot, or feel too ashamed to ask for help, then we encourage you to use the principles above of gradually facing your phobic object/situation in a controlled and graded way, focusing on getting the experience that you need to disconfirm your belief that the feared object or situation is highly dangerous.

Snake phobia

We recognize the practical difficulties of getting hold of a snake and finding someone who is happy to be a supporter. Nevertheless we have included this section on the treatment of snake phobia because it is a common problem, and we hope that therapists and those with a snake phobia will find it helpful to understand the principles and practicalities of treatment.

When the work on treating people with snake phobias began, three snakes in different sizes would be used, for example a corn snake, a python and a boa constrictor, just like using different sizes of spiders. However, because it can be difficult to obtain three different snakes for the session, we currently use only a corn snake that is about four feet long. This is what we suggest you do as well. For your treatment, you should, it goes without saying, only use a non-poisonous snake and the snake should be accustomed to being handled frequently by people. It is best to do this treatment in a fairly large room so that you can be seated in one end when your supporter brings out the snake in the other. It is vital that you have free passage to the door of the room. Knowing that you can leave the room without having to pass by the snake will reduce your anxiety and make leaving the situation less likely.

The first step

The first step of the treatment is that your supporter brings out the snake and holds it in their hands/arms at a distance from you (as far away as the room allows). Your job is to watch the snake at all times, observing its colours, pattern of the skin, movements, tongue, etc. It is also important for you to rate your anxiety at regular intervals. When there has been a reduction in your anxiety and you are ready, you should move about three feet closer. When you are as close as you can manage, you should stay there until your anxiety has decreased further. Continue with this approach until you are sitting down on a chair 2–3 feet away from the snake. After a while you can move the chair closer so that you can reach out and touch the snake. You should attempt this after you have become adjusted to having the snake at such a short distance. Since most people with snake phobia fear the mouth and the tongue of the snake (which makes sense!) you will start by touching the tail. Before you do this, predict what it will feel like touching the snake. Do you think that the snake will be slimy and warm? If so, you will be surprised when you realize that it is dry and cool, the same temperature as the room. The first touch is usually done by your supporter holding the snake's head away from you while you touch its tail. Since you will want to touch the tail only very briefly, you will have to build up to doing it for longer periods by repeating the process a number of times. When this is going well, you should try to touch the snake gradually closer and closer to its head. You should hold one hand around the snake's stomach and let it glide in the palm of your hand as it moves. Then you can hold the snake with both hands and get acquainted with its movements, and how the muscles feel. All the time it is absolutely necessary that you know your supporter is in control of the snake. It is very difficult to do this completely alone because you need to be certain that your supporter will intervene should the snake do anything unforeseen.

Since you are likely to try to avoid close contact with the snake's head it is necessary to build up to this step. First, predict what will happen if you put a finger in front of the snake's mouth. People usually believe that the snake will bite their finger. This should first be tested by the supporter putting his/her fingers in front of the snake's mouth, giving it ample opportunities to bite, while you watch closely. After this you should ask yourself whether what you had thought would happen did really happen. Then you will do the same thing with your own hand, allowing the snake to be so close that you can feel its tongue on the skin of your hand. When this has been done with reduced anxiety you should draw a final conclusion concerning the probability of being bitten by this snake. In this situation it may also be a good idea to discuss with your supporter under what circumstances a snake of that particular species would bite: to kill its prey or if it was threatened, e.g. being trodden on by accident.

The next step

The next step is to gradually let your supporter move the snake onto your lap. Your supporter should enable this to happen in whichever way is necessary to both maintain your calmness and be mindful of the snake (e.g., ensuring the supporter does not accidentally drop the animal and harm it). When you feel fairly comfortable handling the snake in your lap it is time to let it move around more, e.g. crawling around your waist, up one arm, etc.

The final step

The final step could involve having the snake around your neck, feeling its skin against your neck and cheek. If you are willing, you could even put the snake under your shirt or blouse, trying to get it to crawl around your waist. This should, of course, be viewed as an extra step and is not compulsory. Before ending your session, it is important to make sure that all the catastrophic beliefs that you had initially have been tested. If one, or more, remains untested there may be a risk of your starting to avoid snakes again.

Blood–injury phobia

In contrast to people with other phobias, who experience increased heart rate, blood pressure etc., people with blood-injury phobia experience a drop in blood pressure when confronted by their phobia, which can lead to fainting. Many people have indeed fainted when faced with blood or injury. A specific treatment method for blood phobia called *applied tension* has been developed and shown to be effective. This is an intensive five-session treatment which has two aims: teaching you to recognize the first signs of a drop in blood pressure, and teaching you to apply a rapid and effective tension technique to reverse the drop in blood pressure. In this treatment, after practising the tension technique at home you would be shown up to thirty slides of wounded people, blood donation at a blood donor centre, and of a real operation, such as lung or open-heart surgery. The treatment given in this chapter has now been reduced to a one-session format lasting a maximum time of two hours.

The first step

There is a good reason for using the method of applied tension, as it is an effective way of reversing a drop in blood pressure that occurs in phobic situations and will prevent fainting. You will first need to become aware of the first sign of your blood pressure dropping. These signs can be individual to you, but include cold sweat, an unpleasant sensation in the stomach, tunnel vision and singing in the ears. To find out which are the most common signs for you, think back in detail about the past few times you had this experience.

The tension technique

The next step involves learning the tension technique. Ideally, your supporter will be able to demonstrate this. This technique involves your tensing body muscles (arms, chest and legs) as much as possible and to keep tensing for 15–20 seconds. This is followed by releasing the tension and returning to normal, but without completely relaxing. After a thirty-second pause you tense again, and then release the tension, and so on. Continue for about thirty minutes, regularly assessing your blood pressure using a kit purchased from a pharmacy. This should show you that the tension technique leads to an increase in blood pressure, and usually heart rate.

The application training

After the tension technique, have a brief pause and then start the application training. In this phase you should find ten colour images of wounded people, mainly traffic or work-related accidents. You should be able to find these easily by searching for 'images' on your internet search engine. As in the other phobias you should initially predict what will happen when you are exposed to the pictures, and rate the strength of this belief. For example, you might think, 'I will pass out', and believe this 100 per cent. In a formal therapy session, the first picture would be projected on the screen giving a picture size of about 3–4 feet, but this may be difficult to do at home, unless you have a projector. Instead, just sit close to your computer screen and ensure that the picture is as large as you can make it. Watch the picture without screwing up or closing your eyes, or looking away. At the same time, scan your body for the first signs of a drop in blood pressure, and as soon as you notice any drop, apply the tension technique for as long as necessary. The goal is to be able to watch the picture without feeling faint. When you have achieved this, briefly pause before moving on to the next picture, using the same procedure. If you wish, after you have worked through ten pictures you can start to be exposed to other things, for example, pricking of a finger, watching fake blood in a test tube, and fake blood-stained bandages, while applying the tension technique. The reason why this treatment lasts two hours instead of three, as in other specific phobias, is that you would get sore muscles after practising tension for such a long period. At the end of the session, re-rate your belief in the feared outcome, for example, your belief that you will faint. If you have a supporter, they can encourage you to implement the tension technique and continue with the programme.

Injection phobia

The reason you are reading this chapter is that you have a phobia that is interfering with your life. In the case of injection phobia, your anxiety can actually threaten your health by preventing you from getting the medical treatment that you may need. The treatment for this phobia consists of intense prolonged exposure to three procedures that most people with injection phobia find anxiety-inducing: pricking of fingers, subcutaneous injections and venepuncture (drawing blood from a vein in the bend of the arm). The goal is to prick ten fingers, to do 10–12 subcutaneous injections and 2–4 venepunctures.

Understanding why your fear persists

As with the other phobias, it is essential to identify what you think will happen to you if you have an injection, and what you do when confronted with a situation that involves an injection. About 50 per cent of people with an injection phobia have a history of fainting in these situations, and if this has happened to you then it may be that this is what you fear will happen. In this case, you need to use the tension technique described on pp. 111–3 for blood phobia so that you are prepared to act should a drop in your blood pressure occur. On the other hand, it may be that you are mostly frightened of the pain, or of embarrassing yourself, and your thoughts revolve around how unbearable the pain of the injections will be.

Alternatively, it may be you experience a strong feeling of disgust when a needle, or any sharp object, penetrates the skin. Then again you could have a belief that is specific to you, for example that if a blood vessel has been penetrated with a needle it will not stop bleeding and that you will die of blood loss, or that the needle will break. All of these beliefs have to be taken seriously, and you and your supporter need to be creative enough to set up behavioural experiments to test how true your beliefs are in reality.

Where to do this and with whom?

It is very difficult – almost impossible – to do this without professional help. Your professional helper should be experienced in giving injections and qualified to do so. Nurses working in GP practices, or people who take blood in phlebotomy services, can be very helpful. Ideally this treatment will take place in an environment that is as different as possible from the ordinary hospital or outpatient settings in which you have had your negative experiences. Such places tend to have a certain smell that you might associate with anxiety, failure and perhaps fainting. It would therefore be better if your phobia treatment could take place in an ordinary therapy room in which you can feel comfortable. It is important that during this treatment, each small step in the procedure is demonstrated to you and that you then give your permission to your professional helper to perform the particular step. It is extremely important that you can trust them and that nothing is done without your explicit permission. This means that you have to be highly motivated. When you are 'ready', your professional helper should ask you, 'Can I prick now?' If you say 'yes', the professional helper will perform the procedure. If the response is a 'no', then you will need to work with your professional helper to become motivated. It may be that you don't say 'no', but at the same time can't say 'yes' and a non-verbal signal such as a nod of the head may work best.

The first step

As it is likely that you will find venepuncture the most difficult of these procedures, followed by subcutaneous injections, and then pricking of fingers, the first phase will involve you having your fingers pricked. Start by predicting (and rating your belief in your prediction) what will happen if you prick your finger. Your professional helper will demonstrate the lancet and how it works, the grip he/she would want to take of your fingertip, etc. If you are very fearful of the pain you might put a plaster on your fingertip before pricking it, which you may perceive as less painful. When your first fingertip has been pricked, you should rate how anxious you felt and the pain you experience, and compare this to what you predicted. After a brief pause, continue with the next finger, and so on. This phase is over when all ten fingers have been pricked. Before proceeding to the next phase, rate your belief in your original prediction.

The second step

The second phase involves subcutaneous injections in the back of the upper arms, and as always you should predict what you will think will happen and rate your belief in your prediction, after you have understood what is about to happen but before the procedure has started. In this phase you will learn from your professional helper what a subcutaneous injection is, how far the needle will be inserted in the fat tissue, etc. You may not feel the needle prick: if the needle doesn't hit a pain cell or a pressure cell there is no signal going to the central nervous system. Knowing this, you may want to consider the possibility that it is only a matter of chance if the prick will cause you pain or not.

This phase is divided into two parts: the first involves just inserting the needle and immediately taking it out, and the second involves injecting 0.5 ml of saline solution. You will usually need to have 4–6 trials of each. As with the previous phase, you should prepare yourself mentally before the needle is inserted. If you experience too much anxiety at the prospect of getting pricked by the needle, your professional helper will help you to take smaller steps. One smaller step would be to handle the syringe with the needle and 'play' with it for a while. Another step would be to tape a needle on the inner side of the lower arms so that the tip of the needle is close to the skin. Sometimes a piece of cling film can be put between the needle and the skin to make it easier initially. This is then withdrawn gradually. When you are happy, the needle will be inserted and again you should rate how anxious you felt and the pain you experienced. Usually, it is the first trial that is the most difficult, and it gets easier the further you proceed in this phase. Once you have completed 4–6 needle insertions and the same number of actual injections (half of them in each arm), or earlier if your anxiety level has been very much reduced beforehand, this step is complete. As in the previous phase, the last step is to rate your current belief.

The final step

The last phase involves drawing blood from a vein in the bend of the elbow (venepuncture). As in the previous procedures, after the procedure has been explained to you but before it starts you will need to predict what you think will happen and rate how strongly you believe your prediction. Initially, it should be explained how the vacutainer blood collection tube works: you will be shown the two sharp ends of the needle and allowed to listen to the sound when the vacuum is broken; the reason a tourniquet is used will also be discussed. You will then be prepared to have your blood taken. Sometimes it is difficult to obtain blood, especially if the vein is small and deeply embedded, but it may not be necessary to actually take the blood. The important thing is that you give permission to insert the needle. Usually, you will want to have one venepuncture in each arm but, depending on your anxiety it may be that two are needed before your anxiety reduces. This phase will end with you rating the strength of your original belief and discussing with your supporter any remaining beliefs that haven't been dealt with.

Other phobias

The treatment described in this chapter works for phobias of mice and rats, dogs, cats, horses, cows, frogs, worms, hedgehogs, ants and other insects. Besides these animal phobias it has also been successfully used for the treatment of phobias of heights, choking, vomiting, thunder and lightning, and deep water. The principles for using the treatment are the same irrespective of the content of the specific phobia and so the descriptions above should be enough for you, together with a supporter, to adapt and adjust them to any other specific phobias not described. Table 6.1 provides a list of examples of different phobias and related beliefs and behavioural experiments for you to try.

Table 6.1 Examples of catastrophic beliefs and behavioural experiments in specific phobias

Phobia	Catastrophic belief	Behavioural experiment
Snake	The snake will crawl up to me, up my legs, underneath my clothes and bite me. I will die.	Let a non-venomous snake loose on the floor 2–3 metres in front of you and observe where it crawls.
Spider	The spider will crawl underneath my clothes and I will have a strong panic attack and die of heart failure.	Let the spider walk on your hands and arms and observe where it is going.
Bird	The pigeons will fly on to me and through the contact spread a deadly disease.	Stand feeding the pigeons around you. Your supporter scares the pigeons by stamping on the ground and clapping hands. Observe if any pigeons fly on to you.
Wasp	If I am in the same room as a wasp it will fly on to me, sting me, and I will die from the shock.	Be in a room with the door and windows closed. Have the wasp in a glass jar with a screw lid. Remove the lid and observe what the wasp does.

Reproduced with kind permission from *Intensive One-Session Treatment of Specific Phobias*, T. Davis, T. Ollendick and L-G. Öst, New York, Springer, 2012 (Chapter 4).

Lift	The lift will get stuck between two floors, no one will hear the alarm signal, the air will run out and I will die from suffocation.	Enter the lift and press the button that closes the doors, but no floor button. Your supporter should stand outside the lift and spray some deodorant towards the crack where the doors meet. You say aloud when you can smell deodorant inside the elevator.
Heights	If I am on a bridge I will get vertigo, be drawn to the railing, fall over the edge and die.	Walk across the bridge; first with a supporter and then alone. Rate degree of vertigo and observe what is happening.
Injection	The pain from the prick is so strong that it will not pass for several days.	Prick one of your fingers and give a pain rating (0–100) immediately afterwards and then 1, 5, and 10 minutes later.
Injection	The needle will break when it has been inserted in my skin.	Take a subcutaneous needle (30 mm long) in a grip between the thumb and index finger. Bend it 90° and 180° to the right and then 90°, 180°, 270° to the left, etc. to see how hard it is to break it.
Vomiting	If I throw up I will lose control over myself, go crazy, and be locked up at a psychiatric hospital for the rest of my life.	Define clearly what losing control is. Try to make yourself vomit and observe what is happening.

Ending the treatment

When you have worked your way through the one-session treatment, there are two things to bear in mind. Firstly, *you must not avoid/escape from* contact with the previously phobic object/situation in the future. Whenever you encounter it in a natural situation it should be welcomed as a good opportunity to test the skills you have learned during this treatment. Secondly, you should be aware that if you have had a history of nightmares about the phobic object/situation, then you may experience these at an increased frequency during the first week after having done this work, but this is normal and they will fade quickly.

Post-treatment session?

One week after doing the programme described in this chapter, make an appointment with yourself and/or your supporter for a post-treatment session. First review what happened when you followed the programme, starting by describing what your phobia looked like when you started the treatment. Next briefly repeat the different steps included in the treatment and describe thoroughly how your phobia, including the beliefs about the perceived danger, changed during the treatment.

The maintenance programme

Chapter 14 describes relapse prevention strategies to help you maintain the gains you have made. You can think of the analogy of a person learning to drive a car. After getting one's driving licence one is still not a skilled driver. It is necessary to continue driving a car to experience different traffic conditions, and to learn to handle these effectively, progressively refining one's skill. The same principle applies to the skills you have gained through this treatment.

Anxiety is a normal reaction. Anxiety, in its many forms, is a natural part of life (see Part 1), so there is a good chance that you will experience some anxiety in the future and because of this you need to continue to practise the skills acquired during treatment, in order to be better able to use the skills should it be necessary to do so. It is, however, not necessary to practise as much as during the treatment session, just to think about the programme you followed and how you can build on what you have learned.

Setback versus relapse. Many people with anxiety problems tend to think in all-or-nothing terms (see Part 1). If this is true for you, it may make it hard to distinguish between a minor setback and a relapse, or you may believe that having got rid of the anxiety reactions you will never experience anxiety again. If this is the case, try to remember that there is no treatment available today, and there probably will not be one in the future, that can vaccinate a person against all anxiety. Indeed, it is import-ant for you to be able to distinguish between a setback (or a lapse) and a complete 'relapse' or feeling that you are 'back to square one'. Chapter 14 describes a relapse prevention programme to help you maintain all the gains you have made, even at times of setbacks.

Forms for maintenance practice. In Table 6.2, you will see a set of forms for recording the continued maintenance practice over a six-month period. These forms should be filled out and reviewed in a quiet 'self-session' every four weeks for twenty-four weeks either alone or with your supporter. When you go through the forms, think about what has happened in terms of your anxiety reactions and applying the learned skill. This usually takes 10–15 minutes. In the top of the form, fill out (for the first four-week period) what maintenance practice you will use and how often (left column), and what consequences this will have for your daily life (right column). After four weeks, a new form can be filled out so that further improvement after the end of treatment can be incorporated in your maintenance programme. This will enable you to gradually confront more difficult situations. In the middle part of the form, write down your catastrophic belief before the start of treatment and rate how much you believed it. Then write a sentence saying what you think about that particular belief *after* the programme and how much you also rate your belief after treatment.

Table 6.2: Maintenance form used in phobia treatment

Week: 1–4

NAME: _____

IF YOU CONTINUE TO DO THE FOLLOWING EACH WEEK

1: _____

2: _____

3: _____

4: _____

THEN IN THE FUTURE YOU WILL BE ABLE TO:

1: _____

2: _____

3: _____

4: _____

Record the respective number in the columns below each time you have performed the practice task. Make any comments that you may have on the reverse side of the form. Do not skip the practice any week but keep practising regularly. This is particularly important during the first six months after the treatment. Then send your supporter the form in the way that you will hopefully have agreed upon.

My catastrophic belief before treatment was: _____

After treatment I believed: _____

Day	Week 1 Date Activity	Week 2 Date Activity	Week 3 Date Activity	Week 4 Date Activity
Monday				
Tuesday				
Wednesday				
Thursday				
Friday				
Saturday				
Sunday				

Send this form to [insert your supporter, if you have one]: _____

Address: _____

Phone number: _____ Email _____

The final word

Many people's lives are dominated by phobias. This chapter contains a treatment programme that has been shown to work, is brief and can make a difference to your life. It can be a difficult programme to undertake, especially if you are on your own, but we would strongly encourage you to try it so that you can go about your daily life in the way you choose, unrestricted by situations or objects that you happen to encounter.

Table 6.3: Spider phobia questionnaire

The SPQ is a 31 item self-report instrument that measures fear of spiders. Scores can range from 0 – 31 with higher scores indicating greater fear. Answer True (T) or False (F) to the following questions. T= I point, F= 0 points.
1. I avoid going to parks or on camping trips because there may be spiders about. ○   True ○   False
2. I would feel some anxiety holding a toy spider in my hand. ○   True ○   False
3. If a picture of a spider crawling on a person appears on the screen during a film or on TV, I turn my head away. ○   True ○   False
4. I dislike looking at pictures of spiders in a magazine. ○   True ○   False
5. If there is a spider on the ceiling over my bed, I cannot go to sleep unless someone kills it for me. ○   True ○   False

6. I enjoy watching spiders build their webs.

O   True

O   False

7. I am terrified by the thought of touching a harmless spider.

O   True

O   False

8. If someone says that there are spiders anywhere about, I become alert and edgy.

O   True

O   False

9. I would not go down to the basement to get something if I thought there might be spiders down there.

O   True

O   False

10. I would feel uncomfortable if a spider crawled out of my shoe as I took it out of the wardrobe to put it on.

O   True

O   False

11. When I see a spider, I feel tense and restless.

O   True

O   False

12. I enjoy reading articles about spiders.

O   True

O   False

13. I feel sick when I see a spider.

O   True

O   False

14. Spiders are sometimes useful.

O   True

O   False

15. I shudder when I think of spiders.
- O   True
- O   False

16. I don't mind being near a harmless spider if there is someone there in whom I have confidence.
- O   True
- O   False

17. Some spiders are very attractive to look at.
- O   True
- O   False

18. I don't believe anyone could hold a spider without some fear.
- O   True
- O   False

19. The way spiders move is repulsive.
- O   True
- O   False

20. It wouldn't bother me to touch a dead spider with a long stick.
- O   True
- O   False

21. If I came upon a spider while cleaning the attic I would probably run.
- O   True
- O   False

22. I'm probably more afraid of spiders than of any other animal.
- O   True
- O   False

23. I would not want to travel to countries such as Mexico, Australia or countries in Central America because of the greater prevalence of tarantulas.
- O   True
- O   False

24. I am cautious when buying fruit because bananas may attract spiders.
- ○ True
- ○ False

25. I have no fear of non-poisonous spiders.
- ○ True
- ○ False

26. I wouldn't take a course in biology if I thought I might have to handle live spiders.
- ○ True
- ○ False

27. Spider webs are very artistic.
- ○ True
- ○ False

28. I think that I'm no more afraid of spiders than the average person.
- ○ True
- ○ False

29. I would prefer not to finish a story if something about spiders was introduced into the plot.
- ○ True
- ○ False

30. Not only am I afraid of spiders, but millipedes and caterpillars make me feel anxious.
- ○ True
- ○ False

31. Even if I was late for a very important appointment, the thought of spiders would stop me from taking a shortcut through an underpass.
- ○ True
- ○ False

Reproduced with kind permission from R. Klorman, J. Hastings, T. Weerts, B. Melamed, & P. Lang (1974). Psychometric description of some specific fear questionnaires. *Behavior Therapy*, 5, 401

Table 6.4: *IAPT* phobia scales

Choose a number from the scale below to show how much you would avoid each of the situations or objects listed below. Then write the number in the box opposite the situation.

0	1	2	3	4	5	6	7	8
Would not avoid it		Slightly avoid it		Definitely avoid it		Markedly avoid it		Always avoid it

Social situations due to a fear of being embarrassed or making a fool of myself. ☐

Certain situations because of a fear of having a panic attack or other distressing symptoms (such as loss of bladder control, vomiting or dizziness). ☐

Certain situations because of a fear of particular objects or activities (such as animals, heights, seeing blood, being in confined spaces, driving or flying). ☐

Reproduced with kind permission from Department of Health, *IAPT Data Handbook, 2010*, www.iapt.nhs.uk/silo/files/iapt-data-handbook-appendices-v2.pdf (p.24).

7 Panic disorder

Nick Grey and David M Clark

Overview[1]

On p. 9 of Part 1 you read a brief description of panic disorder to see whether this might be relevant to you. This chapter will help you work out in more detail whether panic disorder is the best way to describe some or all of your anxiety problems. If panic disorder is a problem for you, this chapter will help you understand it better, why it hasn't just improved by itself, and how you can take practical steps to stop panic attacks and overcome the fear triggered by particular situations and activities.

The approach in this chapter will help you learn about *your* panic attacks, work out what keeps *your* panic disorder going, and how you can make changes. The strategies in this chapter have been shown to be effective in clinical trials and have helped many people worldwide. Notice that overcoming your panic attacks and other anxiety symptoms is not simply a matter of learning to 'pull yourself together'. If it were that simple you would have recovered long ago. Nobody wants to suffer from panic attacks and worry about them. So overcoming panic and related worry requires an understanding of what happens in panics, plus the application of techniques that will initially help you control your panic attacks when they happen, and later will ideally stop the panics from happening at all.

---

[1] As with all the other chapters in Part 2, this chapter is intended as a self-help guide for individuals with panic disorder and their supporters. It is NOT a therapist manual

Most people with panic disorder have at some stage been sceptical that their problem is one of anxiety rather than a physical health problem, such as a heart or breathing problem, fainting problem, or some other physical abnormality. When you had your first attack you almost certainly thought that some terrible physical thing was about to happen or was actually happening. You may have gone to hospital or to your doctor to get help. It may have come as a shock if they suggested that the problem was really one of panic and anxiety. You may still have some doubts about whether your problem is an anxiety, rather than a physical health problem. This is a typical reaction and not surprising. Presumably you're reading this chapter because you have some belief that your problem may be panic, or others (family, friends, or a therapist) have suggested this to you. As you work through this chapter you will see how panic disorder is both a good explanation for your horrible experiences, and also something that you can overcome.

Note: Occasionally, panic attacks can have a physical cause, for example thyroid problems. Your doctor should check to ensure that your problem is panic disorder. Once your doctor confirms that there is nothing physically wrong with you, then this chapter is for you (even if you still have some doubts at the moment).

What is a panic attack?

People often talk about 'feeling panicky' in a variety of situations, such as a job interview, going on a date, and facing things that have scared them in the past, such as spiders perhaps. This is not necessarily the same as a panic attack, which is defined as a sudden rush of physical symptoms that reaches a peak within a few minutes (certainly fewer than ten). The physical symptoms include: breathlessness, palpitations, chest pain, dizziness, trembling, sweating, a feeling of choking, dry mouth, nausea, feeling unreal, numbness or tingling (especially in the lips and fingers), chills or hot flushes, and fears of losing control, dying or going crazy. At least four of these symptoms need to be experienced for an anxiety attack to be diagnosed as a panic attack.

Dan's account of a panic attack

I suddenly notice my heart racing and my breathing starts to get very shallow. I feel as if I can't breathe properly. I feel frightened and unreal, and I imagine myself gasping for air. I think I might pass out; I get very dizzy and hot, and I start to sweat and feel shaky. My mind is racing, and my thoughts are confused. I think I am losing my mind, that I might lose control and do crazy things. As I think this I get even more frightened, and the symptoms get even worse. My heart is beating like a drum now, and I have pains in my chest, which make me think that my heart can't take any more, that I'll have a heart attack. I think that these feelings will not go away, and that no one will be able to help me. I am frightened that I am going to die. The sensations are so strong and are still getting worse. I want to run somewhere safe, but I don't know where, and my legs have turned into jelly anyway.

Occasional panic attacks are common in all anxiety disorders. For example, a person with spider phobia might experience a panic attack when confronted with a large spider. A person with obsessive-compulsive disorder might have a panic attack after touching a 'contaminated' object. Having occasional panic attacks does not necessarily mean you have panic disorder. This chapter focuses specifically on panic disorder. The main features of this are described below.

What is panic disorder?

The diagnosis of panic disorder is for the people who have *repeated* panic attacks, some of which come on *unexpectedly or out-of-the-blue*. The attacks are not always triggered by expecting a particular situation, entering a particular situation, or a sudden increase in the severity of a particular situation (e.g. a spider moving). The main fear in panic disorder is a fear of having a panic attack and/or its consequences, rather than a fear of a specific situation, activity or object (e.g., heights, public speaking, or small animals).

A panic attack is an unpleasant experience. Small wonder that people who have panicked in a particular situation (such as travelling on public transport, being in a crowded shop or a wide open space) often find that they have difficulty going back into those situations. These people develop what we call 'panic disorder with agoraphobia'. People whose initial attacks were not in a distinctive situation away from home are less likely to develop agoraphobia. However, because they cannot predict when a panic attack occurs, these people often show higher levels of 'background' anxiety between attacks.

Who has panic attacks and panic disorder?

So who has panic attacks? There are several ways of answering the question. First, it is possible to think in terms of how many people suffer from panic. Research has shown that one in ten of us will have at least one panic attack in a year. Think of the people living near you; on average, one person out of each ten has had a panic in the previous year. Often people think this is impossible, and that they would know if a neighbour had panic attacks. However, think how many people in your street know that *you* have panic attacks. Does everyone know? Probably not! Think how many people knew about your panics in the first year. Generally, people do not talk much about panic, so you don't hear about it and will, as a result, underestimate how common it is. Recently several well-known people have spoken out about experiencing panic attacks and panic disorder, including the actress Nicole Kidman, the singer Donny Osmond and the cricketer Marcus Trescothick. Yet it is still massively under-recognized.

So lots of people have panics; but what is it about these people that makes them experience panic? Are they weak or inferior? Are they heading for a nervous breakdown? Are they stupid? Is there something physically wrong with them? The answer to all these questions is **NO**. Absolutely anyone can have panic attacks, given the right combination of circumstances. Here are some examples of people who have been treated by us for panic attacks.

A sister in charge of a general hospital ward had her first panic at home; and within three months she was panicking at least once a day and could not go into town on her own.

A policeman had his first panic when called to a particularly unpleasant road traffic accident; he was able to continue his work, but frequently found himself panicking when driving on motorways.

A 39-year-old former SAS soldier panicked when in town, and became completely agoraphobic within six months.

We can see then that panic can (and does) happen to people from all walks of life. It is not a sign of deficiency, weakness or of any other problem. As you will see, feelings of panic are based on conclusions that initially seem logical, although when you begin to untangle the thinking you will start to see that the logic is not entirely sound. While panic may be more likely at times of stress, stress is not the main cause of panic. Very shortly we will consider what *does* cause panic.

The next attack: not just a disaster

Because the approach described here involves your being able to learn more about the problem, each panic attack will not just be a horrid experience, but also an opportunity. At first it will be an opportunity to learn more about your panic. Later it will be a chance to practise the techniques you will have learned to use to overcome your panics. This may seem a strange idea, but think about it for a moment. What is the best way of learning how to deal with difficulties? If we know how, we can learn from mistakes and difficulties. For example, the best way of learning to deal with a skid is to practise on a skidpan – a slippery area where cars skid very easily. The more instruction people have on a skidpan, the better they will drive when it comes to dealing with skidding. Dealing with anxiety is similar. Until now, you have been at the mercy of your anxiety, so have not learned how to overcome the panic. As you go through this chapter, you will learn more and more from each panic attack and will get better at controlling them. Finally, you will see that you don't even need to try to control these horrible experiences.

Key messages

- A panic attack is a sudden rush of physical symptoms such as palpitations, chest pain, dizziness and breathlessness. It usually reaches a peak within a few minutes.

- Occasional panic attacks are common in all anxiety disorders.

- The diagnosis of panic disorder is reserved for the smaller number of people who have had *repeated* panic attacks (some of which come on unexpectedly or out of the blue) and who are very worried about having more panic attacks.

- Panic disorder is sometimes accompanied by agoraphobia.

- Many people suffer from panic disorder – you are far from alone.

- Having panic disorder is not a sign of weakness or a reflection on you in any way.

Tips for supporters

- As you read through the symptoms of panic disorder, encourage the person you are supporting to think about their own symptoms and how they view their own panic disorder.

- If you feel able, share any experiences you may have had about your own experience of panic attacks or anxiety.

Understanding what keeps your panic going

As you may have noticed in Dan's example above, he mentioned some very frightening thoughts. He thought the pounding in his chest in the middle of a panic attack meant he was about to have a heart attack. Extreme thinking of this sort is typical in a panic. People have frightening thoughts about what is happening to them. The thoughts are closely (and logically) linked to the sensations they are experiencing. Examples are shown in Table 7.1. These aren't the only sensations and thoughts you may have, of course.

Table 7.1 Symptoms of a panic attack and reactions to them

Sensations	Frightening thoughts
Heart racing, pounding, palpitations	I'm having a heart attack; my heart will stop; I'm dying.
Breathlessness	I'm going to stop breathing, suffocate.
Feeling unreal	I'm going to go crazy, lose my mind.
Losing feeling in arms; numbness and tingling	I'm having a stroke.
Feeling dizzy and faint	I'm going to faint, fall over and pass out.
Feeling distant, tense, sweaty	I'm going to lose control of my behaviour and shout out or do something uncontrolled.
Feeling dizzy, heart pounding, chest tight, palpitations, flushed and tingling	I'm dying.

Research shows that these frightening thoughts are the key to panic. This is the *cognitive approach* to panic. So how does it all work?

Quite small things can trigger panic in the first place. These might be a slight bodily sensation, an upsetting thought, or even going somewhere where a panic attack previously happened. Often it all starts with a mild physical sensation, which can lead to worry *if the person believes that the sensation could be the first sign of disaster*. For example, someone noticing their heart beating rapidly after drinking strong coffee might (mistakenly) think that this meant there was something wrong with their heart. Not surprisingly, this thought would make them anxious.

Anxiety itself causes the heart to beat more quickly and strongly, as is usual when we are afraid. The anxiety can also make us feel light headed and produce other symptoms as a normal effect of increases in adrenalin. These changes are there to help us to escape real danger (see Part 1, section on fight or flight, pp. 5–6). However, if you are already worried about physical disaster (such as a heart attack), the increase in sensations seems to confirm the first frightening thought; we think that the fast heartbeats and the feeling of lightheadedness mean that we are actually having a heart attack.

These *catastrophic thoughts* are the key to understanding why you are suffering from panic disorder. As a result of the thoughts, there is a dramatic increase in anxiety, and then there is a big rush of bodily sensations from the extra adrenalin produced as part of the body's reaction to being in danger. You feel terrified, and your body reacts as it usually does when we are terrified, with more sensations, which seems to provide even more evidence that something is badly wrong. The vicious cycle of panic is complete (see Figure 7.1, p. 138).

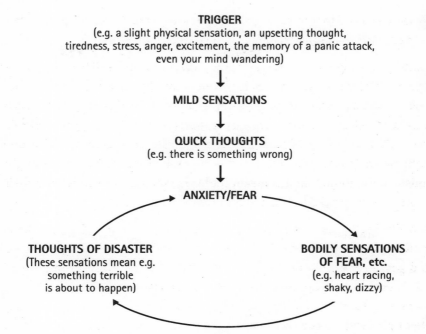

TRIGGER
(e.g. a slight physical sensation, an upsetting thought,
tiredness, stress, anger, excitement, the memory of a panic attack,
even your mind wandering)

↓

MILD SENSATIONS

↓

QUICK THOUGHTS
(e.g. there is something wrong)

↓

ANXIETY/FEAR

THOUGHTS OF DISASTER
(These sensations mean e.g.
something terrible
is about to happen)

BODILY SENSATIONS
OF FEAR, etc.
(e.g. heart racing,
shaky, dizzy)

A real-life example is given below:

Sundee was in a shopping centre, and had a sudden panic attack which appeared to come on out of the blue. Thinking about it carefully afterwards revealed that the first thing she had noticed was that she was 'burning up in the face'. This led her to worry that she might be about to have another panic attack. Because she was afraid she felt rather breathless, and began to gasp for breath. This made her feel a bit light headed, which in turn made her think that she might be about to faint, or even collapse and die. Of course, these thoughts made her feel extremely frightened, which gave rise to even more intense sensations in her body.

Sundee could see how the vicious circle was working, but still wondered why her face had got hot in the first place. Thinking carefully helped her to remember that as she entered the precinct she had noticed some boys staring at her. This had made her embarrassed, which caused her to blush. So for Sundee the vicious circle looked like the figure below.

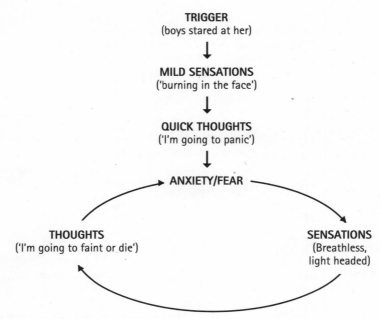

Figure 7.1: The vicious cycle of panic

Key messages

- Research shows that frightening thoughts, which we call 'catastrophic thoughts', are actually the key to panic disorder.

- Something small such as noticing a slight change in your body can trigger a panic attack.

- If you think that the sensation could be the first sign of a disaster, anxiety escalates and creates more sensations which seem to <u>confirm</u> the first frightening thought.

- As a result, there is a dramatic increase in anxiety, and there is a big rush of bodily sensations from the extra adrenalin produced as part of the body's reaction to being in danger.

- You feel terrified which seems to provide even more evidence that something physically dangerous is about to happen.

- This very rapid cycle *is* the panic attack.

Helping you change

Panic is driven by the frightening thoughts that people have about the sensations they get when they are afraid. The approach to overcoming panic that we take in this chapter is based on the treatment called cognitive therapy, but this book helps you to help yourself. This approach focuses on the two alternative explanations of what happens in a panic attack. One explanation is that there really is something seriously wrong with you, and the other (which is supported by all the work we have done) is that there is another, far less frightening, explanation for what is happening, and that you are not in fact in any danger.

In this chapter, we will describe special techniques that you can use to help you identify your own upsetting thoughts, and then you (and your supporter, if you have one) will work to find out how realistic they are. The discoveries you make about these thoughts, and about what is really happening in your attacks, will help to put your mind at rest, and will suggest helpful ways of getting rid of your panic attacks completely.

What is unique about this approach compared with CBT for other anxiety disorders?

The unique aspect of overcoming panic disorder is the aim to change what you think and feel is happening to your body, or what you fear is about to happen, when you have strong physical sensations. You need to understand what is really happening in your body when the sensations are strong. To fully understand this you will need not only to read the information in this chapter, but also to prove to yourself in practice that nothing dangerous happens in a panic attack. This is difficult and frightening for anyone, so if you are a little hesitant that is entirely natural. We hope that this chapter, your hard work, and any available supporter(s) can help you make the changes you want, in order to be able to live the life you want, without being held back in any way.

Starting to overcome your panic: self-assessment

Filling in the panic diary

First, there are some physical causes of panic attacks and your doctor should check these. Once your doctor and you agree that your problem is anxiety you need to find out more about this problem. In order to find out more about how your panic attacks occur it helps to pay close attention to what happens in each attack. There is a diary on p. 186. Each time you have a panic attack, make notes about it under the various headings. These include what you were doing and where you were when you had the attack, how many symptoms you had, and your *thoughts of disaster* – thoughts about the worst things you thought could happen during the attack. If you have a supporter, they can encourage you to keep this diary. You will learn more about how to notice these thoughts in the next section. The section will help you think about the sort of thoughts you are looking out for. Using the diary should help you begin to spot what triggers each attack, and will help you to notice the progress you make during the treatment. It is a good idea to photocopy the diary so you can use it over many weeks.

Don't worry about trying to fill in the alternatives to your thoughts yet. We're coming on to that and you'll soon be able to do this.

Overcoming your panic

Getting started with finding out about your panic attacks

In this section we will introduce the types of questions that you should ask yourself. Get a pen or pencil and write your answers down. You may want to make rough notes first on a sheet of paper, but when you have worked out what you want to say make sure you write it down here so all your work on your panic disorder is in one place. Don't be afraid to go back and alter what you have written if you change your mind. Take your time; the idea is to go through the sequence of questions, then to go back to review what you have written to see that it all makes sense. Your supporter can help you by discussing the questions with you.

It is important to write things down and to spend some time thinking about each step. Panics usually happen quickly, so that it can require careful effort to sort out the way in which a single panic develops. The questions below should help you to sort out what might have previously seemed very confusing:

Think back to the last severe panic attack you experienced. Think carefully about it, and have a specific attack in mind. It's best to choose a fairly typical attack that happened as recently as possible. If you haven't had an attack for a while then take a little longer to really try to fully remember the last severe attack you did have. Take each step slowly, and make sure that you have a written summary of your answers before you move on to the next step. Some people get a few sensations in their body when they remember back to previous panic attacks. This is normal and not anything to worry about. If you can, try to move through this exercise staying focused on this specific attack.

Step One

- When did it happen?

- Where was I just before it began, and when it got going?

- What was I doing?

- Who was I with?

Try to remember the occasion as fully and clearly as possible.

Step Two

Now concentrate on the worst part of the attack.

Think about the sensations you had in your body when the attack reached a peak. Write them down.

- What were the most frightening symptoms that I noticed?

- As I noticed these strong sensations what went through my mind?

- What did these symptoms mean to me at that time?

- What seemed to me at that time to be the worst thing that could happen? (These might be thoughts such as 'I'm going to pass out', 'I'm going to have a heart attack', or 'I'm going to go mad'.)

- Did I have any images (mental pictures) at that time about what was happening, or might be about to happen? (These might be images of what you most fear, such as seeing yourself lying on the ground unconscious or dead, or even seeing images of what you think is happening inside your body such as seeing your heart beating really fast.)

Sometimes, particularly if you have had panic attacks for a long time, the first answer that comes to mind may not be about dangerous things happening to you physically, like having a heart attack or stroke. You may have answered, 'I just thought I might have a panic attack' or 'I just wanted to get out of the situation I was in'. If you did not have that type of thought and have already found one or more catastrophic thoughts, go on to the next section. Otherwise a few more questions are needed.

If your thought was 'I just thought I might have a panic attack' then you need to ask yourself: 'At that time what did I think was the worst thing that could happen if I actually did have a panic attack?'

Write down your catastrophic thoughts about what you would have been afraid might happen.

If your thought was 'I just wanted to get out of the situation I was in', then you need to ask yourself: 'Supposing I was not able to escape, what at that time would I have been afraid would be the worst thing that could happen?'

Write your answers to this question here:

We're looking for the worst catastrophe that you fear could happen *as a result* of these horrible sensations. You should now be ready to go on to Step Three.

Step Three

You should now make a short summary of all the sensations that you had in the worst part of the attack and the catastrophic thoughts you had about them. Write the sensations that you had on the left, and the thoughts that you had about them on the right:

Sensations	Thoughts

We shall come back to this shortly.

Step Four

Now that you have worked out what was happening at the worst part of the attack, go through the attack slowly and carefully in your mind and answer the questions below to see how the attack built up.

Once again cast your mind back to the situation you were in when the panic started. What was the *very first thing* that you noticed as the attack started? A range of things can trigger panic. Often the things that trigger panic attacks can be small things, and usually they are not thoughts. Some of the most common triggers are: returning to situations where you have previously had panic attacks, getting worrying sensations in your body, or feeling anxious or upset, either about panic, or about something unrelated.

Write down the *first* thing that you noticed, i.e. the *panic trigger*:

This trigger is often followed by a quick thought, such as 'I'm going to have a panic attack' or 'Here it comes again'. Sometimes the panic trigger can be followed by a catastrophic thought straight away (e.g. 'I'll collapse, I'm ill, etc.).

Write the sort of quick *thoughts* that you had at this stage in the space below:

Step Five

Now look at the diagram on p. 148 (you will need to flick back and forth here a little . . .). You will see that it is a sketch of what happens in a typical panic attack. Fill in what you noticed in the attack you have been thinking about from what you have written above.

- Start by filling in your own *panic trigger* on the line marked 1) PANIC TRIGGER on the diagram.

- As you began to recall this fear what did you notice happening in your body? Write these *sensations* on the line next to '1st time' under 5) MILD SENSATIONS.

- Next, write in the *thoughts* you had as you noticed the trigger, on the line marked 3) QUICK THOUGHTS.

- Next, think about how you felt as these thoughts went through your mind, and write these *feelings* (e.g. anxious, terrified, worried) on the line under 4) ANXIETY/FEAR, next to '1st time'.

- As you noticed these sensations coming on what sort of *thoughts* went through your mind? Write these thoughts on the line (next to '1st time') under 6) THOUGHTS OF DISASTER.

- As these much more frightening thoughts went through your mind how did you *feel*? You can write your answer on the second line under 4) ANXIETY/FEAR.

- As your fear began to get much stronger what *sensations* did you have? Write these next to '2nd time' under 5) SENSATIONS.

You will see that what is happening is that there seems to be a vicious cycle of *sensations* leading to *thoughts* of danger, which lead to *feelings* of fear, which cause an increase in the sensations, and so on.

You can keep filling in the sequence of sensations – fear – thoughts – sensations – fear – thoughts until you come to the peak of the attack when the sensations and thoughts were at their worst (see Step Three). You can look back at the panic cycle on p. 137. Does yours look similar? If not, then perhaps go through these steps again, with a supporter if that is possible.

This vicious cycle *is* the panic attack. It usually happens very quickly indeed and you may not notice the steps building up in the way we have helped you describe. Don't worry about that. The crucial point is that it is understandable that you feel so frightened in or before a panic attack if you believe something catastrophic is about to happen to you. We are suggesting here that rather than these attacks actually being dangerous, there is an understandable sequence of events that leads to the rapid build-up of these horrible experiences. Well done on completing this! This is a very important step in starting to overcome your panic disorder.

Key messages

- Panic attacks are horrible but not dangerous.

- There is an understandable and rapid sequence of events that leads to a panic attack.

- Understanding the sequence of events by going through the steps above is the first step to breaking the vicious cycle of panic.

- The key to it all is the thoughts of disaster you have when you notice changes in the sensations in your body.

Tips for supporters

- The person you are helping may become distressed and anxious when going through the steps.

- There is no hurry to do this – sitting together in a quiet place, taking your time and taking breaks when necessary can help the person remain calm and complete the steps.

- Let the person take their own time – don't try to complete the cycle for them even if you have had panic attacks yourself, as everyone is different.

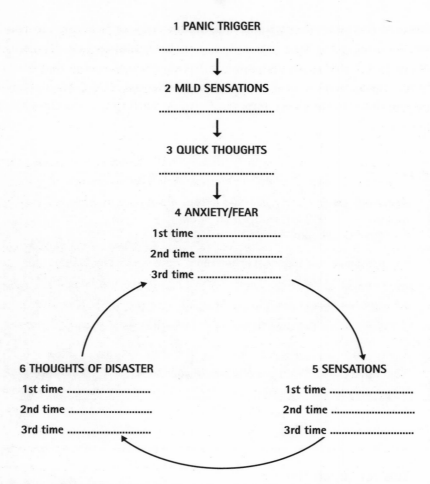

Figure 7.2: Recognizing that the vicious cycle of panic is the panic attack

What keeps the problem going?

As we have seen, the main things driving panic attacks are the fright-ening thoughts of disaster you have. Actually, in a panic attack you are in no danger and no disaster will happen. These thoughts are 'mis-interpretations' of the bodily sensations you get in a panic, i.e. you think the sensations mean one thing ('disaster'), but actually the sensations are your body's natural anxiety reaction. This means that *changing* these terrifying thoughts, by weakening your belief that something terrible is about to happen, should break the vicious cycle and put an end to the panic attacks. But if it is as simple as that, why haven't you been able to do it already? What keeps panic attacks going?

There are several factors that stop the problem going away:

- *Evidence*: People with panic disorder usually feel that they have good reason to believe that the sensations they have in a panic attack are truly dangerous. They have usually not considered other less frightening explanations for what is happening.

- *Attention*: As people with panic disorder think the bodily sensations in a panic attack are dangerous, they are alert to what happens in their bodies. This makes them notice sensations that other people wouldn't notice. Once they notice the sensations, they tend to take them as further evidence for their thoughts of disaster. This process of noticing more sensations is natural and automatic.

- *'Saving yourself' and avoidance*: People with panic disorder understandably begin to *take precautions*, which they believe will save them from disaster. For example, if we believe that our racing heart means we are going to have a heart attack, we will do things to reduce our heart rate, such as sit down, and try to relax and take it easy. In addition people usually try to *leave or avoid situations* where they fear the worst may happen. This means that they never find out whether 'the worst' would ever really happen.

- *Images*: Some people also get brief vivid mental pictures or *images* of awful things that could happen. These tend to just flash through their minds, but can be accompanied by strong emotions. Often people manage to stop them at their worst point, and push them away, but they can still be left feeling shaken and upset, without really thinking it through.

We are now going to look in detail at which of these factors are keeping your panic attacks going, and what you can do to change them.

Examining the evidence carefully

Previous evidence

One thing you may say is, 'I've heard of (or seen, or read about) other people with symptoms like mine, and those people certainly had something seriously wrong with them.' Or you may look back to a time when you had what seemed to be similar symptoms, which then appeared to be serious.

Here what you need to do is to consider carefully whether there are any ways in which the situation during your panic attacks is *different* from the serious situation you have been comparing it to.

In order to get your fears in perspective you may need some information you do not have at the moment to help you tell the difference between what actually *is* happening, and what you *fear* is happening.

Jane had once fainted and felt sick at a wedding reception. After this she had often felt very anxious at work, fearing she would faint there too. In fact, during her treatment she worked out that food poisoning had been the cause of her fainting at the wedding reception, and learned that <u>anxiety alone cannot cause fainting</u> (we return to this later).

A little further below is information on a number of topics that people with panic attacks often worry about. Before you look at this, write out your *worst fears* about what might be about to happen during a panic attack, in the space below. Beside this write a number to indicate how much you believe this *right now*, on a scale from 0–100%, where 0% means you don't believe it at all, and 100% means you are convinced this is true. Then write another number from 0–100% to indicate how much you believe this in the middle of a panic attack.

My beliefs about the worst things that could happen to me during a panic attack	How much I believe them right now (0–100%)	How much I believe them in the middle of a panic attack (0–100%)

Now write some *notes* in the space below about the *evidence* you have that this could happen. This might include things you have heard about, or read about, or an illness you suffered from in the past, or that someone you know suffered from, and so on. Write anything that makes you worry that the worst *could* happen.

Do you have any doubts about this evidence? What would your supporters say?

Is there any evidence that your worst fears won't come true, and that this is best seen as an anxiety problem rather than a physical problem?

Tip for supporters

Look carefully at the evidence that the worst fears might come true. Does it seem convincing? Are there any doubts you have that you can share? Why won't the worst fears happen?

Listed here are some common questions that people with panic disorder ask. Quick answers are provided here. Some further information and ideas to test this out are at the end of this chapter. This will help you assess the evidence for your worst fears.

Question	Quick answer
Will I fall over when I feel anxious and wobbly?	No, this is just a feeling caused by anxiety and overbreathing.
Can I faint in a panic attack?	No. In order to faint your blood pressure has to drop suddenly. In a panic attack it increases.
Why do I notice worrying symptoms much more than I used to, and often when I am relaxing or resting?	When you are not thinking about other things your attention can move onto your symptoms.
Does chest pain mean there is something wrong with my heart?	Chest pain can be caused by tense muscles between each rib. This is made worse by overbreathing.

Why do my hands shake if I'm not losing control?	Muscle tension in the arms and hands can exaggerate the normal, usually unnoticed hand tremor that everyone has.
Is it possible to run out of air and faint or suffocate in a stuffy room?	No. Rooms feel stuffy when the air is warm and humid not because there isn't enough air (or oxygen). Rooms are not totally sealed so air can always get in.
How do I know I won't stop breathing and suffocate if I don't control my breathing?	Breathing is an automatic reflex and can't be suppressed for long. You can continue to breathe when you are asleep, which shows that you don't need to put effort into controlling breathing. The reflex takes care of it.
Why do things sometimes start to shimmer or move in front of my eyes?	It can occur if you stare at objects (which anxious people often do either because it will help them stay in control or because they are checking that things look normal). Also, shimmering movements can be produced as a sort of optical illusion by certain patterns like stripes or by strong fluorescent light.
Why do I get pins and needles in my fingers?	This is caused by blood going to the hands and feet to get ready to fight or flee.
Why do I get so short of breath?	The muscles between your ribs tense up when anxious, making you feel short of breath.
Why do I get butterflies in the tummy?	This is caused by blood not going to the stomach – when getting ready for fight or flight you don't need to worry about digesting any food.

Remember, there are more detailed explanations of these common experiences on pp. 189–96.

Key messages

- What you fear is happening is not the same as what is actually happening. Distinguishing between these is important to helping you overcome your panic.

- It is important to get factual information to help you tell the difference between what actually is happening, and what you fear is happening.

- Identifying the evidence you have for what you fear is happening, and gathering factual information is an important part of change.

Now you have read some information about your worst fears, and learned more about them, please re-rate them below:

My beliefs about the worst things that could happen to me during a panic attack	How much I believe them right now (0–100%)	How much I believe them in the middle of a panic attack (0–100%)

If this helped you, that's good. However, if you still have major doubts, don't worry. Most people need to go over things in a number of different ways before they are convinced. The remaining sections of this chapter will take you through some more ways of working on thoughts of disaster.

Tips for supporters

- The goal of this part of overcoming panic is to help the person with panic disorder distinguish between what they fear is happening and what is actually happening.

- To do this, you will need to help them identify what they fear is happening (e.g. the person is having a heart attack) and what is actually happening (e.g. the person is afraid they are having a heart attack so is very anxious and experiencing a lot of sensations of anxiety).

Having intense symptoms

The thing people with panic attacks often feel is *evidence* that something must be seriously wrong since the symptoms seem so intense. If you sometimes feel this, read through this section. Otherwise move on to the next section which looks at the importance of considering *other explanations* for your symptoms.

So is it always true that feeling strong symptoms means there is something seriously wrong with you? Go over in your mind other times when you might have had the *same* symptoms but not felt frightened. This may not seem very likely at first, but just try to remember the last time you were *really excited*. Perhaps you were watching an exciting football match, or a thrilling film on a huge cinema screen, or perhaps you discovered that you had won the lottery, or went out with your present partner for the first time after you had fallen in love. Write down what the occasion was, and the main physical symptoms you noticed at that time. If you can't remember a time when you felt excited, you can think about a time when you had other strong feelings like being angry, or a time when you had lots of sensations in your body, like when doing exercise.

The last occasion on which I felt excited was (e.g. was angry or doing exercise):

The physical sensations I noticed at that time were:

How similar are these symptoms to the ones I get during panic attacks?

What are the differences?

Usually the symptoms are quite similar, and certainly they are also intense, but the *thoughts* that go with them make them seem different. So why should the symptoms be similar? Read the next section to find out.

Preparing for action

When you get excited or frightened your body starts to get ready to take action. It does this by making your muscles tense up, your heart pound, and so on; this is just what you need if you might have to do something energetic, but it feels strange if you are just sitting still or walking about.

This reaction was useful for our primitive ancestors, because it would make them better at fighting or running away (this fight-or-flight response is also talked about in Chapter 1, pp. 5–6). Athletes and football players need to be ready for action: it usually improves their game. However, if you get a burst of this reaction when you are walking about your house or in the supermarket, it feels very odd.

The body's reactions during an anxiety attack are all appropriate ways of dealing with a real danger. The release of adrenalin and redistribution of blood flow to the muscles are excellent ways of getting one ready to fight or flee. These sensations are not dangerous. Indeed, they are a sign that the body's anxiety alarm system is working as it was intended. The only problem is that the system is being triggered by an imagined danger, rather than a real danger.

So why do you get a feeling of being ready for action when you panic? It's back to those *thoughts* again. If you have a thought about something terrible being about to happen, your body sets off its alarm reaction, and gets you ready for action. The trouble is, there is no action to be carried out! Your heart pounds, you feel dizzy and you are so tense that the muscles in your chest and neck start to hurt, and you feel wobbly. It makes you feel you want to run away – but there is nowhere to run to.

However, this reaction cannot hurt you. In fact, a burst of it can be good for you – it is a bit like starting the car up in the drive and revving it up for a few minutes to get the oil circulating and all the parts in working order. After all, people with exciting jobs, like pilots, racing drivers and stunt artists, don't worry that excitement will damage their health.

The amount that your heart speeds up during a panic attack is almost always less than that caused by running upstairs. In addition we are all encouraged to take exercise that increases our heart rate because it strengthens our bodies.

Not considering other explanations for your symptoms

Another thing that happens to people when they are anxious is that they tend to focus on frightening, dangerous possibilities, and ignore the fact that there may be much less alarming explanations for what is happening. Let's take the example of someone who is afraid they may have heart disease. Every time they notice their heart racing they think there must be something seriously wrong with it. However, this ignores the fact that there are many, many reasons why the heart races, and almost all of them are not serious.

In the list below you will see a few causes of a racing heart:

- Anxiety
- Taking exercise
- Smoking cigarettes
- Drinking coffee
- Looking forward to something exciting
- Feeling embarrassed
- Having a temperature (e.g. if you have the flu)
- Feeling afraid of something
- Being very busy and 'wound up'
- Lifting heavy things
- Worrying about something
- Hurrying
- Falling in love

By now, you will realize that in only a *very few* cases is a racing heart a sign that something is wrong with the heart. Yet often people with panic attacks only consider the very worst explanation if they notice a racing heart.

If there is a symptom that often makes you think of your *worst fears* it would be worth taking some time to try this exercise for yourself.

Worksheet 7.1: Identifying what makes you anxious

Make a list of *all* the possible causes of this symptom. Put the *worst* explanation last on your list. It would also be worth asking your supporter and other people what explanations might occur to them if they had this symptom, and adding them to your list.

The *symptom* you worry about most:

The *possible cause* you fear the most:

Various possible causes of this symptom

1.

2.

3.

4.

5.

6.

7.

8.

9.

The cause I fear the most:

You will probably realize that this symptom has many possible causes, only some of which are frightening. It is also important to remember that sometimes we have symptoms and *cannot* find an explanation for them; this doesn't mean that they must then be serious.

Key messages

One way of answering your negative thoughts about what happens during panic is to carefully weigh up all the evidence, and ask yourself these questions:

- What is my <u>evidence</u> for this belief?

- Are there any <u>other explanations</u> that might be less frightening?

- How would <u>somebody else</u> think about it?

- Am I <u>forgetting</u> some relevant facts?

- Do I need to get some <u>more information</u> to help me put this in perspective, and where can I get it?

Tip for supporters

Encourage the person you are supporting to have an open mind and consider the possibility that there is an alternative explanation for their panic attacks other than that their bodily sensations are signalling impending disaster, or that having a panic attack is dangerous.

Noticing symptoms I would not have noticed before

A lot of people with panic attacks say, 'I get lots of symptoms during the day, not just when I panic; I never used to get so many symptoms before I had panic attacks, so there must be something seriously wrong with me.'

Sometimes it comes as a surprise to discover how much you can be affected by the way you focus your attention. If you have a car, remember what happened just after you bought it. Suddenly it seemed as if there were lots of cars of the same colour and type on the road, many more than before you got yours. Of course, what was happening was that this type of car meant something different and was more important to you, so you noticed it much more.

The same thing goes for symptoms. If you are worried about getting a cold or flu, you may notice that your throat is a little sore, or you have a slight sniffle, although you don't actually get a cold. So if you think you have a serious illness (like a heart condition) think how sensitive that would make you to noticing changes in the way your heart works. Or, if you think you might be going to lose control over your behaviour and go crazy, you might notice changes in the way you think, or a slight trembling in your hands.

This process of noticing things more because they have become important to you works particularly strongly when you have nothing to distract you. This is why people often tend to notice worrying symptoms when they sit down to relax in the evenings. The sensations they notice are probably ones that were around before, but to which they paid no attention because they didn't seem important.

Thinking about it now, do you think any of your symptoms associated with your worst fears tend to be more noticeable at the moment because they are so worrying and important to you?

Now try a small experiment. Think about all the sensations you have in your feet as they press against the floor inside your shoes. Do this for a couple of minutes, really focusing. Do you notice how your feet feel? Were these feelings noticeable to you *before* you began to think about your feet? Another example would be to focus on the sensations you have on the top of your head. How does it feel now you are focusing on it? Are you noticing it getting a bit itchy? Make some notes about this here.

Filling in your diary

Now that you have done quite a bit of work on weighing up the evidence for your thoughts and considering alternative, less frightening explanations, fill in the last column in the panic diary each time you have an attack. This is headed 'Answers to your thoughts of disaster', and it is a space for you to try *challenging* your frightening thoughts and arguing against them. An example is given below:

Description of situation where panic occurred	Number of sensa-tions	Thought of disaster (rate belief 0–100%)	Answers to your thoughts of disaster. Re-rate belief in thoughts of disaster. (0–100%)
Out shopping	5	I'll faint. 80%	I won't faint. My pulse is racing so my blood pressure is up. You need a drop in blood pressure to faint. I feel faint because more blood is going to my muscles, which is a natural response to thoughts of danger, even if as now the thought is wrong. 5%

June was seeing a therapist for help with her panic disorder. Throughout therapy, she wrongly believed she was suffering from heart disease. Negative medical tests and reassurance from her doctor failed to change this belief. When asked what evidence she had for the idea that she had heart disease, she said that she noticed her heart more frequently than did her husband or colleagues at work and she thought this must indicate that there was something seriously wrong with it. The therapist suggested the alternative interpretation that the problem was her *belief* that there was something wrong with her heart. This belief might lead her to selectively focus on her body, which in turn would increase her awareness of her heart.

When asked what she thought of this alternative, she replied, 'You psychologists are very good at thinking of clever explanations and this would, no doubt, apply to some people but I don't think that the effects of attention could be strong enough to account for my sensations.' Rather than argue with this assertion, the therapist said, 'You may be right. Perhaps to get more information it would be good if we did an experiment to see how strong the effects of attention are for you?'

The patient was asked to close her eyes and concentrate on her heart for five minutes. To her great surprise, she found that simply focusing on her heart enabled her to detect the pulse in her forehead, neck, arms, chest and legs, without touching those parts of the body. Furthermore, when she was subsequently asked to describe out loud the contents of the room for five minutes, she ceased to be aware of her heart. This demonstration reduced her belief that she had heart disease. It also increased her belief in the alternative explanation, that it was her belief that there is something wrong with her heart that was increasing her awareness of it.

Key messages

- Remember these sensations may not be very pleasant but they are not dangerous.

- The more you feel worried about something the more you will tend to notice symptoms that support it, particularly if you have no other convincing explanation for your symptoms.

Don't worry at this stage if you cannot yet fill in a completely convincing answer in the 'answers' column. In the next section we move on to other ways of answering your thoughts.

Now re-rate how much you believe that your worst fears could come true. Remember 0% means that you would not believe them at all, and 100% means you would be totally convinced the worst could happen.

My beliefs about the worst things that could happen to me during a panic attack	How much I believe them right now (0–100%)	How much I believe them in the middle of a panic attack (0–100%)

It's fine to still have doubts. You can work on them in the final section of this chapter.

As you continue to fill in the panic diary you can use the things you have learned in this section to help you fill in the 'answers to your thoughts of disaster' columns.

Looking for things that can trigger panic attacks

Earlier in this chapter we mentioned that lots of different things can trigger panic attacks. The two main categories are sensations in your body, and going into a situation where you fear you may have a panic attack.

It is probably clear to you that going back to a place where you have panicked before can make you feel anxious. The anxiety causes various sensations in your body, which you can then misinterpret, which can then spiral into a panic attack.

It is probably also clear that physical symptoms like rapid heart beats (from too much coffee, or from exercise) or dizziness (if you stand up too suddenly, or after a hot bath) can also trigger panic.

It is sometimes harder to see that other emotional events can also trigger panic. This happens especially in situations that are stressful, but in which it is not clear what you can do about the situation, or in which it does not seem safe to look at or express your feelings. Here are a couple of examples:

Kwazi worked in a restaurant with his fiancée, and they both lived in accommodation provided by their boss. The boss exploited them, making them work overtime, never paying their wages on time, and not letting them take holidays at the same time. Kwazi was worried about the possibility of finding another job and alternative accommodation, and did not dare to stand up to the boss. The unexpressed anger would sometimes make him hot, dizzy and shaky. He misinterpreted these sensations as meaning he was ill, or about to pass out or even die. In therapy, Kwazi learned to spot what was triggering the sensations and to challenge the thoughts of illness, passing out or dying. He also began to stand up to his boss, and to explore other possible ways of finding accommodation or employment.

Susie was worried because most of her panic attacks seemed to come on 'out of the blue'. However, when she and her therapist went over some of these attacks very slowly and carefully they noticed that often an emotional event had triggered them off. For example, on one occasion, Susie felt worried and sad when her mother-in-law criticised her for not being able to go into the centre of town, and on another occasion she felt angry when her husband asked her late at night to type a few urgent letters for him. Each of these situations gave her various physical sensations in her body, and she had then focused on them rather than thinking about what had upset her in the first place. Once she realised what was happening she was able to respond that these were <u>normal</u> emotional reactions, to which she had become over sensitive. Realising this was helpful in preventing her reactions from spiralling up into panic attacks

In these two cases the vicious cycle was working like this:

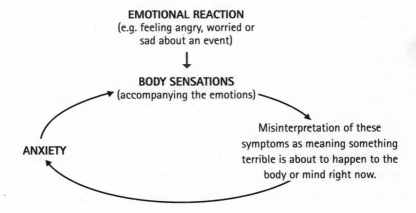

EMOTIONAL REACTION
(e.g. feeling angry, worried or sad about an event)

BODY SENSATIONS
(accompanying the emotions)

Misinterpretation of these symptoms as meaning something terrible is about to happen to the body or mind right now.

ANXIETY

Do you think that some of your panic attacks may be triggered by emotional reactions to ordinary things? If so, make some notes below about recent examples:

Key messages

- It is not always obvious what triggers a panic attack.

- Mild sensations that can then lead to an attack might be caused by things such as stress, tiredness, coffee, standing up too quickly, etc.

- A panic attack can also be triggered by emotional reactions.

- Thinking about the relationship between your emotions and panic attacks can help you understand them better so they don't seem to come 'out of the blue' as much.

'Saving yourself' and avoidance

Finding out what happens if you do not attempt to 'save yourself' and prevent the worst from happening

Often people with panic attacks feel as if the worst *could* happen – but that so far they have been lucky and got away with it. You may say, 'I've had lots of attacks when I have been very close to disaster and just managed to escape it each time.'

Understandably, if you are pretty well convinced that something disastrous will happen to you during a panic attack you will begin to do all you can to prevent the worst from happening. Typical examples of things people fear, and the precautions they take, are given in Table 7.1 (p. 135). These precautions are technically called 'safety-seeking behaviours' (see Table 1.3, p. 11).

Table 7.2 Safety-seeking behaviours

Fear	Precautions/'saving yourself'
Fainting, collapsing	Hold on to something (e.g. a supermarket trolley) Hold someone's arm Sit down Take deep breaths Keep cool
Heart attack or stroke	Attempt to take the strain off your heart by e.g. sitting down, taking deep breaths and trying to relax Focus attention on the body, especially the heart
Falling down	Hold on to something or someone Stiffen legs to keep balance
Starting shaking	Stiffen arms and legs to try to control shaking
Going crazy, losing control	Try to control thoughts, speech and behaviour Check you are 'real' by touching your face or body to see you are 'still there'
Suffocating	Take deep breaths Get out into fresh air
Choking, throat closing up	Keep swallowing to see if throat is OK Eat sweets or sip water

In addition to these precautions that you may take linked to these specific fears, there is also a common further precaution, which is to leave the situation. You are likely to do this no matter what your specific fears are.

First of all, put a tick beside your worst fears if they are listed above. Are these the things you do when you are afraid the worst will happen? Or are there other things you do to 'save yourself' as well as (or instead of) the things listed above? On page 188 and in the appendices there is a brief questionnaire, the Safety Seeking Behaviour Questionnaire. This lists other precautions you might take in order to save yourself. You can use this to monitor how much you are using these precautions.

Write down below all the things you do to 'save yourself' when you are afraid that the worst is about to happen. Remember only to write about your worst fears at this stage.

My worst fears	Things I do to 'save myself'

How 'saving yourself' can make things worse

Thinking about it now, do you think that any of the precautions you take have the effect of making you feel *worse*?

If the answer is 'yes' how would that work?

In fact, taking precautions keeps the fear going in several ways.

One is that it tends to focus your attention on the part of your body that you are worried about, and so make you notice even more worrying sensations. The second is that if you deliberately try to control your reactions, a lot of the things you do make the sensations worse. Here are some examples:

Precautions	How it can make things worse
Checking your body for any 'worrying' sensations	You notice more sensations
Taking deep breaths	Makes you feel more dizzy and more breathless
Stiffening your legs	Actually makes you feel more wobbly
Trying to stop yourself from shaking	Actually makes you more shaky
Swallowing a lot	Makes it more difficult to swallow
Checking that you are real by touching your face and body	Can make you feel less real as you stay focused on this fear and keep doubting yourself
Trying to control your thoughts	The more you try to keep a particular thought out of your mind the more it simply comes back (this is normal and known as the 'rebound effect')

In the example from earlier, Sundee was in a shopping centre when she had a sudden panic attack. As she started to notice feeling breathless she believed that she would stop breathing. As well as making her feel anxious she tried to 'save herself' by breathing deeply to make sure she 'got enough air in'. This breathing made her feel more light headed. Sundee then thought that she might be about to faint, or even collapse and die. Of course, these thoughts made her feel extremely frightened, which gave rise to even more intense sensations in her body.

Here, the way Sundee was breathing in order to save herself from stopping breathing was actually making the situation worse and led to a full panic attack.

From now on, it is important to work on reducing your belief in your frightening thoughts still further, by giving up the precautions you have been taking, so that you can find out what *really happens*. This can be scary. It is important to remember all of the information and evidence, and things you have learned so far in this chapter. As we have said in other parts of this chapter, a panic attack can't cause you to pass out, go mad, have a heart attack, etc. You will of course feel anxious, but the more often you try to stop using your precautions the less anxious you will feel as your body learns through experience that it is in fact safe.

To fully prove to yourself that the sensations in a panic attack are not in fact dangerous you will need to experience that even when the sensations are very strong and your worst fears are activated, the disaster doesn't occur. You also need to discover that you don't need to save yourself. When you really understand and believe this then the cycle that currently keeps the panic going will be broken. The problem will be beaten.

This will, of course, feel horrible, but it is not dangerous. If you have a supporter it would probably be helpful to try not using your precautions ('save yourself') with him or her first so they can give encouragement and support.

A note on 'controlled breathing' or 'breathing retraining'

You may have read or been told that learning to control your breathing is an important way to overcome panic attacks and panic disorder. This is a common part of some treatments for panic disorder. Although smooth, shallow breathing is sometimes given as a way to control breathing, we have found that this may become a precaution (a safety-seeking behaviour) in itself. You may still fear panic attacks and worry what would happen if you didn't do your controlled breathing early enough or well enough. You need to learn that your sensations are harmless even if you don't control your breathing in any way.

Of course, when under stress, such as before a job interview, breathing slowly and smoothly can help you feel calmer. But in those situations, it is not being used as a precaution to save yourself like in panic disorder.

However, in this approach, to fully overcome panic disorder, there is no need to learn how to control your breathing, and no need to try to do so when you have a panic attack. Even without controlling your breathing nothing bad will happen.

Tip for supporters

Try controlling your own reactions, too, and discuss with the person you are supporting what it felt like for you.

Overcoming avoidance of feared situations and activities, and agoraphobia

Many people who have panic attacks start to change their lifestyle in order to avoid the unpleasant sensations that they fear will lead to a panic attack. Typical changes that are driven by this fear of further attacks include reducing or stopping exercise, stopping drinking coffee and/ or alcohol, and stopping having sex. Even if you don't stop doing these things you may find that you will only do them once you have checked how you are feeling, and judge that you are feeling well enough.

We have found that a good place to start overcoming avoidance is to try to get back to doing the things you used to do in your life but have given up because of the fear of having a panic attack. All of these are activities you may have avoided as they can cause changes in your body, which you may then fear will develop into a panic attack that leads to physical disaster. To take this further you can try to do these activities on days when you aren't feeling so well, too, just to show yourself that it is still safe to do so. In time you will learn that you don't need to check how you are feeling, but can simply do what you want when you want to.

You may also have tried to keep a firm lid on your emotions to prevent the normal physical sensations that come with strong emotions. This is the time now to allow yourself to become excited about things (or angry, or any other emotion you have been trying not to feel), so you can learn there is no physical danger from such feelings.

In addition, people with panic disorder avoid places where they fear they may panic. In this way what we call 'agoraphobia' starts to develop. Once you have understood what is happening in panic attacks you are in a good position to tackle any situation you have been avoiding. You may have already started to do this.

You will probably have read or heard that the best way to overcome agoraphobia is to repeatedly go into the situations you fear, until you no longer feel afraid of them, starting with the least frightening.

We now know that there is a better way to work on overcoming agoraphobia. When you put yourself into frightening situations what you need to do before you are in the actual situation is:

1. Notice what frightening thoughts are going through your mind.
2. Do your best to reason with yourself and answer these fears. You may find it helps to write brief answers to your thoughts on cards (or similar, like having a note on your phone), which you can read through just before entering a feared situation.
3. Notice whether you are making predictions about what will happen (e.g. I'll fall down if I let go, I'll faint if I stay here, etc.).
4. Then try to *test the predictions* by deliberately not taking precautions, and even by testing things further, by doing things like swaying around or standing on one leg (to be certain that you *will not fall*) or running up and down the stairs if your heart is racing (to be certain you will not have a heart attack). The more daring you can be, the quicker you will feel confident again.

It is usual to go into situations that are only slightly frightening first, before going into more scary ones. However, we would encourage you to go into the most difficult situations that you are willing to try out, rather than building up too slowly or gradually. The aim of this approach isn't to learn that you can gradually get used to situations. Rather the aim is to learn that the worst fears you have about your physical sensations will not occur at all. The best way to find this out is to make sure that you go into situations in which these fears are properly activated, to not use precautions, and to discover that nothing catastrophic happens.

Recording what you do

When overcoming avoidance and not 'saving yourself' you will learn the most, and make the quickest progress, if you record what you do. We have found that this is best done in a structured way. In the following pages there is a worksheet for recording the times you test out your thoughts of disaster. There is also an example of an experiment that Sundee did to test out her fears of fainting and dying (below).

Sundee's experiment

Date and situation	Prediction	Experiment	Outcome	Learning
	What do I think will happen? What are my worst fears? How much do I believe this (0–100%)?	What can I do to put this to the test? What precautions do I need to drop?	What actually happened? Was the prediction correct?	What have I learned? How likely is my worst fear to happen (0–100%)? Any 'Yes, but's? How can I further test my worst fears?
Saturday: go to shopping centre	I'll have a panic attack. I'll faint (99%). I'll collapse (99%). I'll die (50%).	Go to the shopping centre. Go to the busy shops that I really would like to get back to. Rather than hold on to things or someone, make sure I am in the middle of the centre of shop so I don't use my precautions.	Well, I felt very lightheaded, breathless and anxious. But I didn't faint, collapse or die.	Maybe when I get the very strong sensations in these attacks nothing bad will happen. I think I know this logically now but it still feels very scary. Also the centre wasn't as busy as it usually is so my panic attack wasn't as strong as it can be. Maybe these things would happen if it was busier and the sensations stronger. I'll faint (50%). I'll collapse (50%). I'll die (10%).

Worksheet 7.2: Prediction experiment outcomes and learning

Date and situation	Prediction	Experiment	Outcome	Learning
	Prediction What do I think will happen? What are my worst fears? How much do I believe this (0–100%)?	**Experiment** What can I do to put this to the test? What precautions do I need to drop?	**Outcome** What actually happened? Was the prediction correct?	**Learning** What have I learned? How likely is my worst fear to happen (0–100%)? Any 'Yes, but's'? How can I further test my worst fears?

As you can see from Sundee's worksheet she found that she did not faint when she went to the shopping centre but that she still had some remaining doubts.

There are a number of questions you need to ask yourself. You should then fill these in on the sheet on p. 177.

- What are your worst fears of disaster?

- How will you test these?

- What precautions do you usually use? You'll need to *not* do these to fully test your fears.

After you have put your worst fears to the test you can complete the final two columns of the sheet.

- What actually happened?

- What you have learned?

- Any 'yes, but's? What could you do to really convince yourself that your worst fears won't happen?

These can be called 'behavioural experiments'. This form of behavioural experiment is one in which you test out your predictions. These are used in treating all anxiety disorders (see pp. 62–4 in Chapter 1). An alternative behavioural experiment worksheet is provided on p. 65 in Chapter 1. These worksheets are different ways of recording the same information. You can use whichever form you prefer.

If you follow the above guidelines you will find that the process of making your reactions to perceived threats more manageable will go more quickly and easily for you. Good luck!

Convincing yourself

We wouldn't expect that doing a single experiment will suddenly convince you that your worst fears won't happen – and hence break the panic cycle and make the panic attacks stop. This didn't happen for Sundee in the example on p. 176. We expect that you can put things to the test in more and more situations and reflect on what you learn. From this you can learn through experience ('in your heart and body') what we hope you already know logically ('in your head') – that panic attacks are horrible but not dangerous, and your worst fears won't come true. Each time you think 'yes, but' this is a chance to try to do another test in a new situation.

Ultimately the very best test of this is to have a panic attack without using any of your precautions and finding that your worst fears don't occur – or even try to make the worst fears happen and find that you can't! We know this can be hard to do. It will help to remind yourself of the other information you have learned from this chapter and from your supporter(s). It can help to have this information written down for yourself (like you have been doing on the panic diary) and to keep it with you as a reminder when you put your worst fears to the test.

Key messages

- If you fear something bad is going to happen it makes sense to try to prevent it.

- These precautions ('saving yourself') can make the sensations worse, and they also stop you learning that the worst fears won't occur without the precautions.

- To fully learn your worst fears won't happen, you need to go into situations in which they typically occur without using your precautions.

- You may need to do this several times in different ways or situations to fully convince yourself. The situation you avoid is less important than the sensations you feel and what you fear is the worst that can happen in an attack.

- Using the behavioural experiment record sheet will help you learn the most by structuring what you do.

- The very best test is to 'make' a panic attack occur, try to make the worst fear happen, and find that you can't!

Tips for supporters

- This is usually the hardest part of overcoming panic and people need lots of support and encouragement. You will also need to remind the person with panic disorder that panic attacks are not dangerous (although they are horrible), testing the worst fears out is not in fact risky, and that this is the key to fully beating panic disorder.

- It's also possible that you may become a precaution yourself and that the person you are supporting won't go into certain situations without you – that you are the way the person 'saves themselves'. This is normal and understandable, and this is where you need to encourage the person to test out strategies alone.

Now rate your worst fears again:

My beliefs about the worst things that could happen to me during a panic attack	How much I believe them right now (0–100%)	How much I believe them in the middle of a panic attack (0–100%)

We don't expect that these beliefs will change easily. The next section on images may provide extra help. The best way to further change these beliefs is to continue to test them in the ways described above.

Dealing with images

Many people have images that pop into their mind in the middle of a panic attack. These images usually involve seeing in their mind what they most fear will happen. For example, people afraid of passing out may have an image of themselves lying unconscious on the floor; or someone afraid of dying of a heart attack may see a picture of their heart exploding or their body lying in a coffin. Research shows that images are more frightening than words. So, seeing a picture of yourself collapsing can be even more scary than just thinking it.

Steve was a 26-year-old working in a call centre. In his panic attacks the strongest physical sensations were chest pain, racing heart and dizziness. At these times he also had a picture come into his mind of a large clot of blood circulating in his body. It was so real he described he could feel it. As the attack got to the worst point he saw this clot moving towards his heart or his head. This made him strongly believe that he was going to have a heart attack or a stroke, caused by the clot. Even though he knew in reality that he was experiencing a panic attack and that he was perfectly safe, this image was very powerful. In order to fully overcome his panic disorder he needed to change his image to better fit with what he knew – that there was no danger from a blood clot in his body. He did this by imagining the clot harmlessly dissolving and in fact coming out of his body. By practising changing the image in his mind when he was not in panic-attack mode, he was then able to change it when it occurred in the midst of a panic.

In order to deal with your images and the fear that comes with them, there are a few steps you need to follow:

1.   Identify the image or images you have in the middle of a panic.

2.   Work out what this image means – what you think is the worst that is

going to happen. Often this is what is happening in the image itself, such as collapsing. This is almost certainly one of the worst fears you have already worked on.

3.   Remember that this is just an unrealistic image and nothing dangerous can actually happen. Remind yourself of all the work you have already done on this worst fear.

4.   Think about how you might change the image in your mind so that it better fits with reality – i.e. showing that your worst fear won't happen. Remember, they are only images, not reality, and you can change them however you like. This could be you jumping up from the floor or out of the coffin!

5.   Practise changing this image first when you are not feeling very anxious. Bring the frightening image to mind. When it is at the worst point (and your anxiety might be raising now . . .) change the image in your mind to show that your worst fear doesn't happen.

6.   When you get this image during a panic attack, try changing it in the way you have already practised.

Sometimes this seems a little strange – to play around with changing the picture in your head. But this is something that professional sportsmen and women practise repeatedly before their race, football match, etc. It helps change how they feel, *and* improve how they actually play or perform. Just give it a try and if changing the image in one way doesn't seem to work then simply try changing it another way. This is something you have to experience rather than read about.

Key messages

- Pictures or images can be as frightening as thoughts.

- The images are usually related to your worst fears of disaster.

- These are just images and can be changed with practice.

- You can change the image to further show that the worst fears won't happen.

Preventing a relapse

Preventing relapse is important for all anxiety problems and you can read more about this in Chapter 14 in Part 3. As you regain your confidence in overcoming your panic disorder it is a good idea to look into the future and think about situations that might stir the problem up again. Then try to think through what you could do to prevent yourself from developing panic attacks and starting to avoid things.

Write a list below of any problems you anticipate in the future, and any ideas you have about how you could avoid developing panic attacks:

At this stage it is often useful to make a list of all the things you have learned so far about your panic attacks, what has kept them going, and how to overcome them. You can use the space below to write short notes about the different things you have learned.

Below you will see someone else's notes on what they learned about panic. The notes need only be brief, like those in the example.

You cannot faint when your pulse is racing.

Panic attacks can happen to anyone.

One in ten people suffers one attack each year.

They are caused by fear of something and are kept going by adrenalin being released into the bloodstream causing a high pulse, sweating, and breathing harder due to extra work by the heart affected by this hormone.

Light headedness is caused through more blood going to the muscles for either fight or flight to happen.

Focusing your attention on your symptoms makes them worse, causing a belief that there is something seriously wrong. The more you worry, the more symptoms you notice. Positive thinking and knowledge of panic attacks can bring them to an end when you acknowledge them as sensations caused by the mind.

During an attack, it is best not to 'save yourself'. Instead, press on and try not to focus your attention on the attack.

Conclusion

We hope you have found this account of the nature of panic and what you can do about it helpful. It is not a magic wand and it requires lots of hard work from you, and often those supporting you. Once you fully believe (in your heart and body as well as your head) that panic attacks are only horrible rather than dangerous then there will be no need to fear them. Then they will stop, not come back, and allow you to live your life as you want.

Key messages

- Panic attacks and panic disorder can happen to anyone.
- The key to panic disorder is that you believe the bodily sensations you have in a panic attack mean something awful is about to happen to you (I'll faint, I'll go mad, I'll die). These worst fears often come along with images that reflect and reinforce your fears.
- There is always a good reason why you believe something awful is going to happen – usually the fact that the sensations are so strong is an important part of this.
- Although panic attacks are horrible they are not in fact dangerous. Your worst fears of disaster won't happen.
- The understandable precautions you take to stop the worst from happening actually keeps the problem going.
- You need to learn both 'logically' and through your own experience, that the sensations in a panic attack won't harm you, even if you don't use your precautions.
- To overcome panic disorder you have to do things and put yourself in situations that will make you anxious. You can't simply do it from reading a book.
- With hard work and support you can overcome your panic disorder. Good luck!

Worksheet 7.3. Panic Diary

						SYMPTOMS								
OVERALL ANXIETY		PANIC ATTACKS												
	DAY	DESCRIPTION OF SITUATION WHERE PANIC OCCURRED	Breathlessness	Palpitations/heart racing	Choking	Chest tight/uncomfortable	Sweating	Dizziness/unsteady/faint	Unreal/distant feeling	Nausea	Hot or cold flushes	Trembling/shaking	Numbness or tingling	Fear of dying/going mad/loss of control

FULL ATTACK	LIMITED ATTACK	RATING OF SEVERITY	PANIC FREQUENCY (per day)	LIMITED ATTACK FREQUENCY(per day)	Main bodily sensations / thoughts of disaster (rate belief 1–100%)	Negative Interpretation of the sensations/ thoughts of disaster rate belief 0-100%	Rational Response / answer to thoughts (re-rate belief 0-100%)

Table 7.3: Safety-seeking behaviour questionnaire

When you are at your most anxious or panicky, how often do you do the following things?

Try to think about other things	Never	Sometimes	Often	Always
Hold on to or lean on to something	Always	Often	Sometimes	Never
Hold on to or lean on someone	Never	Sometimes	Often	Always
Sit down	Always	Often	Sometimes	Never
Keep still	Always	Often	Sometimes	Never
Move very slowly	Never	Sometimes	Often	Always
Look for an escape route	Never	Sometimes	Often	Always
Make yourself do more physical exercise	Always	Often	Sometimes	Never
Focus attention on your body	Always	Often	Sometimes	Never
Try to keep control of your mind	Never	Sometimes	Often	Always
Try to keep tight control over behaviour	Always	Often	Sometimes	Never
Talk more	Never	Sometimes	Often	Always
Take medication	Never	Sometimes	Often	Always
Ask people around for help	Never	Sometimes	Often	Always
Change your breathing	Always	Often	Sometimes	Never

Reproduced with permission from *Panic Disorder Therapist Manual for IAPT High Intensity Therapists*, Clark and Salkovskis, 2009.

Longer answers to common questions

Will I fall over when I feel anxious and wobbly?

People feel unsteady when they are anxious, because they breathe rapidly and this can make them feel wobbly and shaky. However, it can't lead to falling over; it is just a feeling.

When we are having a panic attack the symptoms come on very quickly at first, and we become afraid that they will carry on increasing quickly until something awful happens, e.g. collapsing or falling over.

But many of the symptoms can be caused by the way we breathe in a panic attack to try to keep the problem under control. For a few minutes breathe in the same way that you do in a panic attack. Remember to do it the same way you actually do in a panic attack, rather than how you would like to do it. What do you notice?

Many people notice the symptoms of a panic attack starting to build up. If you then start to feel wobbly and believe you will fall over it is common to try to sit down or keep still. But you'll never find out what would happen if you carried on – would you really fall over or is it just a horrible feeling? It's also common to walk differently if you start to feel wobbly. Many people walk with their legs slightly wider apart as they think this will stop them falling over. But if you try this now you will find that this can actually make you feel more wobbly. Once again the things you do (understandably) to save yourself can be making the symptoms and the panic worse.

You may *feel* wobbly when you are anxious, but this will not lead to your falling over.

Can I faint during a panic attack?

People who panic often fear that they may be about to faint. In movies, people are often shown fainting away if they receive a bad shock. In fact panic *itself* cannot lead to fainting.

Why is this? In order to faint you need to have a drop in blood pressure. When you are anxious, what happens to your blood pressure? It temporarily goes *up* and your heart beats faster, as part of your body's 'alarm reaction' to danger. This actually has the effect of *protecting* you from fainting.

You can check whether this is true for you. Next time you have a panic attack and fear you may faint, *take your pulse*. Count the number of times your heart beats in one minute. (If you don't know how to take your pulse ask someone to show you how.)

You cannot faint unless your pulse falls to below 40 beats per minute.

If you take your pulse a few times when you are anxious or panicky, and a few more times when you feel fine, you will probably find that your pulse will be a little higher when you feel nervous. It will never drop as low as 40 beats per minute, unless something else is going on (see below):

* Being physically ill (e.g. having flu)

* During hormonal changes (e.g. a period, pregnancy, menopause, puberty)

* Having sunstroke (not just being hot). It is the *light* that gives you sunstroke.

* Seeing a lot of blood, or other injury to the body.

This last reason affects about 10 per cent of people, who experience a blood pressure drop in this situation. If you are one of these people, and it is a problem to you, there is a simple technique to increase your blood pressure and put your heart rate up to normal. This is called applied tension (see p. 111–13). Essentially you tense your muscles, such as in your fists, arms and legs, when you see blood or an injury, or when you expect it.

So why do people sometimes *feel* faint when they are anxious? This is because when you fear you are in danger, blood surges to your muscles to get you ready to run away, or to fight. This means a little less blood goes to your head. However, as your overall blood pressure doesn't drop there is *no danger of you fainting.*

Will I faint if I get very hot in the shops?

Remember what you have already learned about fainting. In order to faint you need to have a *drop* in blood pressure. If you are anxious in a situation you will feel hotter, but this is because your blood pressure increases slightly for a while, so you will not faint. To test out whether feeling hot *can* make you faint you could try the following little experiments:

a) Try to make yourself very hot at home, where you can test out what happens in privacy. Put on a lot of clothes, including a scarf or a heavy coat, turn up the heating, drink a hot drink, turn on an extra fan heater or hair dryer, and keep the windows and doors closed. Stand up to see what happens. Make some notes below on what happened:

b) Next time you go somewhere hot (e.g. a big department store) wear some extra clothes. Once again to test that being hot (and anxious) can't make you faint, although you may feel uncomfortable. What happened when you tried to do this?

Now you will realize that heat alone cannot make you faint. Firemen face intense heat, and can still do their jobs. The same is true of people who work near furnaces making metal or glass objects and people who live in hot countries.

Why do I notice worrying sensations much more than I used to, and often when I am relaxing or resting?

You may notice sensations more than you used to because you think they are a sign that something bad will happen, and you want to avoid that happening. Sensations are more noticeable when you pay attention to them. So that when you are not thinking about other things you will become more aware of them. The following exercise demonstrates the effects of attention on how noticeable sensations are:

a) Sit quietly and focus on your body. Make a note of the sensations in your legs, arms, shoulders and body. Were you aware of all of these sensations before doing this?

b) Now look around the room, and describe one of the objects in it out loud. How many sensations were you aware of when you were paying attention to something else?

Doesn't chest pain mean there is something wrong with my heart?

Some people with chest pain have heart disease. However, we are assuming that if you are reading this you have been checked out by your doctor who has confirmed that you do not and that your problem is anxiety.

When you have been tense for a while do you ever notice pain or discomfort in your chest? This may make you worry that there is something wrong with your heart. But this type of pain is due to harmless muscle spasm. There are lots of muscles in your chest, between each pair of ribs. These muscles can start to ache if you breathe in a tense way.

To see if this is true for you, try this small test:

Take a deep breath, and do not let it out again. *While holding this air in your lungs* take short breaths in and out for two minutes, if you can manage it.

What do you notice happening?

Most people get uncomfortable sensations in the chest when they are anxious because they breathe in a tense way. This tends to persist for a while even when they relax. This is something like a cramp in the muscles between the ribs. Any muscle held tensely for any length of time tends to ache. If we sit in a chair with one leg stuck out in front of us it would start to feel uncomfortable quite quickly. We also get aches and pains when we exercise muscles we haven't used for a long time (e.g. if we carry a heavy suitcase).

This sort of pain does *not* mean there is something wrong with our heart. When we are anxious we probably do not relax our chest between breaths, but breathe in and out in a tense way.

Try to notice how you are breathing next time you feel a pain in your chest when you are feeling tense. Then try letting your breath out fully as you breathe out, and wait a moment for the next breath to come in. This gives the muscles a chance to relax, and will probably feel more comfortable. Remember, even if you don't try to breathe differently nothing bad will happen to your heart or anything else.

Could these strong sensations really be caused by anxiety?

Many people who have panic attacks doubt that strong sensations can be caused by anxiety. If you share this view you could try the following brief experiment:

Sit in a place where you won't be disturbed and remember a recent severe panic attack. Close your eyes and picture where you were, what was around you, and how you were feeling in your body. Try to recall all the sights, sounds and smells as if it were actually happening again now.

Make some notes about what you noticed below:

Most people who have panic attacks worry about the sensations they get, and whether they may mean that they are ill in some way. Remembering past attacks is often enough to bring on worrying thoughts, and the anxiety generated can sometimes bring on strong sensations in the body.

If this happened to you, doesn't this suggest that strong sensations really *can* be caused by anxiety?

It if didn't happen, read on.

You have probably had other experiences which demonstrate the connection between feeling anxious and getting strong sensations in your body.

Think of a time when you knew you would have to do something that frightened you, like giving a talk or going on an aeroplane. Or think of a time recently when you woke up in the middle of a nightmare.

- What was the situation?

- How did you feel? (e.g. anxious, nervous, terrified, embarrassed)

- What kind of strong sensations did you notice in your body? (e.g. heart racing, sweaty, upset stomach, feeling sick or shaky)

- To what extent were they *similar* to the sensations you get when you have a panic attack?

Really strong sensations *can* be caused by anxiety, and are not dangerous.

Why do my hands shake if I'm not losing control?

Muscle tension in the arms and hands can exaggerate the normal, usually unnoticed, hand tremor that everyone has. If you are trying to control shaking by tensing your muscles you are probably making it worse. In order to prove to yourself that other people have hand tremors you can do the following test: ask your supporter to stretch out one arm, and then place a sheet of paper on the palm of their hand. Can you see the paper quivering?

Now try the following experiments to see whether tensing your muscles is making the shaking worse:

1. Place a sheet of paper on your own hand with your arm out-stretched. Notice how the paper moves. Now tense the muscles in your arm and hand to try to stop it moving. What do you notice?

2. When you are next in a situation where you notice yourself shaking do not try to control it. Just let it happen. Did this make the shaking better or worse?

If tensing your muscles is making the shaking worse the answer is to relax, not to try to control the shaking.

Is it possible to run out of air and faint or suffocate in a stuffy room?

When a room is stuffy it is *not* because there isn't enough air (or oxygen) in the room. Rooms feel stuffy when the air is warm, and contains quite a bit of water vapour (i.e. it is humid). Stale odours can also hang around and make a room feel stuffy. None of this means that there isn't enough oxygen around. Even if a small room were *completely* sealed the air in it would last for a few days before you would pass out.

Actually rooms are never totally sealed. Tiny draughts of air pass through cracks and gaps around doors and windows, so it would never be possible to run out of air in an ordinary room, even if the doors and windows were closed.

You can prove this to yourself with a small experiment:

Get an aerosol of scented air freshener. Get a friend to squirt it into the air a few times on one side of a closed door while you stand on the other side of a door. How long is it before you can smell the air freshener?

This experiment shows how quickly air spreads from room to room, bringing with it fresh oxygen for you to breathe. You can also notice that if you are cooking something smelly, like fish or cabbage, people are able to smell it in the next room, even if you have the door closed.

Why do things sometimes start to shimmer or move in front of my eyes?

Something appearing to move or shimmer in front of a person's eyes is a common experience. Ask someone you know if it ever happens to them. It is caused by a number of things. Firstly, it often occurs if people stare at objects (which anxious people sometimes do if they believe this will help them to stay in control, or keep their balance). Secondly, shimmering movements can be produced as a sort of optical illusion by certain patterns. Striped patterns of lines close together, which are sometimes found on floors or ceilings in shops, can produce this effect. Strong fluorescent light can also make things look unreal and unsteady.

The following experiments show these effects:

---

1. To show how staring can produce visual disturbances, try the following: fix your gaze on a specific spot in front of you on the wall. Stare at the spot. What happens to your vision?

2. To show how some patterns can produce unpleasant visual effects, try gazing at the illusions at this website: www.psy.ritsumei.ac.jp/akitaoka. What happened?

Some people are particularly sensitive to visual effects caused by certain patterns, and others feel unsteady in certain types of fluorescent light. However, although this feels strange, it is not harmful. You will not lose your balance and it doesn't mean there is something wrong with your eyes or brain.

8 Generalized anxiety disorder and worry

Kevin Meares and Mark Freeston

Richard's story

Richard could not relax. He felt tense and anxious the whole time, so much so that he started to worry about his health. He enjoyed his job, but he found it stressful and from time to time felt that he just couldn't cope with it. He headed up a small but talented team. Despite this he found it hard to delegate and so did too much of the work himself, so adding to his stress. It was not that he doubted the quality of his colleagues' work but he knew that even good people might make mistakes. He checked his own work repeatedly and never sent emails without reading them several times first. He always phoned his girlfriend to check that she was on her way home, and he worried if she was late. Often he imagined horror stories as his worries took hold, such as terrible car accidents, train wrecks or abductions – checking the internet for any news of these imagined events while at the same time imagining how he would manage work while caring for his girlfriend as she recovered from serious injuries. His girlfriend found his constant checking very difficult, sometimes ignoring his calls. His family and friends loved him but they also got annoyed because he was overprotective and often needed reassuring that they were OK. He started to suffer with tension headaches and began to drink a little too much. His worry was so much part of his life that he hardly noticed it, but he did notice feeling tense, exhausted and deflated.

Overview

We all experience bouts of severe worry from time to time. Some people, like Richard, however, experience excessive and distressing levels of persistent worry. In this case it is likely that they are suffering from a disorder called 'generalized anxiety disorder' or GAD. The most important feature of GAD is that people experience quite severe anxiety and worry about a wide range of things over long periods of time. Other symptoms of GAD include:

- Finding it difficult to control the worry.
- Restlessness or a feeling of being keyed up.
- Getting easily tired.
- Difficulty concentrating, or feeling that your mind has gone blank.
- Irritability.
- Tension in the muscles.
- Sleep disturbance, so that we have difficulty falling or staying asleep, or wake up feeling unrefreshed by our sleep.
- Finding it difficult to function normally at home, at work, or elsewhere, because of the extent of the worry.

Because of the importance of worry to GAD, we are going to spend the rest of this chapter talking about worry, and how you can understand and learn to overcome it.

Some people may feel that there is nothing that can be done about worry, or that it's just 'them' – part of their personality that can't be changed. But even though you may always have had a tendency to worry – maybe your parents did, too – you can still learn to understand it and get on top of it in a different way. Excessive worry is not a part of your personality, and it's not something that you should accept as inevitable. The other thing to note is that it is normal to feel anxious and worried at times, so we are not saying that you will never feel like this, but you can definitely learn to keep it in proportion, and to deal with it differently.

The ideas found in this chapter are the product of several different groups of researchers from around the world who have studied worry, some of them for nearly thirty years. Their work has contributed to the development of a better psychological understanding of worry and to a specific and effective cognitive behavioural therapy. Currently this treatment is one of the most effective and widely tested treatments for worry, and we describe its techniques in this chapter.

Is this chapter for me?

To help you to see if this chapter is for you here are some simple questions:

Have you always been a worrier?	Yes ☐ No ☐
If there is nothing to worry about, do you still find yourself worrying?	Yes ☐ No ☐
Do minor everyday things spiral into major concerns?	Yes ☐ No ☐
Once it starts, is your worry hard to stop?	Yes ☐ No ☐
Does worry stop you enjoying life?	Yes ☐ No ☐
Do your friends or family often suggest that you worry too much? Or, do they often tell you to stop worrying?	Yes ☐ No ☐

If you answer 'yes' to at least two of these questions, and if the worry is making it difficult for you to function properly at work, at home or in social situations, then it is likely that this chapter is for you.

Section 1: Understanding worry

In the explanations below we have added questions to help you to think about your experiences, and how the explanations apply to you.

You might find it helpful to make notes as you go along, so that you can collect your thoughts about the different aspects.

There are three important aspects to understanding worry, which we will describe in turn:

- Understanding uncertainty.

- Distinguishing between real and hypothetical worries.

- The importance of ideas about worry.

Understanding uncertainty

Uncertainty is a state almost all of us find unbearable at some point. Imagine a family waiting in an A&E department for news of a loved one involved in an accident, and not knowing whether they will survive or not; sometimes the uncertainty, or not knowing, is the hardest thing to bear. But this is a major and terrible situation. For most of us, even without realizing it, uncertainty is a constant feature of our lives, and we tolerate it without even noticing. We cannot know for certain whether there will be an accident on the road or the train; we cannot know for certain that our children aren't getting into trouble when they are out of our sight, but usually we are able to go about our business without much more than a passing thought about these possibilities. We have learned to tolerate this uncertainty. For people who worry excessively, though, even small daily events can produce a level of anxiety and worry on a par with the A&E situation.

So worry and uncertainty are intimately linked. For people who are worried, it is the feeling that you get when you are faced with uncertainty and start to think about what might happen. You worry because you don't know what is going to happen, and you start to imagine or fear the worst. You start to ask yourself *'what if?'* questions. Typical examples include: 'What if my partner has an accident on the way home?'; 'What if my report is useless and my boss decides I should get the sack?' This *'what if?'* question then triggers a whirlwind of worry. For instance, someone who worries might notice a headache, and start to think, 'What if I get sick and I can't look after my kids?' Then the questions get worse: 'What if my kids get put into care?', 'What if they start to take drugs and become criminals?' These worries might then lead to worrying about something completely different. So the person may move on to worry about their finances, and then to worry about how they will be able to pay the legal fees for their 'criminal' children, even though their children are still under five years old and have not done anything wrong yet!

People who worry tend to get caught up with these overwhelming thoughts about bad things that might happen. Like the example above, the worries that come into people's minds are usually highly unlikely but seem very real at the time. Consequently, worriers tend to be concerned by the unpleasant events they imagine in the future, rather than what is actually happening in the present.

'*What if?*' questions can be triggered by events that anyone would find scary, such as being referred to a specialist doctor, or hearing about redundancies at work, but for people who worry excessively they are also triggered by everyday situations, such as a minor disagreement or having a routine appointment with the doctor, visiting friends or shopping.

Do you have lots of 'what if?' type questions that go through your mind? How do you feel about or react to uncertain situations?

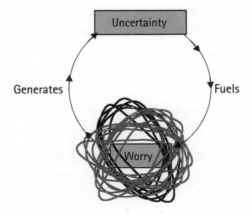

Figure 8.1: Worry and uncertainty

The impact of worry about uncertainty

Worriers tend to run on safe and familiar tracks to try to avoid uncertainty, but this can also place *real* limits on them by taking away new opportunities, new beginnings, new relationships, or by keeping people stuck within unhelpful situations, roles or relationships. Another possible consequence of this limited lifestyle is low mood and depression, especially when people are stuck in familiar but unrewarding situations, roles or relationships.

Distinguishing between worry about real things and 'hypothetical' things

There are two types of worry. There are some problems that we worry about which really exist; these problems could be called 'real event worry'. For example, if I worry about the size of my credit card bill, then this problem exists and my worry is based on a real and present problem. So rather than just worrying, it would make sense to try to do something about my spending – to put it another way, to engage in problem-solving. We will come back to problem-solving later in this chapter.

There are also worries about problems that haven't happened yet, but *which might*. These kinds of worries are known as 'hypothetical event worry'. For example, while many of us would dream about winning the lottery, worriers would also *worry* about winning it. They might worry about what to buy, how to deal with all the requests for money, even what to do when all the money had gone! In this hypothetical event worry, they may have not even bought a ticket yet, let alone won the life-changing jackpot.

Because it is about something that only exists in our imagination, we cannot 'problem solve' this kind of worry. Despite the worry being based on an imagined event, it still produces severe anxiety and fears. We need to learn that the things we imagine in our hypothetical event worry are only thoughts and nothing else, and approach them in a different way.

Spiralling from real to hypothetical worries

Real event worry can sometimes spiral and evolve into hypothetical event worry. So from a real concern that is here and now, the worrier may end up worrying about something completely different but set in the future. In Richard's example at the beginning of the chapter, notice how if his girlfriend was late (a real event) this led him to worrying about her having an accident (hypothetical event) and how he would cope with her serious injuries while managing work (hypothetical event).

Sometimes it can be hard to tell the difference between real and hypothetical worries, so Table 8.1 gives some more examples.

Table 8.1 More examples of real event vs. hypothetical event worries

Real event worry may spiral to →	Hypothetical event worry may spiral to →
My wife is late home from work and we have some tickets for a show later	My wife could have had a car accident
I have a fever and feel dreadful	I might become seriously ill and die alone
I've lost the passwords to my internet banking account	Somebody will 'hack' into my account and take all my savings
My child has a temperature	I will be interviewed on local television about how I failed to spot a serious illness

(continued)

My neighbours are noisy	I'll never be able to sell the house; I'll be stuck here for ever
My car was stolen	It will be used in a bank raid and I'll be prosecuted for this and end up in jail alone
I fell out with my neighbour	They will make a complaint and I will get in trouble with the police and be forced to move
My child is disobedient	I will be visiting him in prison; how will I fit the visits in with work?
I can't concentrate on work	I will lose my mind if I keep worrying
I have too much work to do	I will lose my job and end up on the streets

The importance of ideas about worry

Without being consciously aware of it, we have ideas about worry at the back of our minds that can help to keep worry going. There are two broad groups of ideas or beliefs that both tend to make us worry more. The first group could be called 'positive beliefs' about worry. Examples of positive beliefs would be *'worrying shows that I care'* or *'worrying motivates me'*. These ideas 'set us up to worry'. The second kind of thought could be called 'negative beliefs' about worry. These ideas appear once we have started to worry and add an intense element of anxiety to the whirlwind of worry. A typical thought might be *'worrying so much means I am losing my mind'*. When these thoughts appear, they feel very real and are so believable that they bring with them severe levels of anxiety or panic, which stoke up worry all the more. We could describe these beliefs as 'turbo charging' anxiety.

Exercise: Look at the list below, and see if you recognize any of these ideas.

Positive beliefs about worry

1. *Worry helps me to find solutions to problems*: This belief is based on the idea that worry is a useful strategy that helps to find solutions to problems. The belief suggests that worry enables us to look ahead and prepare for what might go wrong, or that worrying can help us to decide what we should do if our fears happen.

2. *Worry motivates*: This is one of the most common beliefs in people with excessive worry. In a recent tutorial a student said, *'My worry motivates me to work; if I didn't worry then I wouldn't work.'* This belief is only helpful if it does just enough to get us working; it then needs to 'leave us alone' to let us get on with the job in hand.

3. *Worry protects:* This idea means that the person who worries believes that if they worry before a difficult event, then they will be prepared for the worst, so that if something bad does happen they will be able to cope with it better.

4. *Worry prevents:* In this kind of belief, there is a strange kind of logic. The idea is that if you don't worry you are somehow tempting the fates, who will get back at you by making bad things happen.

5. *Worry shows I care:* This belief is very common. Here the beliefs centre around the idea that worrying means that the worrier is a thoughtful, caring or loving person; and, by implication, if they didn't worry this could mean that they were inconsiderate, careless or unfeeling.

The problem with these positive beliefs is that, although on the face of it they look sensible, in fact they make things worse. We will show you how to tackle these beliefs in the Treatment section.

Spotting your positive worry beliefs

Instructions: Think about something you worry about and try to answer the following questions. In the blank spaces below insert a description of what your worry is about. It might be the name of a loved one, a child, a family member, a colleague or a friend. It could be an event like an exam or a meeting. It could be a general concern like work, or money or health.

Supposing I didn't worry about _____, then what would that say about me?

Supposing I worried less about _____, then what would that say about me?

How does it help to worry about _____?

Supposing I stopped worrying completely about _____, would I be bothered by this? If so why?

If I worried less about _____, would anything happen?

Does worrying about _____ help in any way? If so how?

I should worry about _____ because _____

_____

Does it help you to understand why you worry in certain situations? Does it help you to understand what makes you more inclined to worry? Have you discovered any of your worry beliefs?

Negative beliefs about worry

People tend to believe that once they have started worrying, their excessive worry will lead to a number of unpleasant and distressing outcomes, like losing their mind or losing control. These thoughts 'turbo charge' worry – they could be called 'worry about worry'. We have listed some common ones in Exercise 8.1.

Exercise 8.1: Worry about worry

Consider each belief in the table below and ask yourself which of these beliefs applies to you?

Worrying excessively means that	How strongly do you believe this thought?
	Not At all true 0%------------------------100% Totally True
I am out of control	.........................%
I will be overwhelmed	.........................%
I will go crazy	.........................%
I will be unable to focus or work or perform	.........................%
I will be condemned to a life of anxiety	.........................%
I will become ill	.........................%
I lack confidence	.........................%
I am weak	.........................%

We have talked about uncertainty, types of worry, and beliefs about worry. Although these three ideas are key to understanding worry, there are also a number of other aspects to it that are important.

Worry and physical symptoms

When people are caught in the spiral of worry, they often feel tense, nervous or panicky, and experience a variety of other signs of anxiety, such as the symptoms described at the beginning of this chapter, or in the first part of this book. It might help to make a note of how you are feeling, so that you can use these symptoms to help catch yourself starting to worry.

What kinds of feelings and physical sensations do you experience when you worry?

Worry and coping

If you are a worrier, you may also have an overriding sense that you cannot cope with the everyday problems or situations you face. You may feel overwhelmed by them, or think that you lack the confidence to solve life's problems. This can result in avoiding or putting off dealing with problems, leaving them unsolved, which in turn triggers more worry.

Do you worry about your ability to cope with life's problems?

Worry, distraction and avoidance

Trying to distract your mind away from your worries might work for a short time but it can be difficult, particularly when the unpleasant sensations mentioned above are there to remind you of them. Also, trying not to think about worries means that you think of them all the more (see the white bear experiment on p. 373 in the OCD chapter). Despite using distraction and trying to avoid thinking about your worries, they have a tendency to continually return to the front of your mind.

Are your worries so upsetting that you try to avoid thinking about them? How do you distract your mind from your worries? Do you try hard to keep busy or overwork to keep your mind off your worries?

Worry and control

Our thoughts race when we worry and the speed of thought can sometimes give the impression that our thoughts are chaotic and lack any pattern or order. This sense of chaos further adds to the idea that our thoughts are out of control, causing us to worry all the more.

Do you have difficulty controlling your worries? When you start worrying about something do you have difficulty stopping? When your worry is racing do you ever feel like you are losing control of your mind?

Worry and other people

Worry is a private experience. Even our close friends may be unaware of our worry – we try to hide how bad it gets in case people think we are crazy, or pathetic. Often we worry in the early hours of the morning or at other times when we are 'alone with our thoughts'. These hidden and private worries can have a profound impact on our actions and on how we relate to others. For example, our worry may motivate us to be overprotective, or we may continually check on our loved ones, which may be experienced by others as intrusive or nagging, as was the case with Richard (see p. 197). Sometimes our worry drives us to seek reassurance from those around us, 'checking out' our fears with others in subtle or more obvious ways. If we do share our worries, we may be dismissed or told, 'Don't worry about it', but we still feel someone has to do the worrying.

How does your worry influence how you relate to others? How does your worry influence how you act? How does your worry interfere with your life?

Worry and enjoyment

Worriers also tend to focus on *what may happen* and so 'live' in the future. This prevents them from enjoying life in the here and now. For example, at a football match, rather than enjoying the game, the worrier may think about whether they will be able to get their bus home and what may then happen if they can't. Living in this way has a profound effect on an individual's capacity to simply live and enjoy life. If this goes on for a long time it can lead to depression.

Do you find it hard to enjoy the moment? Do you spend a lot of time in an imagined and anxiety-provoking future?

What happens when worry stops

In the middle of all these worries, the overriding feeling is anxiety, but even when the storm eases off you might not feel much better. You might find that you feel demoralized and exhausted. You might 'beat yourself up' mentally after the whirlwind has passed, or you might feel useless and low if your worry has got in the way of solving a problem or stopped you from doing something important.

How do you feel once a bout of worry has passed?

We can try to show how some of these things fit together by using the diagram below:

The **situation** in Figure 8.2 now finds Richard getting ready for work. The uncertainty found within a news bulletin about the weather is turned into a *what if?* type question by Richard. This then triggers a **whirlwind of worry** that produces **anxiety** that manifests in strong negative feelings, distressing bodily sensations and unhelpful actions. Once the worry has passed Richard feels **exhausted and demoralized**.

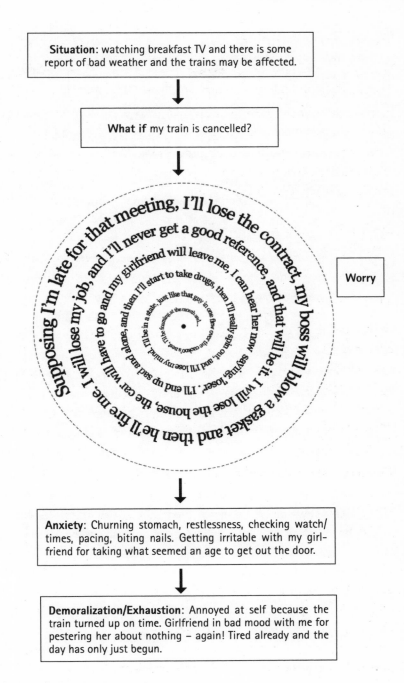

Situation: watching breakfast TV and there is some report of bad weather and the trains may be affected.

What if my train is cancelled?

Worry

Anxiety: Churning stomach, restlessness, checking watch/times, pacing, biting nails. Getting irritable with my girlfriend for taking what seemed an age to get out the door.

Demoralization/Exhaustion: Annoyed at self because the train turned up on time. Girlfriend in bad mood with me for pestering her about nothing – again! Tired already and the day has only just begun.

Figure 8.2: Richard's worry spiral

Key messages

- GAD is a condition in which people worry excessively.

- Worrying can generate strong feelings of anxiety and distressing physical symptoms.

- There are three important aspects to understanding worry:

  1. *Understanding uncertainty*: We worry in response to life's uncertainties. People who worry find it hard to tolerate uncertainty and spend a lot of time asking 'what if' questions that make the anxiety worse.

  2. *Distinguishing between 'real event' and 'hypothetical event' worries*: Some worries are realistic and need to be dealt with using problem-solving techniques or by finding practical solutions to the problem. Some worries are about things that may never happen, and need an approach that tackles the worry itself.

  3. *Understanding our beliefs about worry*: Without realizing it, we have ideas or beliefs about worry that help to keep it going. These can be either 'positive beliefs' about worry (which cover the way in which people think worry might be helpful and therefore they need to keep doing it) or 'negative beliefs' about worry (the ideas that worry is dangerous, which make people more anxious and therefore prone to worry more).

- Worry also has other consequences for us. It can make us experience physical symptoms of anxiety, and can interfere with our relationships and our ability to function in some important way.

Broadening your understanding of worry

How many people suffer from excessive worry?

To worry is to be human – we all worry, some more than others. Research in many different countries has suggested that somewhere between 2 and 4 per cent of a population have enough symptoms to get a diagnosis of GAD in one year. Playing it safe, that's roughly about one person in every twenty-five. Next time you are sitting in a café watching the world go by (or sitting worrying . . .), think about this: one in every twenty-five.

When does GAD usually begin?

Worry can occur at any time, and this is also true for the onset of GAD. We tend to be more likely to start worrying at times of change and stress. If our lives have changed in a major way, or if we have more responsibilities, we will become more susceptible to worry.

Often people start to have problems with worry relatively early on – between the ages of eleven and the early twenties. These early phases of our lives are important as we lay the foundations for the years to come and try to establish a sense of who we are. It is a time of heightened uncertainty coupled with changes in responsibilities and independence. At this time, worry can appear owing to many subtle influences. It doesn't need a major life event or trauma to trigger it.

The other time that worry tends to appear is much later in the lifespan, during middle age. This is the time of life that is often typified by stability in a number of areas of our lives. We may be more certain of who we are, and where we fit in the world. We may have an established career and home life. When worry appears later on, it is usually linked to some significant change, such as children growing up, a breakdown of a relationship, bereavement, an accident or illness, or a major shift in the way we live our lives, such as retirement. This might challenge the status quo and generate doubt and uncertainty.

It is important to remember that excessive worry can appear at any point in a person's life, but is often linked to heightened levels of uncertainty.

When did your worry become problematic? Was life more uncertain than usual at this point?

What causes GAD?

A precise cause of GAD is not known and there may be several factors involved in its development. In our clinical experience, there are many pathways to worry. Some people might be more likely to experience anxiety because of their genetic or physiological make-up, or because they have had a lot of insecurity in their lives. These experiences are likely to make it harder for people to tolerate uncertainty, and to start the chains of thinking that keep worry going.

What was your experience of uncertainty growing up? Did anyone or anything make life overly certain or overly uncertain at some stage of your life?

What do people worry about?

People with GAD tend to worry about the same kinds of things as people without GAD – only they fall into worrying more easily and tend to spend more time worrying. Regardless of whether you worry a little or a lot, research suggests that our worry tends to cluster around particular themes. These include our health, finances, relationships, family, work or study, and finally worrying about worrying. Because they are worrying so much, worriers tend to start to worry about what their worry may be doing to them. So, although worry feels like a whirlwind with an unpredictable course, there are patterns and it tends to swirl around a number of themes that reflect the things that are important to us. These worry themes typically mirror the stage of life we find ourselves in.

What are the things that you worry about most? Which worry themes are most common for you?

Difference between excessive worry and everyday worry

Worriers tend to worry more often and for longer periods of time and believe that their worry is more out of control than people with everyday worry. However, and as we have said, it would appear that a worrier's relationship with uncertainty helps explain most about why they worry so much.

Does a little bit of uncertainty start you worrying?

Worry and other psychological problems

A large number of people with GAD will have more than one psychological problem. The most common problems that co-exist with worry are depression and the other anxiety disorders, such as social anxiety, panic attacks or health anxiety. About 70 per cent of people with GAD report depressive problems at some point in their lives.

What else might be going on for you? Are there other key chapters in this book that might be helpful to read?

Tips for supporters

- Go through this chapter together to help the person you are supporting – and you – understand how they are worrying and how it affects them.

- When we have asked a question in this chapter, encourage the person you are supporting to think about how it applies to them.

- If you have seen them do any of the things we ask about, use these examples to help them understand what is going on.

- Talk to them about how you might be able to help them as they go through the book. Can you meet once a week to discuss their progress? Help them to make a plan of what to do? Can you offer a thoughtful, compassionate perspective on their worry?

- Ask them if they want you to remind them to complete their diary.

- Ask if they need help separating the types of worry outlined in this section.

- Help them to figure out what might be an early warning sign of their worry.

Section 2: Become more aware of your worry

Now that you have read the first section of this chapter you understand more about worry, and you will have had the chance to make notes of how the ideas we have discussed apply to you. If you have not done so, then it might be an idea to go back over the section now. If you have a supporter, then ask them to help you think about how the questions apply to you.

Some people find the diagram that we showed of Richard's worry spiral helpful in understanding what happens to them (see Figure 8.2). Look at the exercise below and see if you can create your own diagram (there is a blank version underneath the completed version below).

Exercise 8.2: Questions to help develop your worry diagram

Thinking about a recent bout of worry, can you use Figure 8.2 to help track how your worry develops? Use the following questions to help you to complete this.

1. Situation Date and time	Where were you or what were you doing just before you started to worry? What were you thinking about just before you started to worry?
2. 'What if?'	Can you spot the 'what if?' statement/s that triggered your worry? What was uncertain about the situation? What went through your mind just before you started to worry?
3. Worry	Did 'what if?' questions lead to others, possibly more serious? Did the worry start to spiral out of control? What themes did you worry about? Health, finances, relationships, family, work or study? Worrying about worry?

4. Anxiety Feelings, bodily sensations and actions	What physical sensations did you experience? What emotions?
5. Demoralization/ exhaustion What were your after-effects of worrying?	How did you feel after you stopped worrying? How strong was this feeling (0 = not very strong, 100 = intense feelings)?

You could use the blank sheet below to help you complete the questions.

Worksheet 8.1: Questions to help develop your worry diagram

1. Situation Date and time	
2. 'What if?'	
3. Worry	
4. Anxiety Feelings, bodily sensations and actions	
5. Demoralization/ exhaustion What were your after-effects of worrying?	

Keeping track of your worry

Some people find it helpful to keep a diary of their worries. If you would like to do this, then it is most helpful if you write things down as soon as you can. So when you start to worry, get out your notebook, your phone or your tablet, and make a note of what is going on in your mind. This can have a lot of different purposes. For one thing, if you make up your mind that every time you start to worry you will write it down then it might help to break into the spiral of worry. And for another, it might help you to see that as you progress through the stages of treatment in this chapter, things start to improve and you make fewer entries!

Try to keep a diary of your worry over the next week or two. You can use the information you gather for other exercises later in this chapter. If it's possible to write things down as soon as you notice you have started to worry then that would be good. But sometimes it's not practical to do so, so work out two or three times a day when you can sit down undisturbed and think back over the past few hours. It might help to ask yourself the questions from Worksheet 8.1 when you realize that you are worrying.

When you have recorded your worry for a week or so, you could ask yourself the following questions:

- When and where do you worry the most? Are there particular situations that tend to trigger your worry?

- What are the things that you worry about most often? Are there recurring themes in what you worry most about? Using your worry themes, now go back to the questions on p. 205: 'Spotting your positive worry beliefs'. Does this help you to understand why you worry so much about these things?

- Do your worries represent real events or are they hypothetical worries?

What are your goals?

When you are trying to make changes, it can help to try to be clear about what you would like to achieve, or what your goals are. We talked in Part 1 of the book about how to frame your goals (p. 24). Just a quick reminder – goals should be **SMART**:

Specific

Measurable

Achievable

Realistic

Time limited

So don't make your goal 'I want to be free of anxiety for evermore!' Think about how worrying is affecting you at the moment. Does worry stop you doing things that you'd like to be able to do?

For instance, you might worry so much that you won't let your children go on school trips. So, a goal might be: 'I will let my children go on the school trip and find a way to cope with my worry while they're away.' Richard's goal might be: 'I will delegate more to my colleagues'; 'I will not ring to check where my girlfriend is.'

You could also make goals about how you will carry out changes: for instance, a realistic goal might be: 'I will catch myself asking "what if?" questions and make sure I stop.'

You could look at the questions below to help you to formulate your goals:

- How does worrying make you feel?
- How would your relationships/friendships/work life/social life/school, etc., be improved if you worried less?
- What would you notice if you worried less?
- What things could you do with your time if you worried less?

Use these questions to help you think about what you would like to change if you worried less, and how these changes could become your goals.

Section 3: Treatment

By now you will know if worry is a significant problem for you. We have used a diagram to help you to track how your worries develop and have described how important the intolerance of uncertainty is when you worry. We started you thinking about whether your worry is based on real or hypothetical events, and whether you have ideas about worry that keep it going.

Based on these ideas, we will introduce four treatment approaches:

1. Helping you to tolerate uncertainty.

2. Solving life's problems: dealing with real event worry.

3. Overcoming avoidance: dealing with hypothetical event worry.

4. Dealing with beliefs about worry.

Remember **one size does not fit all** and some things we describe may not be relevant to you. Read through and see which of these ideas will help you most.

1. Helping you to tolerate uncertainty

Before we start, think about how worry or uncertainty has limited the way you live your life. What could be the advantages of accepting a little more uncertainty into your life? Could there be any disadvantages? What are the advantages of letting go of certainty and having new experiences?

We have seen that uncertainty plays an important part in worry, and that people who worry find it extremely difficult to tolerate this. So we need to find a way to help people to get used to the idea of uncertainty, and to stop asking the 'what if?' questions that fuel worry. This is done by gradually increasing their exposure to uncertainty, and by introducing more flexibility into how people live their lives.

But this can be difficult, and you may need to think about preparing yourself to change. One way to do this is to recognize that there is almost always a cost associated with the strategies that you use to manage uncertainty.

Exercise 8.3: How the intolerance of uncertainty influences our actions

The table below highlights the costs associated with how worriers manage uncertainty. Complete the questionnaire, and then choose one or two items and think about the gains or benefits you would get if you could tolerate the uncertainty and do things in a different way. Maybe completing this questionnaire will give you some ideas about what needs to change in your life.

Actions and costs	Rating
	Very unlike me Very like me
To what extent do you do the following ?	**Please circle**
Ask for reassurance on a decision you have made, and then feel stupid for having asked in the first place because you knew you were right.	1 2 3 4 5 6 7
Check e-mails, letters or cheques several times before sending them, and then get behind on other jobs.	1 2 3 4 5 6 7
Not allow your kids to do things for themselves in case they don't get it quite right. And then feel annoyed that you have to do everything yourself.	1 2 3 4 5 6 7

Want to know where everything is, and feel unsettled if things are out of place, even when you don't need to use them right now.	1 2 3 4 5 6 7
Need to have the plans for an evening clearly laid out beforehand and get upset when they don't go as planned, even though everyone is having fun.	1 2 3 4 5 6 7
Do things in the same routine and complicated way for fear of going off track and then complain how boring life is.	1 2 3 4 5 6 7
Avoid committing yourself to something just in case it might go wrong.	1 2 3 4 5 6 7
Find good but imaginary reasons for not doing things and then realize that you have missed out on something you would have enjoyed if you had taken the chance.	1 2 3 4 5 6 7
Avoid (or keep contact to a bare minimum with) people who may act unpredictably, thus missing out on other aspects of their company.	1 2 3 4 5 6 7
Get lots and lots of information to help you make a decision, and then be incapable of making sense of it all.	1 2 3 4 5 6 7

Having reviewed the exercise above – are you now ready to learn how to tolerate uncertainty better? Changing your behaviour is about finding out something new, by doing something differently. This means rather than avoiding uncertain situations, you will need to begin to seek out increasingly uncertain situations on purpose to see what happens. We do not expect you to dive into the deep end of uncertainty. To begin with, it is much better to think about small, manageable and realistic steps. Expect to feel anxious and underconfident, and expect to worry more when trying new things out. We all do! But also, look for the hidden benefits, such as greater variety or better relationships.

Take a moment to think practically about what you could do to introduce a little uncertainty into your life on purpose so that you can learn to tolerate it a bit better.

Exercise 8.4: Some ideas about what you could do to help yourself experience a bit more uncertainty

See the table below for some ideas about what you could try. Highlight those that are relevant to you and then decide to take a risk and try something new. Or make your own list from things that you know you would like to try in your own life if you could.

To help you decide where to start, give each 'new' thing a rating of 0 to 10 about how much worry it would cause you (0 is none at all; 10 is the most worried you can be). Then choose something that you have given a rating of 3–4, and start there. When you have managed that new activity, you will ideally feel more confident to try items with a higher rating.

Don't ask for reassurance on a decision you have made.	Stop checking e-mails, letters or small cheques before sending them.
Take a gamble; go and see a film you know nothing about.	Buy food you have never bought before.
Arrive ten minutes later than you normally would at an informal social occasion.	Take responsibility for something small and time limited – go ahead; don't ask for reassurance.
Go to a different shop for your groceries.	Delegate small jobs at work or at home.
Order something you have never tried in a restaurant.	Go to a restaurant you have never been to (and don't read the reviews).
Allow your kids to do age-appropriate things for themselves.	Once you have bought something new, use it and keep using it.

Stop asking others to check your work.	Make a smallish, impulsive buy.
Put a cap on the amount of time or information you need to make a decision.	Stay in the here and now; go with the flow when in familiar settings.
Take opportunities to meet new people.	Try out new activities; take a taster session for a club or a hobby.
Within your acquaintance circle, let people get to know you.	Sit still in social occasions; lose the butterfly wings.
Book a visit to your GP, accountant, dentist or bank manager, or anyone else you are avoiding.	Move things around in the home – break your patterns and order.
Ask your loved ones to **not** tell you exactly where they are, or exactly when they will be home.	Don't stick rigidly to a plan; act spontaneously if an opportunity presents itself.
Break your routines and go 'off track'.	Let others drive if you always drive yourself. Drive yourself if you always let others drive.
Make a minor commitment.	Find good reasons for doing things instead of not doing things – then do them.
Act while the problem is still small.	Do the task that needs your attention and not the thousands of others that get in the way.
Be generous and less critical of yourself.	If you make too many snap decisions, take time to have a coffee to think things through.
Find your own path; don't follow the crowd for the sake of it. Do your own thing.	Say yes more often to small invitations.

When you start to make these changes you are likely to feel quite nervous and worried. Try not to let the worry stop you from doing what you have decided to do – we know that anxiety does wear off if people can just sit tight and expose themselves to the things that frighten them. We have talked about this in other sections of this book, including Part 1 and Chapter 6 on specific phobias. Make up your mind what you are going to do, and then do it!

And, as a popular contemporary writer (Susan Kennedy, aka SARK) suggests, 'make friends with freedom and uncertainty'.

Key messages

- The way the worrier ends up managing uncertainty 'costs them more' than they had bargained for.

- Slowly increasing your exposure to new things and adding flexibility to how you live your life will help you to enjoy life more and worry less.

- Start to expose yourself to situations of uncertainty and remember that the anxiety you feel *will* wear off.

Tips for supporters

- Don't expect big changes to start with.

- If someone is intolerant of uncertainty, even small changes will take them out of their comfort zone.

- Encourage them, but let them set the pace.

- You can model trying new things, but they have to do it for themselves.

2. Solving life's problems: dealing with real event worry

Go back and have a look at Table 8.1 on pp. 203–4 about the difference between real and hypothetical worries. Do your own 'real event' worries escalate into much more catastrophic fears about what might happen in the future?

To overcome your worry it is important to become much more aware of when your worry starts to spiral from real to hypothetical.

Separating real event and hypothetical event worry

For now let us consider how we can separate out the two types of worry. The questions below should help you to recognize when your worry has become much more hypothetical.

Exercise 8.5: Using your worry diary, or thinking about the last thing you worried about, try to answer the following questions:

- Is the thing that I am worrying about something that *actually exists now*? Can I describe the issue that I am worrying about in concrete terms with a time, date and a place? Would someone else be able to 'see' the issue, e.g. the credit card bill, the disgruntled partner, the pile of work to do, the kids being difficult, and so on?

- How far into the future has my worry taken me? A day, a week, a month, three months, a year, five years, fifteen years?

- Could something be done about it? Could someone else solve this? (In theory, is this issue solvable?)

- If yes, then could I do something about it (even though I may worry that I may not be able to do it right)?

If this bout of worry is about a real current problem, then the next step is to think about how to solve it – the pages below give tips on how.

If not, then this must be a hypothetical worry, and you can try to manage this differently (see pp. 202–4).

Dealing with real event worry: approaching and solving problems

Worriers tend to see problems as *threatening*, *doubt their ability to cope* with problems, and tend to be *pessimistic* about the outcome even if they engage in problem solving. *Is this true for you?* These beliefs then set up vicious cycles since failing to engage in solving problems tends to reinforce these ideas. There is no evidence to suggest that worriers are worse at problem solving than non-worriers; it is only their *beliefs* about their problem solving that are different, not their skills.

Worrying is not problem solving

Sometimes, worriers can confuse worrying with solving problems. While it sometimes feels like we are doing something about our problems by worrying about them, in reality, we are usually not. Problem solving requires a very different style of thinking from worrying. For instance, problem solving is characterized more by questions that begin 'how', 'when', 'where', whereas worry questions tend to begin with 'why' or 'what if'. Another way to check the difference is to ask yourself, 'Have I come up with a solution, or am I just going over the same problems again and again?'

Problems are a normal part of life: we encounter them all the time and we successfully solve many of them without realizing this. But sometimes we approach problems in an unhelpful way. Have a look at the list below and see if any of these relate to you. Each item in the list is followed by a question or suggestion to help you think about how you might approach problems differently.

1. Do you avoid or delay solving the problem? Worriers tend to avoid or delay solving problems. As a result of this, what could be a minor problem to start with gets progressively worse, leading to more severe problems and stimulating even more worry (for example, avoiding paying credit card bills, leading to charges and increasing debt).

Can you start to face the problems before they escalate?

2. Do you try not to think about problems, or put them to the back of your mind? As long as a problem is still a problem, it will butt in until we deal with it.

Starting with the easiest, can you make a list of problems that need to be solved and start to solve them?

3. Do you ask others to solve problems for you? If we continually ask others to solve problems for us, then this means we deny ourselves the opportunity of finding out that we could manage the problem for ourselves.

Can you start to solve problems for yourself?

4. Do you solve problems impulsively? Another way of dealing with problems is to respond impulsively to them, without thinking things through. Often, attempting to solve problems in this way leads to hurried or incomplete solutions, or solutions that make the problem worse.

Can you slow your problem solving down and think things through?

5. Do you try to solve too many problems at once? Worry has the tendency to multiply and expand, and this pattern echoes in problem solving. Often worriers will partially engage in trying to solve one problem, and then flip-flop between this and other problems. As their attention is divided, this can mean that nothing gets done and all of the problems remain in a semi-solved state.

Having made a list of problems, start with one – solve this before moving on to the next.

6. Do you flip-flop between approaching a problem and then avoiding it? This is another common kind of pattern that worriers unwittingly fall into: they approach a problem and then flit between trying to solve the problem by doing something purposeful and then avoiding the problem.

Can you keep engaged with a problem until it is solved?

7. Do you pre-judge the outcome of your problem-solving efforts? Often worriers will think that whatever they do, the problem will turn out badly; they are, in essence, negatively pre-judging themselves.

Remind yourself of all the problems you have solved; how is this problem different?

8. Do you over-analyse things? A worrier might think of all the possible ways that the problem could be solved and the outcomes of each solution, with each solution generating more problems, which require more solutions, and so on. This results in the worrier getting lost within the labyrinth of alternatives, getting overwhelmed, and never solving the problems.

Can you limit the time you need to solve a problem?

Use your worry diary to help you think about the types of problems that triggered your worry. How did you respond to the problem? Having read the above list, has it suggested how you might do things differently now?

Problem-solving skills

Research tells us that people who worry excessively do possess problem-solving skills: their skills are as good as anyone else's. In case you are not confident about your skills, here is a quick refresher based on what works well in most circumstances. It may be beneficial to spend time focusing on developing your problem-solving skills.

Exercise 8.6: Quick problem solving

Use the guide in the table below to help you solve a minor problem first and see how you go. Then, try another one, and then work up to starting to solve the more major ones.

- What's the problem? Choose a problem that is
  - not life changing (i.e. relatively simple and small);
  - not involving or depending on others;
  - one where you can see the result quickly.

- Describe the problem in practical terms.

- Break it down into mini-steps – can you separate out a series of things that would need to be done to tackle the problem?

- What is the first step in the sequence? What is the first thing you need to do?

- At this point, what are the options? Think of all the possible things you could do to tackle the problem, even if some of them seem a bit unrealistic. Just let yourself 'brainstorm' everything that might change things.

- Spend a bit of time thinking about each of these solutions or options.

- Choose the one that seems slightly better than the others. Slightly better in this case means real, the simplest, most likely to succeed, with minimum cost (time, effort, money, etc.) and with a good result.

- Act on it.

- Review what happened. Was the outcome at least 'OK'?

- If not, then try another option. If it did work, then go on to the next step.

- Think about what happened to your worry about this problem. Ideally, as you engaged in more active problem solving your worry became a bit more manageable.

Key messages

- Worrying is not problem solving.

- The worrier's attitude to problems is the issue, not their skills.

- Think carefully about how you approach problems – what needs to change?

- Use problem-solving skills to deal with life's problems rather than worrying about them.

Tips for supporters

- Help the person you are supporting to notice the (many) problems they *are* probably solving successfully – despite the worry – and to realize that they do have problem-solving skills.

- Help the worrier notice whether they are approaching problems in an unhelpful way, as outlined in the list above.

- Help them choose the right (in other words, small) problems to start with, not necessarily the one that is bugging you the most!

- Provide support and encouragement, but not advice; worriers need to do it by themselves.

3. Overcoming avoidance: dealing with hypothetical event worry

Now, we turn our attention to the type of worry for which we cannot use problem solving: *hypothetical event worry*. In this type of worry, we tend to imagine scenarios that would be catastrophic if they happened. Then we react emotionally as if these imagined, or hypothetical, scenarios are real. We feel as terrible as if the things had really happened, even though they haven't.

Hypothetical worries typically involve themes of loss of loved ones, rejection by others, breakdown of important relationships, loss of financial security, illness and suffering, and the inability to face or cope with any of these. At the heart of these worries lie our dreams and aspirations, like wanting to be a good parent, or to be in good health, or to have financial security. All of us are afraid when the things we value are threatened. Can you return to the themes of worry that you discovered in Exercise 8.2 question 3? What are your aspirations? What does your worry threaten?

For worriers, the things that threaten these aspirations are *hypothetical event worries – things that could happen, haven't happened yet, and in all probability will never happen – but if they did, it would be terrible.*

As you have learned, *real event worry* about everyday problems can soon turn into *hypothetical event worry*. If we are able to track a hypothetical worry back to a real event then we can use problem solving to help. If, on the other hand, the worry is more hypothetical, we cannot solve a problem that only exists in our imagination; in this case we need to learn to face our fears. Working on *hypothetical event worry* is about learning to face the real **thoughts and images** within the worry itself.

Fear keeps us safe and motivates avoidance

When we were children, we believed that there were monsters under the bed. You may have done as well. If so, what did you do to keep yourself safe from the monster? What went through your mind as you lay in bed? Did pictures flash into your mind, which then triggered worry? For instance, *'what if it gets me'*, *'what if no one hears'*? Does this sound familiar? How did these imaginings affect your behaviour? Did you run and jump into bed for example, or pull up the bedclothes, keep the light on, and keep your arms and legs inside the covers?

Exercise 8.7: Identifying your avoidance technique

To solve the problem of the monster under the bed we have to overcome the natural avoidance of the monster. There are different types of avoidance; some are more subtle than others. Review the following list – which ones do you use when faced with your worries?

1. **Suppression**: This is a way that worriers try to avoid worrying thoughts and images by pushing them to the back of their mind or by trying not to think about them. Unfortunately, this rarely works for long, as trying not to think about something will tend to make us think about it all the more.

Can you see how this might apply to your worry? What happens when you try to push worrying thoughts or images out of your mind?

2. **Distraction:** This is when we give ourselves mental or physical tasks so we don't have the 'space' to worry. For example, cleaning the house or putting things in order, like grocery cupboards or toolboxes. Once the distracting activity stops, the worry creeps back in as it is more than likely linked to some unfinished business that will keep demanding our attention until we deal with it.

Do you distract yourself from your worries?

3. **Avoidance of mental pictures in worry:** We mostly worry in words not pictures. When images do appear in worry, they tend to 'pop up' in our minds, appearing and disappearing very quickly.

We want to escape the images because of what they show, namely raw, awful and horrible things that no one would want to dwell on. The images provoke strong feelings, physical sensations, and other streams of worry. To help you understand this, consider the following: hearing someone recount the storyline of a horror film will never be as scary as watching it – the bare facts of the story you listen to don't have the atmospherics that a skilful director creates with images.

If you have images that pop up, do you try to move away from them in your mind?

4. **Mental gymnastics; changing the detail of our worry:** Many people try to twist and turn away from the images or thoughts in their hypothetical worry. For example, we may try to dilute the awful worry by thinking about something else, or replacing negative images or thoughts with positive ones. The overall impact of all these mental gymnastics is that the worrier fails to face their fear, which maintains their worry.

Do you try to take the sting out of the scary parts of your worry by getting caught up in minor details like watching a horror film, concentrating on what the villain is wearing rather than the weapon he is carrying?

5. **Avoidance of situations:** The worrier tries to avoid situations or events that match closely with what they imagine in their *hypothetical event worry*. For instance if you imagined that your partner might have a car accident, you may pressure them into taking the train or using the bus, not based on anything other than what you have 'seen' in your hypothetical worry.

Do you avoid situations or events (or ask others to) that match or could trigger what you see in your worry?

Learning to face our fears

In the 'monsters' metaphor on pp. 232–3, in order to overcome the fear, the bottom line is that the child needs to face the fear to learn that there is nothing under the bed. With *hypothetical event worry* this would mean facing the content of our worry while also dropping our efforts at avoidance: namely, suppression, distraction, pushing images away and mental gymnastics.

You may feel daunted by this, which is entirely understandable. You may say to yourself, '*This will make my worry much worse!*' Remember that you probably experience these nightmarish daydreams at least every day and often for prolonged periods of time, and that trying to avoid them or not thinking about them has made no difference.

It is normal to feel upset when you start to face your fears because the ideas in our worry can be really terrible. It is precisely because *you really care* about the things you worry about that it is so upsetting. Being able to tolerate upsetting thoughts and images will not make you insensitive or uncaring. It will mean that you can, in fact, start to tell the difference between thoughts and reality. Imagine not being terrified by your worry, but being able to participate and enjoy the moment, living, not worrying.

In general, to help someone overcome their fear we would get them to confront it, or expose themselves to it. In order for this exposure to work they have to stay with the thing they are frightened of until their anxiety comes down naturally – which it will. You will probably be concerned that the anxiety will not reduce and that it will spiral out of control, but this just isn't the case. Our anxiety does come down, even without us doing anything to make it come down. We have to learn to allow the wave of fear to wash over us, letting go of all our attempts to avoid or control it, in order to find out that nothing bad will happen.

To work with your *hypothetical event worry*, it is important to sit with the feelings without doing anything to make the situation or your feelings better. Learn that hypothetical event worry is a stream of thoughts.

These thoughts do not describe real events. *They are not facts*. They are not premonitions. They are *just thoughts*. They are the by-products of your imagination, revolving around things that are important to you.

Exercise 8.8: Writing down your hypothetical event worry

Choose a quiet moment, a time when you know that you will not be disturbed – it's probably better not to do this late at night, when worries can get magnified and can be harder than usual to switch off. Choose a *hypothetical event worry* from your worry diary. Imagine that you had to help someone to make a movie of your worry and think of all the details they would need to know. Think about when the worry is happening – next week, next year, or at some indeterminate time. Describe what is happening, what you think, feel, do, see, hear, etc. Do not censor yourself; everything needs to go down on the page.

Sometimes it might feel like the worry has no ending. Keep writing until you have passed what might be the worst moment, or if you notice that you are going around in a circle. We are also trying to help you to learn to 'sit' with uncertainty, in other words, to learn to tolerate it better, and so it is not about finding a good ending; actually it is better if the ending is left hanging, with a question such as *'when will this ever end?'* or *'who knows where this will lead?'* Endings like these are designed to trigger uncertainty and so maximize your exposure to it.

Review what you have written. Have you avoided including anything?

Take the final and detailed version of your *hypothetical event worry* and read and re-read it for up to thirty minutes a day. It can help to make an audio recording of it on an MP3 player or a CD and listen to it. Use the form below to record the experience of reading through it. Note that the form asks you to rate your anxiety before, during, and afterwards, using the scale provided. You should find that once you have let yourself concentrate on the worry in this way, your anxiety will start to wear off, and you will find it much easier to think about the worry. Once you have done this with one worry, choose another, until your worries will feel much more manageable.

When you have done this you should find that your relationship to your *hypothetical event worries* has changed, and that you recognize them for what they are. Can you recognize them sooner now? Are you able to interrupt them, or have you found things that you can say to help you to 'put the brakes on'?

Facing your fear

Fill out this worksheet each time you face your hypothetical event worry. Use the scale below to rate your anxiety or discomfort. Remember you need to work with your worry for long enough for the feelings to reduce.

Worksheet 8.2: Rate your anxiety/discomfort

Anxiety/discomfort scale

None		Slight		Moderate		High		Extreme	
1	2	3	4	5	6	7	8	9	

Session No._____

Day or date _____ Start time ___:___ Finish time ___:___

Place _____ Worry _____

Anxiety/discomfort   Before _____   During (max) _____   After _____
(please use scale)

Did you use any avoidance strategies? No _____ A little _____ A lot _____

How did you avoid?_____

Key messages

- To overcome worry, we need to face the things we 'see' in our hypothetical worry.

- Avoidance does not work as a way of managing the fears that are at the heart of our worries.

- Worries are thoughts based on what is important to us, but they are not predictions or premonitions. They are simply thoughts.

- We can learn this if we are prepared to face the awful things we imagine in our worries.

Tip for supporters

This may be hard for you, too. The horrible things they may imagine are because they care so much. If you are supporting a close friend or relative, then sometimes the hypothetical worry will be about you or someone you care about. If you share some of the concerns that the person you are supporting has it may be harder to help them to see that the worry is just a thought. Just remind yourself of the ideas in the section above, and make sure that you know the difference too!

4. Dealing with beliefs about worry

Go back to the description of the beliefs about worry on pp. 205–7. The basic idea is to begin to see that the rules about worry actually make you worry more. The two kinds of beliefs – positive and negative – require slightly different approaches.

Dealing with positive beliefs about worry

We have seen that positive beliefs about worry make you think that worry is useful. The beliefs make you feel that worry helps your motivation, show that you are a decent person, help you to prepare for bad things that might happen. So, one way to try to reduce the amount of time you spend worrying in this way is to think about other ways in which you can achieve the goals.

Are there better ways than worrying to show that you care?

How else could you motivate yourself to work hard?

You could also try talking to other people to see what they say. Would they agree that worrying beforehand prepares them for the worst? Or might they think that worrying in this way makes them feel so bad that they actually feel too stressed out to cope with anything?

It could also be helpful to work out exactly how worrying might have an impact on events. For example, how does worrying about the kids keep them safe?

Below are some examples of worry rules to help you think about how you can learn to work with them and learn to bend and break them.

Belief/rule	Questions to help you challenge your rules and beliefs
Worry helps me to solve problems	Does worrying actually solve your problems, or do you just get stuck going over and over problems in your mind? Does the anxiety you get with worry help or hinder problem solving? Are there problems you have solved that you did not worry about?
Worry helps to motivate me	Do you know any successful or motivated people who aren't worriers? Is worry the best way of motivating yourself?

I worry to pre-pare me for bad things happening	If bad things have actually happened – did worrying about it beforehand help? Can you really prepare for all the eventualities? How many times have the bad things you worry about actually happened in the way you imagined?
I worry to prevent some-thing bad from happening	If you worried about something good happening – e.g. winning the lottery – do you think this would make it happen . . . what does this suggest about bad things? Have there been times when you have not worried and the bad thing happened anyway?
Worry shows I care	If you were running a class to teach people how to care, would you teach people how to worry? If not, why not? What other things do you do that show you care? Has this kind of worry backfired as others become annoyed by your worry?

Dealing with negative beliefs about worry

We talked about some of the negative beliefs about worry. These would be things like 'worry will drive me insane' or 'I will lose control'. These beliefs actually make you feel more anxious and drive the worry on and so it is a good idea to try to tackle these ideas. One way to do this is to think about what has happened in the past. You have worried a lot. But have you ever gone insane or lost control?

How did you stop yourself from going insane or losing control (e.g. counting, making sure you can still read, doing sums in your head, etc.)? Do you feel able to drop this and find out what happens? Focus on a smaller worry to start with and see if you can actually drive yourself insane or lose control (we wouldn't be suggesting this if we thought it might work!). Then pick a larger worry and do the same. And so on.

It might help to go back to Part 1 to remind yourself how to tackle anxious thoughts.

Key messages

- Worriers have beliefs about worry that make it harder to stop worrying.

- *Positive* beliefs about worry can be dealt with if we can find better ways of achieving the things we want rather than simply worrying about them.

- *Negative* beliefs about worry can also make us worry more. These thoughts can be dealt with using techniques to challenge thoughts, such as those described in Part 1.

Tips for supporters

- Often people don't realize that they have these beliefs, so helping someone to look at the lists and recognize the beliefs can be a really important first step.

- Try to help the person you are supporting to find different ways of achieving the positive results they think worry brings.

- Try to help the person to challenge the negative beliefs about worry by looking for evidence and using other techniques used in the thought-challenging section of Part 1.

Conclusion

Reading this chapter is only the start. These ideas and techniques now need to become part of the way you live your life: welcoming uncertainty into your life and taking small risks, solving life's problems rather than simply worrying excessively, and recognizing that your worry is only just that – worry.

Final word for supporters

- Although it is difficult, adopting an understanding and supportive stance that encourages trying new things is likely to be the most successful in the longer term.

- Remember that the worrier needs to learn to do things for themselves.

- Remind the worrier that doing new things is likely to make them feel anxious and frightened, but the anxiety will wear off once they start doing things differently.

- Although the upheaval may be uncomfortable, there will be rewards. Not only will the worrier be less caught up in worry, but also more open to new experiences as they learn to first tolerate and then embrace uncertainty.

- Remember that change takes time, particularly if people have been worrying for a long time. For most of us, change takes place in very small steps, not in one dramatic quick episode. So help the person you are supporting to notice small changes, and to feel proud that they are trying so hard!

9 Social phobia

Gillian Butler and Freda McManus

What is social phobia?

Social phobia (also known as social anxiety disorder) is natural, because everyone – or nearly everyone – suffers from it occasionally. Most of us can remember a time when we have felt embarrassed by something we have done, or have made fools of ourselves in public. But social phobia is a more extreme and persistent kind of social anxiety that interferes with people's lives, sometimes in serious ways. When suffering from social phobia people feel apprehensive or nervous interacting with others, or uncomfortable in their presence. This makes it hard to feel at ease around other people, and to be spontaneous and natural in conversation. Talking to people, or knowing that they are being observed, can be enough to make someone with social phobia feel worried and self-conscious. Common fears are that they will do something embarrassing or humiliating and that others will then make critical judgements about them. So they will end up feeling rejected and inadequate. Socially phobic people do not have to do something embarrassing or humiliating to feel upset and anxious – they just have to think that they might, or that they already have, and that others have noticed, or think that they soon will. No wonder that at times they want the floor to open and swallow them up.

There is no hard and fast way of making the distinction between social phobia and common, manageable social anxiety. This is important as it means that no treatment will get rid of the problem altogether. The main aims of treatment are therefore different: to help people feel less distressed by social anxiety, and to stop the anxiety interfering with their lives. Then they can make friends, build families, go to work, and do other things they want to do, including allowing others get to know them more easily. When you have social phobia it is hard to feel at ease in the company of others, and to 'be yourself'. This means that the people we meet may not be able to discover how interesting, or thoughtful, or energetic or generous we can be. One of the rewards of learning to overcome social phobia is that you can then express yourself in ways that may previously have been stifled by feeling anxious: to enjoy, rather than to fear, being yourself.

Four aspects of social anxiety

Social anxiety affects our body, our feelings, our behaviour and our thinking, but it does not affect everyone in exactly the same way. Think about what you notice happening to you when you are anxious in social situations; if the things that you notice are not on the list below, then add them for yourself.

Examples of effects on your body:
- Shaking or trembling
- Sweating
- Blushing
- Tension
- Racing heart

Examples of effects on your feelings or emotions:
- Panicky feelings
- Fear, apprehension, nervousness
- Frustration, irritation, anger
- Shame
- Sadness, depression, feeling hopeless

Examples of effects on behaviour:
- Avoiding people, places or activities
- Escaping from difficult situations
- Protecting yourself from things that you fear
- Trying not to attract attention

Examples of effects on thinking:
- Worrying about what others think of you
- Becoming painfully self-conscious and self-aware
- Dwelling on things that you think you did wrong
- Believing, or assuming, that you are inadequate

The four kinds of symptoms are closely linked. For example you can't **think** what to say, so you **feel** upset and self-conscious, look away (**your behaviour**), and start to blush (**a bodily change**). Then you are so aware of blushing that it gets even harder to think what to say, and you feel desperate to get away. These close links are made so fast that it can be hard to work out what happened first.

Different kinds of social phobia

- Gemma's biggest fear was that if others got to know her they wouldn't like her. She was relatively comfortable with her immediate family, but she had never made close friends at school, and in her late thirties she still felt lonely and isolated.

- Tom was unable to do things if other people were watching. He found it hugely difficult to use his mobile phone when with his friends, or to fill in a form if someone was watching. He could not order a round of drinks in a quiet bar, or eat out comfortably in a restaurant.

- Ed found it excruciatingly embarrassing to talk to anyone whom he perceived to be physically attractive. He had not had any lasting close relationships by the time he asked his doctor for help when he was in his mid-forties.

- Kim was extremely successful at work as a solicitor, but found parties and informal gatherings impossibly difficult. James was the opposite. He could tell jokes and play around with people his own age, but became tense, anxious and self-conscious at work. He found it especially difficult to talk to anyone in authority, such as his boss.

tried to prepare himself for meeting people during the lunch break by rehearsing things to talk about. He had been unable to accept promotion as this would involve speaking up in meetings, and organizing and reviewing the work of others.

Social phobia affects men and women roughly equally. It often starts around adolescence. Speaking in public, or speaking up in front of others, is the most common difficulty. Social phobia occurs all over the world, though the precise form that it takes varies from culture to culture. The things that will embarrass you, and make you feel that others are judging you negatively, will occur differently in different cultures. In some cultures it is acceptable to talk about money, or to make direct eye contact with someone of the opposite sex. In others, it is not. When socially phobic people feel anxious they (naturally) try to protect themselves from the disasters that they fear. The things that they do in these situations are called their safety behaviours (see Chapter 1). We all know that alcohol oils the wheels of social interaction, and socially anxious people can come to depend on it. When this happens, it makes sense to try to tackle both problems at once.

Social phobia and shyness

The vast majority of people all over the world go through a stage of being shy and most of us grow out of this during childhood. Many people feel shy at times all through their lives. They may be 'slow to warm up', but feel fine once they have got to know people. Feeling shy feels similar to social anxiety, and some people think of social phobia as an extreme form of shyness. The steps taken during treatment for social anxiety are also helpful for shy people, and it may not matter therefore which word you use to describe your problem. What matters is not whether you call it 'social anxiety' or 'shyness', but whether it causes you distress or interferes with doing what you want to do – if it doesn't then that's fine. But if it does, then it may be something that you want to change.

Key message

Social phobia is a more extreme form of normal social anxiety. It makes people think that they have done or will do something embarrassing or humiliating and that other people will judge them harshly as a result. So they try to protect themselves by doing things to keep themselves safe. What they do to keep safe can sometimes end up exacerbating the problem, thereby creating a vicious cycle. Each person with social phobia experiences it slightly differently. It helps to identify how it affects your body, your feelings, your behaviour and your thoughts.

Tip for supporters

It is hard to overcome social phobia, and also hard to ask for help – especially for those with social anxiety! So encourage the person you are helping to talk about it. Remind them that it is worth trying to change even though it can be difficult. When they are ready, help them to think about the ways in which their social fears and worries cause them distress or interfere with their lives, and to identify as many aspects of their social anxiety as they can.

Understanding what keeps social phobia going

Thanks to the research of two clinical psychologists, David Clark and Adrian Wells, we now know that there are three aspects of social phobia that keep the problem going. These are:

- self-consciousness;
- patterns of thinking;
- safety behaviours.

So these are the things to focus on during treatment.

Of the four aspects of social phobia listed in the box on pp. 244–45, the effects on your body and your feelings are usually the things that socially anxious people notice most, and that they are most concerned by. So these are usually the things that people try to change by themselves, before they decide to ask for help. Knowing where to focus that effort instead, so as to work on self-consciousness, on the way we think, and on safety behaviours, makes all the difference.

The new theory, supported by findings from research studies, is mapped out in the diagram below. The main aspects of social phobia are shown in the written parts of the diagram, and the cycles that keep the phobia going are shown by the arrows linking these aspects.

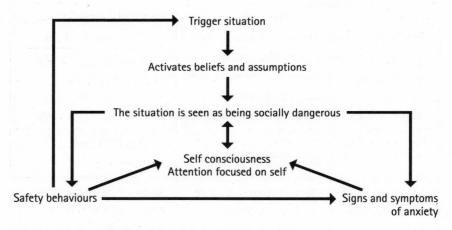

Figure 9.1: The Clark and Wells (1995) model of social phobia

If you look carefully at this diagram you will see that self-consciousness appears in the middle, at the bottom, and it is linked to everything else. The patterns of thinking are hidden in the beliefs and assumptions ('I'm useless'; 'you've got to be outgoing for people to like you'), and in the thoughts that make a social situation seem to be dangerous ('this is horrible', 'I can't think of anything to say', 'everyone's looking at me'). The safety behaviours include all manner of ways of protecting ourselves when this happens – from keeping quiet for fear of saying something wrong, to chattering on and on so there aren't any embarrassing silences. The signs and symptoms of anxiety are all the horrible things you feel – and no longer want to feel – when this happens.

Some examples of the main elements in the model are shown in Table 9.1. Read through these and then fill in the blank table, starting with a recent example of one of the situations that you find difficult – a trigger situation for you. Later in the chapter we will ask you to put these into a diagram like the one on p. 248.

Table 9.1: Understanding social phobia

Aspect of the model	Gemma	James
Trigger situation	A neighbour comes to the door	His annual review at work
Beliefs and assumptions	I'm not confident like she is I must be polite and friendly	My manager is unfriendly I mustn't be nervous
Seeing danger	She will expect me to ask her in	He doesn't like me He'll complain
Self–consciousness	Notice the shaking inside 'I'm losing it already'	Aware of getting muddled, and of not being able to concentrate
Safety behaviours	Pretend to be going out Say very little	Avoid eye contact; try to say the right things; agree with him
Symptoms	Panicky feeling, heart racing.	Tense, sweaty, fidgety

Here is a blank one for you to complete for yourself:

Table 9.2: Understanding your social phobia

Aspect of the model	
Trigger situation	
Beliefs and assumptions	
Seeing danger	
Self–consciousness	
Safety behaviours	
Symptoms	

Links between the main elements of the model on pp. 248, shown by the arrows in the diagram, help to explain why social phobia persists. The ways in which each of these main elements keep the problem going are described next. Use these descriptions to help you think of the ways in which these links work for you.

How self-consciousness keeps the problem going

When anxious, socially phobic people focus in on themselves, self-consciousness fills up their minds, leaving little room for other things. So they find it hard to hear what others say, or to notice the expression on their faces. Instead they become painfully aware of themselves: of the sound of their own voice, or their feelings, or of what they think they are doing wrong – their shaking hands or muddled speech. That's why they sometimes do exactly what they hope not to do, and knock over the coffee mug, or stumble over their words, or can't think of anything to say. It is hard to pay full attention to what's going on if we are constantly preoccupied with ourselves and our shortcomings. And of course these are what we remember later.

Self-consciousness comes from focusing our attention inwards, on ourselves, so that we become hyper-aware of what is going on inside us. It keeps the problem going because:

1. It inhibits our performance. When we are preoccupied with ourselves we may come across to others as distant or self-absorbed, or even as unfriendly or uninterested.

2. It prevents us picking up information about what is happening. There is no brain-space left for noticing important things, especially those things that can be read in people's faces. So when we get positive responses from others we may not even notice.

3. It creates a vicious cycle. Being self-conscious makes us even more aware of what is going on in our mind and body. This makes the situation we are in feel even more dangerous, so that the desire to protect ourselves or keep ourselves safe also increases.

Key message

Self-consciousness and focusing inwards on what is going on in your mind and body make you feel worse in social situations, and make it harder to interact naturally with others. See if you can find an example from your own experience.

How patterns of thinking keep the social phobia going

Patterns of thinking keep social phobia going because they set in motion vicious cycles of thoughts, feelings and behaviour. If we see a situation as socially dangerous we might think: 'I don't belong here. Nobody here really likes me.' So we might feel sad and anxious, and find it hard to relax and to talk freely. Then the interaction we have becomes stilted or awkward, confirming our impression that we don't really belong. Many of the ways people think are reflected in the predictions they make about social situations, even if they haven't put those predictions into words. Here are some examples of common predictions:

- I won't be able to keep the conversation going.

- They will see how nervous I am.

- I'll do something stupid.

- No one will want to talk to me.

These negative predictions explain why social life feels so threatening, and why socially anxious people want to protect themselves by using safety behaviours. The more you protect yourself the harder it is to build your confidence, and this keeps the fears and anxious predictions going, too, in another vicious cycle.

Underlying the thoughts that make social situations seem dangerous and threatening are often more longstanding ways of thinking that many people never put into words. These are beliefs and assumptions, and they also create cycles that keep the problem going. A belief reflects fundamental attitudes, for example about oneself, 'I'm different from others'; or about others, 'people always judge me' . . . negatively of course. Assumptions reflect the (unwritten) rules that people live by, and they fit with their beliefs. If we believe that we are fundamentally different from others we might assume that if we try to be like them, then they might like us. If we believe that people always judge us (negatively), then we might do our best to make sure that they never really get to know us, and go through life trying to hide our real selves from other people. But this sort of behaviour is likely to keep our anxiety going, and to strengthen the underlying beliefs and assumptions.

Key message

Different levels of anxious thinking can contribute to keeping the social phobia going as they interact with feelings and beliefs (see Chapter 2 for a more detailed explanation). See if you can find some examples of your thinking that contribute to your social anxiety.

How safety behaviours keep the problem going

The natural thing to do if we are facing a threat, or a risk or a danger, is to try to keep ourselves safe. But if we protect ourselves we never get to find out that maybe the situation is not as dangerous as we thought it was, or to build our confidence. Once again, vicious cycles, as reflected in the arrows in the diagram on p. 248, keep the problem going. The box below shows some examples of how safety behaviours can keep social anxiety going.

Examples of how safety behaviours can keep social anxiety going

- You say little, so people you are talking to ignore you, and you feel left out and think they are rejecting you. Feeling rejected makes it feel only sensible to keep quiet next time, too.
- You know that when you are nervous your hands shake. But you don't want people to notice this, so you tense them up, and hold your arms in tightly, to prevent them shaking. But tension makes it harder, not easier, to stop shaking. Besides, the effort to hide the shaking makes you self-conscious, and then you feel more, not less, nervous that others will notice your shaking.
- Many people who don't want to attract attention to themselves speak quietly. But then those around them can't hear what they are saying, and try harder to hear. They may come closer, or look at them carefully, or ask them to repeat what they just said. Again the attempt to keep safe backfired.

It makes sense to try to keep yourself safe if you feel anxious, or think that you are at risk of being rejected, embarrassed, or humiliated. The safety behaviours and avoidance link up with the feelings and thoughts, and all together they become like bad habits: they make the problem worse, not better. The way to make your social life feel safe is just like learning to feel safe in a swimming pool – to get in there and splash around, enjoy yourself and then learn to swim.

> ### Key message
>
> Trying to protect ourselves from the threats and dangers we anticipate, by avoiding things and using safety behaviours, keeps us thinking that this is what we need to do to feel better. It keeps the thoughts and feelings going even when it brings temporary relief, and sometimes it makes things worse not better.

Three other things that perpetuate the problem

1. *The post-mortem.* Just as it sounds, this involves thinking about (dissecting) a social situation once it is over: something like a meal with friends, or a recent conversation. This is when all the things you think you did wrong come to mind, bringing embarrassment or even horror with them. The post-mortem is quite normal. It happens to all of us – when we cringe as a memory comes back to us, even if it's the middle of the night. The trouble is that the post-mortem is no help to us at all. It comes with a delay, so prolongs the agony. It brings bad feelings with it all over again, and it adds feeling bad about ourselves to all the other bad feelings: 'I'm hopeless . . . useless . . . completely unacceptable.' The other problem with the post-mortem is that our memory is affected by our anxiety: we remember what we think happened, not what actually happened, and so we reinforce our negative views of ourselves in social situations.

If this happens to you, try to recognize it as unhelpful and turn your mind away from it. Distract yourself by doing something, or thinking about something interesting or pleasant instead.

2. *Low confidence.* If your social phobia has gone on a long time it is not surprising that it has undermined your confidence, or begun to do so. This makes it hard to do new things. The less you do the harder it is to remember that confidence comes from doing things and not worrying too much about the mistakes that you make along the way. It is impossible to learn without making mistakes. So try not to be held back by feeling unconfident. If you have a go, your confidence will start to build up in all sorts of ways, and working on your social phobia, especially as described in the section on Doing Things Differently pp. 278–80 is especially helpful in building social aspects of your confidence.

3. *Feeling low and depressed.* Social phobia gets people down. That is hardly surprising as it interferes with doing the things that you want to do, and with being the sort of person you would like to be, and know that you could be when with others. For this reason the last chapter of this book explains what to do if you are depressed as well as anxious. Our research has also shown that working to overcome their social phobia generally makes people less depressed as well. This is especially true if the social phobia began *before* they became depressed rather than the other way round.

Helping you change: a treatment overview

First you will need to plan how you want to approach the work of overcoming your social phobia. The next step is to make sure you understand your social phobia: how it works and how it affects you personally. Assessing yourself, and setting your personal goals, comes next. Then you will be able to focus on the three central parts of the work:

1. Reducing self-consciousness: working to shift the focus of attention.

2. Changing thinking patterns: identifying and re-thinking your thoughts and expectations.

3. Doing things differently: devising experiments to find out what

happens if you test out your expectations without using safety behaviours. Use the information that you pick up in your experiments to help you to re-think your old patterns of thinking.

Following these steps has an excellent chance of bringing about valuable and lasting change. They are described in the following two sections: 'How to approach this self-help programme' and 'Treatment'.

How to approach this self-help programme

It is probably best to read the whole chapter right through first, and then to go back to the beginning and work through it at your own pace. Working steadily, doing something every day if possible, is particularly helpful. You will need to set aside a regular time to work on your social phobia: ideally about an hour once a week and a much shorter time every day (or most days). This time is for planning the work and for thinking about how it is going.

Your first step should be to decide how you are going to keep track of the work that you do and how it goes. So get a special notebook, or make a new file on your computer. If you have a supporter, set aside times for regular meetings or conversations, and start these by deciding what to talk about, or 'setting an agenda'. Each time, decide what your priorities are, and make sure that you always end the session with a clear understanding of the tasks that need to be completed before you talk next.

Tip for supporters

Read this chapter all the way through. Then ask the person you are helping when, and how frequently, they would like to talk to you about their efforts to change. Be guided by them. Think of yourself as helping to make specific plans about what to do, helping them to feel in charge of the work they are doing, so as to build their confidence. Encourage them to write down the reasons it is worth trying to change, and to make a list of the specific things that they would like to be able to do more easily. These are the goals for both of you to keep in mind.

Understanding the unique aspects of CBT for social phobia

You will use the main CBT methods as well as some special ones designed to tackle the unique features of social phobia: self-consciousness and concerns about how you are perceived by others. Self-consciousness is a natural human emotion that we all feel when we become aware of the scrutiny of others but when it is excessive it can seriously inhibit social performance and enjoyment of social interactions. CBT techniques can help you to learn what you can do to reduce this self-consciousness.

CBT will also help you to become less concerned about how you think you are coming across to others – about what you think they are thinking about you. Mostly, when something scares you, the fear dies away when you face your fears. But in social phobia this seems not to happen. Most sufferers have already, to a greater or lesser extent, confronted the source of their phobia – other people – on a daily basis. It is after all, impossible to avoid them. But facing others appears not to reduce the fear of meeting them or interacting with them. This is because the underlying fear is about what others are thinking about you, which you often can't know for certain, as it comes from a kind of guesswork. In tackling your social anxiety you will discover how to approach situations that you would normally avoid, and how to find out what you need to know once you are in them.

Understanding how social phobia affects you personally

Start by thinking about why exactly you want to change. Try to be clear with yourself, as this helps you to keep in mind why overcoming the problem is important. For example, Shireen was prompted to tackle her social anxiety when she noticed her children were learning to do some of the same things and seemed to be 'catching' her social anxiety. Gemma realized that her biological clock was ticking and unless she was able to socialize outside her immediate family she might not be able to find a lasting relationship or to have children of her own. James was prompted to seek help when he took on a new role at work that meant he had to engage in more formal business situations. He felt that he was 'too old' to still be so shy.

In your notebook or on your computer, write down the main reasons why it is important to you to be less socially anxious. Make sure you can find your notes easily so you can refer back to them if at times it seems like a struggle to persevere. Even if all goes smoothly there are likely to be times when it is easier to rely on old habits than to push yourself to face situations you instinctively avoid.

Assessing yourself

It is helpful to get an idea of how severe your social anxiety is at the moment, as this will help you to measure your progress as you start to make changes. There are some self-report measures that are freely available for this purpose, which you can access on the internet. One of these is the Social Phobia Rating Scale (SPRS) which can be downloaded from: www.goodmedicine.org.uk/stressedtozest/2008/11/handouts-questionnaires-social-anxiety and is included in the Appendices. Fill this in before you start, and do it regularly during treatment. You can decide how often: for example you could do it weekly, or monthly, or before each meeting with your supporter.

Setting goals

Next think about exactly what you want to achieve. These aims can then be refined into Specific, Measurable, Achievable, Relevant, Timely (SMART) goals. In setting your personal goals for overcoming your social anxiety, questions to ask yourself will include:

- What exactly do I want to be able to do differently?
  - ° In what circumstances? With whom? When? How often?

- How will I know when I can do that?
  - ° What might others notice is different about me?
  - ° How would I know it was different?

- How do I want to feel differently?
  - ° What is it realistic to expect?
  - ° How will I know if I do feel that way?

Tom worried about his hands shaking noticeably in front of others. His goals for treatment focused on being able to do things that he currently avoided:

- Complete a form in front of other people, e.g., in the post office.

- Use his mobile phone on the bus or in the street, then with groups of friends.

- Eat in a nearby café, and then in other restaurants.

- Order beer in a bar (he currently chose drinks that were not filled to the top of the glass) and carry it to a table.

- Be able to concentrate on speaking to another person while his hands were on show.

Goals will often focus on helping you to engage in situations that you have previously avoided, but they may also be about what you do in such situations.

Gemma wanted to be more open with people and to express her opinions even if she thought others wouldn't share them. Her goals were to begin doing this with those she felt most secure with (close family and friends) then work up to the scarier situations – with more casual acquaintances and then in more public or formal ones such as complaining about poor service in a restaurant, or returning something to a shop. In particular, she wanted to stop preparing for conversations by rehearsing what she could ask the person about, and instead just talk about whatever came up.

Ed specifically wanted to stop avoiding certain people that he feared would trigger his blushing (people that he found attractive). Ideally he would have liked to be able to engage such people in conversation without any fear of blushing, but thought that a more realistic goal was to be able to talk to the person irrespective of whether he blushed.

It is unlikely that you will ever be totally free of any social anxiety or self-consciousness at all (and it wouldn't be desirable to be completely immune to the opinions of others), but what exactly would you like to be able to do?

Key message

Think carefully about what you want to be able to do. Make a list that includes small things as well as big ones. The more specific your goals are, the easier it will be to see your progress towards them.

Tip for supporters

You could help the person you are supporting to make a list of their goals – help them to identify why it is important to them to tackle their social anxiety, what benefits it would bring and what they might reasonably expect to be different once they have had a go at overcoming social anxiety.

Working out what is keeping your social anxiety going

It can be hard to work out exactly what is keeping your social phobia going, so it is a good idea to set some time aside and find a quiet place to sit down and do this. The aim is to work out your underlying fears and to be able to pinpoint the various ways in which you try to protect yourself, or the safety behaviours linked to your fears.

A useful first stage is to draft your own version of Clark and Wells's model of social phobia (see Figure 9.1). Earlier (p. 249) we asked you to work out the main elements of the model starting from a specific difficult situation. Now the task is to fill in the blank boxes in the diagram below. Some questions have been added on the table to help you to identify what might be relevant in those boxes, and a blank flow chart has been provided in the Appendix. The boxes and questions are numbered as a rough guide to the order but you might prefer to complete them in a different order.

Now you can use the information you have collected to work out how the different aspects of the problem link together for you. Think about how your thoughts influence your feelings, physiology and behaviour; about how your behaviour links back to the way you think about yourself; how self-consciousness affects what you do and what you think and so on. This work can give you some clues about what you should do to bring about change. What most people who experience excessive social anxiety want is to *feel* better, to feel less anxious and experience fewer physiological symptoms of anxiety. But as it is difficult to change feelings directly, it is more useful to look instead at the things that lead to the feelings: the self-consciousness, thoughts and safety behaviours.

Tip for supporters

You could have a go at this, too – then compare notes to see if you can add anything to each other's versions.

Figure 9.2: Flowchart to help you map out your social anxiety

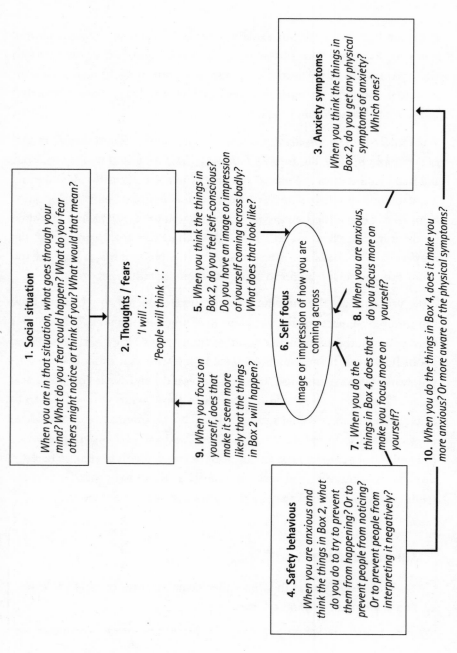

1. Social situation

When you are in that situation, what goes through your mind? What do you fear could happen? What do you fear others might notice or think of you? What would that mean?

2. Thoughts / fears

'I will . . .'
'People will think . . .'

3. Anxiety symptoms

When you think the things in Box 2, do you get any physical symptoms of anxiety? Which ones?

5. *When you think the things in Box 2, do you feel self-conscious? Do you have an image or impression of yourself coming across badly? What does that look like?*

6. Self focus

Image or impression of how you are coming across

8. *When you are anxious, do you focus more on yourself?*

9. *When you focus on yourself, does that make it seem more likely that the things in Box 2 will happen?*

7. *When you do the things in Box 4, does that make you focus more on yourself?*

4. Safety behaviours

When you are anxious and think the things in Box 2, what do you do to try to prevent them from happening? Or to prevent people from noticing? Or to prevent people from interpreting it negatively?

10. *When you do the things in Box 4, does it make you more anxious? Or more aware of the physical symptoms?*

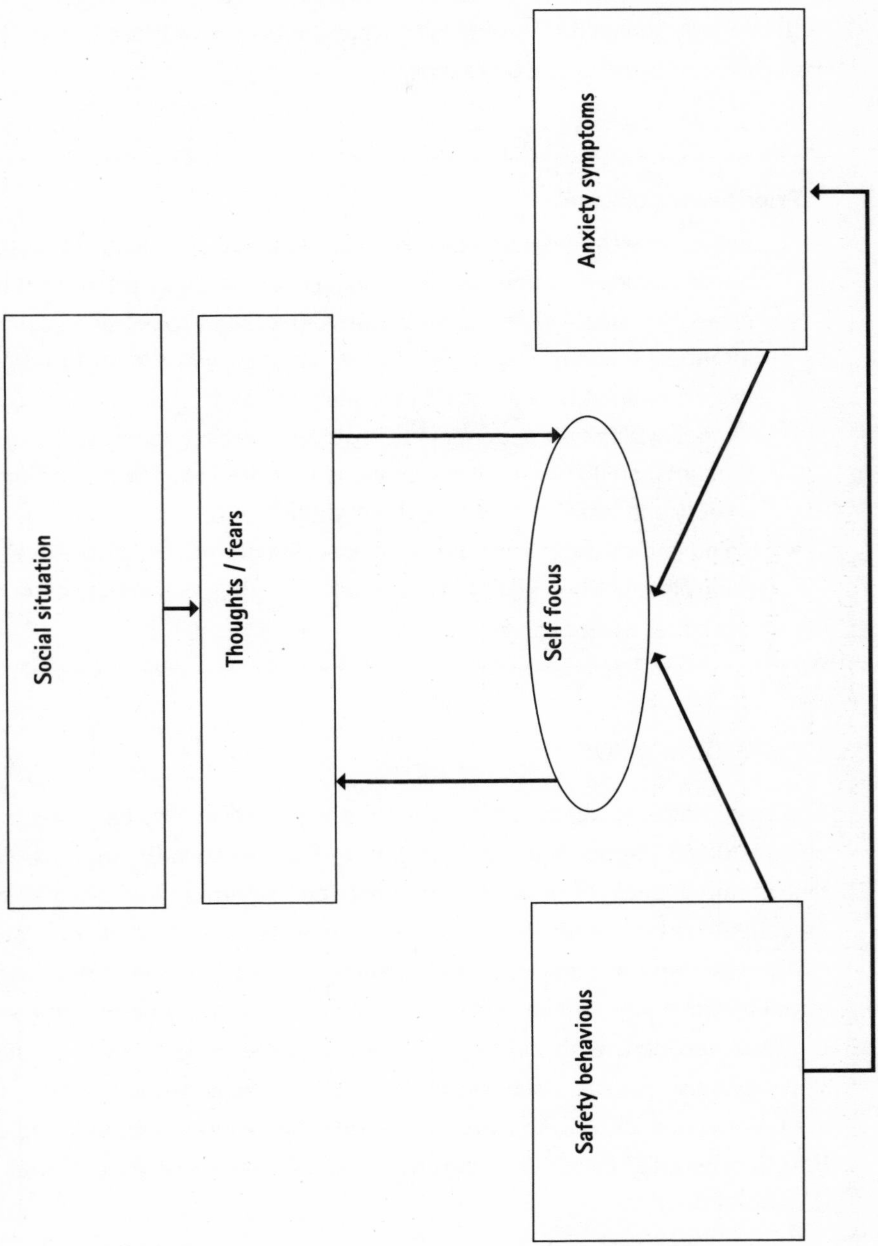

Figure 9.3: Blank social anxiety flowchart

Treatment

Once you understand more about what keeps your problem going you will be ready to use the strategies for changing some of those things. The priorities are listed in the box below.

Priorities for change

- Reducing self-consciousness: The main strategy is to learn to focus outside yourself so that you are no longer constantly aware of what is going on inside – or self-consciousness. This means practising paying attention to what is going on in the situation you are in, to other people, to what they are saying or doing and so on.
- Changing thinking patterns: This involves thinking again about the thoughts, predictions and assumptions that are linked with fear and anxiety and learning how to re-think these things.
- Doing things differently: Planning experiments will help you to do things in new ways and to work out what this tells you about yourself and about other people.

Psychoeducation

The next stage of treatment is to learn about and to practise the strategies and techniques that will help you to feel less socially anxious. The three main aspects of treatment are described separately on pp. 255–85, as you should do them in that order. Indeed this could be useful, especially when you are learning about exactly what to do. Once you know about all three you will be able to combine the methods. For example you might experiment with talking to some people who make you feel nervous; practise paying attention to them and to their feelings while you are talking, and think afterwards about whether you were right to expect that they would reject you. Learning how to do each of these things is described next.

Reducing self-consciousness

The aim is to learn to forget yourself in order to be yourself, just as you would if you were running downstairs. If you tried to tell yourself exactly how to do this you would probably trip over, as too much self-awareness interferes with performance. So what you are going to practise is switching your attention. Learning to focus externally is not a new skill – you probably do it all the time, for example when you lose yourself in a film, book or piece of music, and fail to notice what else is going on around you; or when you are so engrossed in answering your emails that you don't notice the television in the background any more. So you should practise giving more attention to the person or people that you are interacting with. Eventually this will enable you to become more fluent and attentive, and to feel more comfortable.

Focusing externally is a big effort at first, but over time it should become habit. The first thing to practise is switching attention from internal to external, and back again, in non-threatening situations. For example, you could do this while watching television, or on the bus, or walking the dog. First pay attention to what is going on in your body (focusing internally), and then switch your attention to what is going on around you (focusing externally). When inwardly focused you are paying attention to how your body feels on the inside, and what is going on in your mind: noticing how hot you feel or worrying about how you are coming across. When you are externally focused you will notice what you can see, hear, smell and feel around you, such as the colours in the sky, wind on your face, and feel of the ground under your feet as you walk the dog, or exactly what is happening in a television programme as you watch it. Notice the contrast between the two kinds of attention: being involved with a television programme as opposed to noticing that you feel hungry, or worried about something, or annoyed with someone else.

Some useful points to remember about attention switching:

- Attention naturally wanders, as things around you grab your attention. So you will not be able to keep it fixed in one place. Don't worry about that, and just turn it outwards again if you notice yourself becoming self-conscious.

- In an un-self-conscious conversation, as you probably know, attention naturally moves between other people, the things around you, and your own feelings and ideas. So don't try to fix on something, like the other person's face. Let your attention wander about, and move it outwards if you notice your signs and symptoms of anxiety.

- The more interested and curious you are the more you will pay attention to what you are talking about, and to other people, and the less attention will be left over for your anxiety and worrying thoughts. So give yourself something to find out from the other person, or talk about something that really interests you.

One strong motivator for focusing internally in social situations is the perceived need to monitor how you feel in order to estimate how (badly) you are coming across. But self-perceptions of this kind are terribly inaccurate – you do not appear how you feel. People cannot see how you feel – if they could you wouldn't have to explain it to them. You will get a much better sense of how you are coming across by focusing externally and by finding out more about other people – collecting the kind of information that passes you by when self-consciousness dominates. This helps you to notice, for instance, that not everyone is staring at you even when it feels as if they are, or that the person that you are speaking to is enjoying the conversation.

First practise switching your attention in non-threatening situations and then try doing it in social situations. Start with relatively easy ones, such as speaking to people you feel relatively comfortable with, then move on to more threatening situations. If you find yourself becoming self-conscious try not to worry about it, and just move your attention outwards once more. Practising switching your attention back and forth will make this easier to do.

You might find it helpful to compare the effects of being internally or externally focused in social situations – so try a few minutes' conversation each way and see which you think makes you (i) feel more comfortable and (ii) perform better in the situation.

Key message

Learning to switch your attention is like any other skill – it takes practice. Start by practising switching from internal to externally focused attention in non-social situations and then move on to practising focusing externally in social situations. Shift your attention outwards again if you start to feel self-conscious.

Tip for supporters

You can help the person you are supporting 'compare and contrast' the effects of being internally or externally focused. Get them to practise a pretend social situation with you, e.g. having a chat over coffee for five minutes. Ideally it would be a situation that will make them a little anxious. For the first role-play ask them to focus on themselves, and in particular on what is going on inside their body and mind, as much as possible. In contrast, in the second one ask them to try to focus externally – on you and the conversation. Immediately after each conversation ask them to rate, from 0–10, how anxious they felt, how anxious they think they looked, and how well they think they came across. This will enable them to compare directly the effects of focusing internally to externally. You could also give them feedback as to how they came across in each version.

Changing thinking patterns

In this section you will learn how to re-think the patterns of thinking that otherwise contribute to keeping your social phobia going. These patterns include your expectations, predictions, assumptions and beliefs, and these will be different for different people. Gemma thought that if she revealed her true self to people they would reject her for being boring and dull. Tom's concerns centred on his assumption that people would know how anxious he was, and think him odd if they saw his hands shaking. Ed worried that he might blush when speaking to someone he found attractive, and that the person would then think he was coming on to them and think him a *sad old letch*. Kim knew that she was unable to make small talk and believed that others found her dull and uninteresting. James usually felt OK in informal social situations but struggled at work or when speaking to people in authority as he believed he was not bright enough to be doing this job, and assumed they would discover how stupid he was. Joe, whose social anxiety affected all situations, believed that he would be revealed as generally inadequate in every way, whatever he did.

Having negative predictions in mind drives the anxious feelings. If you think that you are coming across as a total idiot, and think that others can see how anxious you feel inside it makes perfect sense that you feel anxious. Thus an obvious way forward is to use CBT techniques to help recognize your patterns of thinking, and then to examine the validity and helpfulness of these thoughts and predictions.

Key message

Thinking about how badly we are coming across, and about the terrible impression we must be making on others, will make anyone anxious in a social situation. CBT helps you to identify your thoughts and to find out if there are other ways of seeing things.

The first stage is to tune in to exactly what you are saying to yourself in social situations. When you notice yourself becoming anxious stop and ask yourself, 'What is it I am most bothered about? What is the worst that

I am fearing could happen?' It is useful to keep a chart like the one below to keep a record of your thoughts.

Table 9.3: Social phobia thought record

Situation	Feeling (intensity %)	Thought (belief %)
Getting ready for team meeting on Friday	Dread (70%) Anxious (40%)	I'm going to make a fool of myself (50%) I'll look like I don't know what I'm talking about (70%) I'll shake (100%) They'll think I'm an idiot (60%)
Waiting to meet Sally at bus stop	Self-conscious (80%) Anxious (40%)	Everyone's looking at me (80%) Bet they wonder what I'm doing here (80%) They'll see I'm shaking (90%) They think I'm an idiot (90%)
Talking to Sally's colleague	Self-conscious (100%) Anxious (70%)	I can't think of anything to say (90%) I'm not making sense (80%) He must be desperate to get away (80%)

Tips for supporters

You can help by putting questions to the person you are supporting when they are beginning to get anxious about a social situation. The following list of questions might be useful in helping them to identify clearly what they are thinking:

- What is going through your mind right now?

- Is there something that you are predicting will go wrong?

- What's the worst that could happen in this situation?

- Is there a particular symptom or symptoms that you are worried about other people seeing?

- Do you have any image or impression of how you are likely to come across?

Once you have tuned in to what you are thinking, the next step is to begin to examine the validity and helpfulness of these thoughts. Thoughts are our opinions, not necessarily facts. When we are anxious our thinking often becomes distorted, and overly black and white. We tend to make negative predictions about how we are coming across that may not be justified. So when I feel as if I am blushing, I may think I have gone bright red, and that everyone has noticed and thinks I am an idiot but this isn't necessarily the case. Firstly, I may not look as red as I feel and, secondly, even if I have gone red, others may not be paying attention to that, or may view it much less harshly than I imagine.

There are many ways of re-thinking old patterns of thinking. The one described next uses an expanded version of the chart above, and the work is done by re-thinking old habits of thought, either by yourself or with the help of someone else. Another way, described in the next section, is to experiment with new ways of doing things so that you can collect some new information relevant to the kinds of situations that trouble you.

In order to examine the validity of socially anxious thoughts you need to examine the evidence for them, and the extra columns added to the chart on pp. 272–3 help us to do this. First, decide which of the thoughts to evaluate – the one that bothers you most is likely to be most useful and this thought has been emboldened in the chart. Then start to look for the evidence that supports this thought. When you have found all you can, turn your attention to the evidence that does *not* support this thought. With both kinds of evidence in front of you think them through and see if you can come up with a realistic, and balanced conclusion. Finally, think about how to take the issue forward. You might even be able to make a definite plan of action.

Tips for supporters

You can help at all stages. In particular by helping them to:

- Be specific about exactly what they are predicting in a given social situation.

- Find any evidence that *does not* fit with their negative predictions or beliefs.

- Make a plan of action for what to do differently in the light of any changes in their thinking about a particular situation.

When and how to use thought records (also see Part 1)

Try to complete thought records when the issue is 'live': as soon as possible after something that made you anxious. It gets harder to 'catch' the thoughts the longer it is since the situation happened. At first, completing thought records as shown above may seem laborious and inconvenient. Like any skill it requires practice, and it helps to write things out in full until you feel you have got the hang of it. Your helper, if you have one, may be able to assist with particularly tricky thoughts, or when you are struggling to find anything that does not fit with the thought. Over time you should be able to spot repeating patterns in your thinking and thought records, and it will get easier as you will have addressed that type of thought many times before. With practice you will get better at thinking things through in this way in your head and may only need to write down the most difficult issues. An example is given on the next page, and a blank form for you to complete follows, and is in the appendix.

Table 9.4: Social phobia thought record

Situation	Feeling (intensity %)	Thought (belief %)	Evidence for the thought	Evidence against the thought	Balanced view and/or action plan
Getting ready for team meeting on Friday	Dread (70%) Anxious (40%)	I'm going to make a fool of myself (50%) I'll look like I don't know what I'm talking about (70%) I'll shake (100%) **They'll think I'm an idiot (60%)**	I always feel like I look like an idiot, and I may not be able to present my points as fluently and articulately as some people are. I might look anxious.	My boss has already expressed appreciation for the work I've done on the project. Others sometimes appear anxious in meetings and nobody thinks they're an idiot so why should it be any different for me?	I can bring my notes with me to refer to and even if I am not the most articulate, I do actually know more about the subject than anyone else there. Even if I am not the most articulate, they won't necessarily think I am an idiot.
Waiting to meet Sally at bus stop	Self-conscious (80%) Anxious (40%)	Everyone's looking at me (80%) Bet they wonder what I'm doing here (80%) **They'll see I'm shaking (90%)** They think I'm an idiot (90%)	I can feel myself shaking and I've seen my hands shaking when I look down.	There are plenty of things I don't notice about other people at bus stops so it may be that they aren't paying that much attention to me anyway. Even if	It doesn't really matter what strangers think of me. I should check out how much attention they actually are paying to me.

Talking to Sally's colleague	Self-conscious (100%) Anxious (70%)	I can't think of anything to say (90%) **I'm not making sense (80%)** He must be desperate to get away (80%)	It certainly feels like I'm talking nonsense and it's coming out as gibberish. I did get confused and stumble over words.	they are looking. Sally says the shaking isn't anywhere near as noticeable as I think. Also it could be medical or a medication side-effect. And does it really matter what strangers think anyway?	I should judge whether or not I'm making sense on whether the other person appears to understand me rather than on how I feel I'm coming across. And remember, that I only have half the responsibility for the conversation.
				Normal conversations do fumble about – it shouldn't be like reading the news. He did seem to understand what I was saying and didn't seem to be in any particular hurry to get away, even though I tried to give him the opportunity.	

Worksheet 9.1: Social phobia thought record

Situation	Feeling (intensity %)	Thought (belief %)	Evidence for the thought	Evidence against the thought	Balanced view and/or action plan

Four typical themes that arise in thought records about social anxiety

The following four themes are such common ones that it helps to be aware of them as you start this aspect of the work.

1. *Taking too much responsibility.* People with social anxiety often take 100 per cent of the responsibility for how any social interaction goes. If it doesn't go well they assume it is their fault, and that they messed it up. It is worth remembering that you only ever *share* the responsibility for a social interaction – if it doesn't go well maybe it is because the other person isn't very easy to talk to! Or because they have something else on their mind at the moment that is distracting them. Or perhaps you just don't have a lot in common. Or is it the situation that is difficult? People with social anxiety tend to blame any social failure on themselves while really responsibility is shared.

2. *Emotional reasoning.* This means using your *feelings* as evidence of how you are coming across. It happens because when socially anxious we become hyperaware of what is going on in our body, and much less aware of what is going on around us. This influences the judgements about how it is going because the main thing the socially anxious person is aware of is their own feelings of anxiety. It is natural to assume that this is what dominated the situation for others, too, but it isn't. People with social anxiety often feel that their anxiety is completely obvious to others, but it isn't. Other people can't see your feelings – if they could no one would ever have to ask how you are because they'd be able to tell from looking. Just like people can't tell if you are hungry or thirsty from just looking at you, they can't tell how you are feeling. They may be able to make a guess on the basis of what you do, if you laugh or cry for instance, but it will still be a guess. We all learn to behave in ways that disguise our feelings. Switching your attention outside of yourself will help you to be less hyperaware of your anxiety and be better able to observe how other people behave and react. Then you can draw conclusions based on

what is happening in the social situation and the interaction with the other person, rather than on how you feel inside.

3. *Overly high standards for social performance.* People with social anxiety often have very high standards for their own social performance, such as feeling that they should be fluent and interesting all the time, or that it is totally unacceptable to forget what one was saying, and to dry up in the middle of a conversation. In reality all these things are common. Conversations often meander around, or become repetitive and stilted. It is worth paying attention to the times when other people make these 'social mistakes' and observing how they are responded to. For example, if someone repeats themselves, or forgets what they were saying, does anyone really seem bothered by it?

4. *Believing you are boring, unlikeable or uninteresting.* People with social anxiety may believe that they are socially unattractive, for a variety of reasons, such as not being interesting or witty enough. However, it is worth remembering that acceptability is much more to do with the match between two people, and whether they like each other, than with the characteristics of either of them. There will always be people that you don't like, or have a lot in common with, and others will feel the same about you. This doesn't make you boring or unlikeable; it just means that you are not well suited to each other. If you are not interested in golf, then you may find the conversation boring, but other golfers won't. Indeed, the people most likely to be experienced as boring by others are those who don't show any interest in the other person, and just bang on about whatever it is they want to talk about, and this is far from what most people with social anxiety do!

Key message

Many people with social phobia have similar thoughts. Four common themes are taking too much responsibility, emotional reasoning, using overly high standards, and thinking badly of yourself.

Tips for supporters

You might be able to help the person spot themes in their thought records:

- Do they seem to be taking too much responsibility for social interactions?

- Are they basing their conclusions about social situations solely on how they felt in the situation?

- Do they seem to have very high standards for their own social performance?

- Do they seem to be consistently overly critical of themselves?

Doing things differently

There is no way round it: the way to build confidence is to face the things that you fear. In this section you will learn how to stop doing the things that feel as if they will protect you: avoiding difficult situations and keeping yourself safe. These behaviours contribute to keeping the problem going. Instead you will discover how to do things differently by planning some mini-experiments. First you will need to identify your personal self-protection strategies: what you avoid and how you try to keep yourself safe. Then you can use this information to plan some experiments, to test out some of your fears. Thinking the experiments through, before and after you have done them, brings the three parts of the treatment together by linking the new behaviours to new ways of thinking.

Start by thinking about, and trying to recognize, the ways in which you try to protect yourself. Avoidance is not doing something because it would make you anxious. Safety behaviours involve doing something to make you feel less anxious. They both work in the same way, and both of them keep the problem going, so make as long a list as you can of all these things. Prompt yourself by answering the questions below.

Avoidance: not doing something that would make you anxious

1. What social events do you avoid going to?

2. What social interactions would you never join in with?

3. Are there times when you make excuses or find a way of making your escape? If so, when does this happen?

4. Do you refuse invitations? Which sorts of invitations?

Some examples of avoidance: saying no to social invitations, arriving late or leaving early to limit the time; refusing to try new things or places because of fear of embarrassment; not speaking in front of others; staying away from certain people or situations; avoiding speaking to someone you find attractive.

Safety behaviours: doing something to protect yourself

1. What do you do that makes anxiety-provoking situations feel safer?

2. How do you try to make sure that nothing too bad happens?

3. Are there ways in which you try not to attract attention?

4. Do you do anything in social situations to try to prevent yourself coming across badly? Or to prevent others from noticing?

Some examples of safety behaviours: looking down so no one can catch your eye or see your face; not wearing bright-coloured clothing, or clothes that make you feel hot; being careful about what you say; handing stuff round at a party so you can move on easily; taking a friend with you if you feel too nervous on your own.

Avoidance and safety behaviours often overlap. For instance, you might avoid speaking up in front of a group, or keep yourself safe by saying very little. The important point is to be aware of both of these ways of protecting yourself. They can both be tackled using mini-experiments to test out the consequences of behaving differently.

Gemma didn't avoid conversations but she avoided expressing her true opinions in those conversations for fear that it would make people dislike her. Her new boyfriend had noticed that she always made sure she was behind him if they ever entered a bar or restaurant, and she would make sure she did not arrive before he did by waiting in her car nearby until he texted her. Tom didn't avoid going to the pub with friends, but his main safety behaviour involved keeping his hands out of view so people wouldn't notice if they were shaking. Ed was aware that he tended to avoid eye contact when talking to anyone he found attractive. He also tried to keep himself cool to limit any blushing and sweating. So avoidance is not just about avoiding going into the situations, but also about what you do once you are there, for example, for Tom, carrying a round of drinks from the bar, and for Gemma, expressing opinions, especially disagreement.

Key message

Both kinds of self-protective strategies – avoidance and safety behaviours – perpetuate social phobia. Recognize what you do, then you will know what to change.

Tip for supporters

You can help the person you are supporting to draw up a list of the self-protective strategies that they use. You might be able to spot things that they hadn't even noticed themselves – situations they are avoiding or the subtle things they do to protect themselves in those situations. Encourage them to begin to change these behaviours by reminding them that facing fears helps to build confidence.

Once you begin going into social situations that you have previously avoided it is important that you get the most out of them. To do this you can treat each time as an experiment – a chance to discover how realistic your social fears are, or to discover what happens if you behave differently in the situation. So it is important to think in advance about how you will get the information to answer your questions. So for Tom, whose primary concern was that others would notice his hands shaking, it was important to work out how he would know if they did notice his hands shaking. Tom was confident that if the friends whom he went to the pub with noticed his shaking, they would comment. So when he went to the pub and reduced his avoidance by ordering drinks that were full to the top and carrying them back from the bar, he paid attention to whether anyone commented on his shaking. He was even able to ask one of his closest friends if they had noticed anything.

Similarly for Ed, who was concerned about blushing if he had to speak to someone attractive, it was important to be able to tell if he had blushed, and what, if anything, the other person had made of it. How would he know if they did indeed think he was a 'sad old letch' as he feared? He thought that if a girl had noticed his blushing and thought him a sad old letch, then she would make every effort to end the conversation as soon as possible. So he used this to judge whether his fears were being realized or not. In this way it is possible to treat every situation as an 'experiment', helping you to discover more about your social anxiety, and about how you actually are coming across. No single experiment will fundamentally change your perception, but each one is like a pebble on the beach, and over time the pebbles accumulate to change the shape of the beach – in this case to change your thoughts and feelings about how you come across to others. For this reason it is important to keep detailed notes of the outcomes of your experiments (See Chapter 5, p. 62–7, for behavioural experiments and worksheet). These are used to record (i) what you feared in advance of the situation, (ii) what you did to test that fear, (iii) what the outcome was and (iv) what you concluded from it.

Key message

Reducing your avoidance of social situations can be combined with setting up experiments to test out your social fears and collect information about how others respond to you in social situations.

Tip for supporters

You can help the person you are supporting to identify what it is they fear most about the situation, and by devising a way of testing that within the situation. You may even be able to collect 'data' for them – for example by monitoring and observing how other people react to them in social situations.

Experiments for trying out new ways of doing things

Experiments take the sting out of facing your fears. The whole point of them is to find out something you want to know. That means that as well as being anxious or nervous about doing them you soon become interested in what you are going to discover, or curious about what you will find out.

For instance, many people avoid talking about social anxiety for fear of what other people might think of them. But a degree of social anxiety is natural so everyone knows how it feels. An early experiment you might start with is to ask one or two people that you know if they ever get anxious in social situations, such as when speaking up in public, or when meeting new people. If they say yes, then ask how it affects them. What do they worry about? How do they make sense of their anxiety in that situation? Once you have a few findings, stop and think about them. What did they say? Did their fears seem realistic?

And what does it tell you about the normality of social anxiety? Think, too, about how you felt while collecting this information? Were you as anxious as you expected to be?

This is an important point. Making a prediction before you try doing something new helps you to collect a lot more information than you might otherwise be able to. The steps to go through when you are planning these are:

1.   Identify what you do to protect yourself.

2.   Find out what happens if you give up protecting yourself in this way by making a specific prediction about what will happen if you don't do it (or even do the opposite).

3.   Draw conclusions from what you have done.

Examples of experiments

Gemma's main fear was that people wouldn't like her if they got to know her. So to protect herself she always avoided talking about herself, and expressing her opinions. So one of her main experiments was to go into social situations and talk about herself, and express her opinions. She tried this out by going into work on a Monday morning and instead of just saying 'yes, thanks' when colleagues asked if she had a nice weekend, she actually told them about her weekend. She predicted that they would quickly lose interest and would not ask about her weekend again. What she found was quite the opposite – most people seemed genuinely interested in what she had been up to and she discovered common interests with some of her colleagues, which made it much easier to talk to them in other situations, too.

Doing experiments like this made it easier for her to develop confidence and drop other safety behaviours, such as always making sure her husband was with her or entered a social situation first. She had predicted that if she met her boyfriend in the pub, and arrived first, everyone in the pub would stare at her as she came in and think she was some kind of weirdo. To begin to test this out first she went to a pub with her husband and just observed whether other people were on their own, and if they seemed to be the focus of other people's attention. What she found was that plenty of people were on their own, particularly early in the evening. Some appeared to be waiting for someone, and others didn't. Noticing this helped to plan her next experiment – going into the pub to wait for her husband by herself. What she discovered was that no one paid her any attention.

In contrast, Tom was fine about going to the pub, but it was what he did when he was there that he needed to experiment with. He predicted that his friends would notice his hands shaking if he carried full drinks back from the bar and that they would realize how anxious he was and make fun of him for it. What he found out was that in fact all they did was complain about how long it had taken him to get served!

Using surveys

Sometimes it isn't possible to know what others are thinking, or how they view something simply by observing their reactions. So it can be useful to ask them. For example, Ed was concerned that if people noticed he was blushing they would think he was a 'sad old letch' or at the least lying to them. Before he even put himself in the situation it seemed important to find out more about what people generally thought when they noticed someone blush; so he asked a female friend what she would think if, when she was talking to a man of a similar age to herself, he started to blush. Would she necessarily think he was lying or coming on to her? He was surprised to discover that she would only have thought that maybe he was hot or self-conscious. However, this was only one person's view so he needed to ask a few more people to get a sense of how people generally viewed blushing.

Once Ed discovered that people didn't automatically conclude that you were coming on to them, or lying, if you happened to blush when you were speaking to them, it was easier for him to begin to tackle the list of situations that he avoided, and to ensure that he wasn't avoiding aspects of those situations, such as speaking to women he perceived to be attractive, or avoiding showing his face when speaking.

Gemma was concerned what people would think of her if she went into a pub on her own. To find out more before doing the experiments above she asked a few female friends if they ever went into pubs on their own, even just to wait for someone. She was surprised by the range of responses – one friend who travelled a lot with work was used to going to pubs and restaurants on her own and felt no anxiety about it. Others did go into pubs on their own but some of Gemma's friends also said that it made them slightly anxious, particularly at first. And one even used Gemma's tactic of always waiting outside.

Key message

Using your day-to-day experience as an opportunity to carry out experiments to test out your social fears will maximize the progress you make in overcoming social anxiety. Try to treat any social interaction as an opportunity to collect data about the accuracy of your negative predictions.

Tip for supporters

You can help the person you are supporting to construct and carry out surveys by helping them to identify what it is they need to find out in relation to their social concerns. Once you have identified which questions to ask, the sufferer may have a limited pool of people to ask, or be too embarrassed to ask people, so you may be able to extend this by asking your acquaintances their opinions – either face to face or via an email survey. An advantage of an email survey is that the responses can be passed on to the person you are supporting directly so they get the full range of other people's views.

Relapse prevention

Because social anxiety is such a usual phenomenon you can't expect to ever reach a place where you don't ever feel it again. What you are aiming for is to be able to enjoy doing the things you want to be able to do without being distressed by worries about how you come across, or being overwhelmed by the physical sensations of anxiety. This is the same as with the other anxiety disorders, and techniques to address it are found in Chapter 6.

The future

It is important to remember that social anxiety is usual, so you shouldn't expect to ever be completely free from any social anxiety whatsoever. What we hope is that the techniques outlined in this chapter have helped you to get your social anxiety to a manageable level – so it no longer stops you from living the life you want to live or causes you significant distress. We hope that learning about what keeps social anxiety going – the thoughts, self-consciousness and self-protective behaviours – has helped you to understand how social anxiety escalates. And that learning what to do about it has helped you to change your thinking, reduce your feelings of self-consciousness and experiment with behaving differently in social situations. Just as these different components combine to create vicious cycles that escalate anxiety, they can be used to create 'virtuous cycles' to reduce anxiety. Being less self-conscious helps you to notice positive feedback from others and engage in the situation, which gives you the confidence to test out your predictions and behave differently. So the key task in the future is to continue to use the techniques so you can keep the cycles turning in the virtuous direction. And to remember that *some* social anxiety is usual and even useful!

10 Health anxiety

Nicole M. Alberts, Shannon L. Jones
and Heather D. Hadjistavropoulos

Overview

Almost every adult at some point in their life has experienced at least a brief moment of health anxiety. If you find that you're constantly worried about your health or frequently have periods of anxiety that are focused on your health, then working through this chapter can help you better understand your health anxiety – including how it may have developed and what is maintaining it now. The chapter will also provide you with simple and straightforward ways to manage your health anxiety. Some people find that change comes from reading and understanding health anxiety better. Other people, however, may have to try new strategies for managing health anxiety. Many research studies have shown cognitive behavioural therapy to be an effective way to reduce health anxiety (see the references for further information). Research suggests that even when delivered in a less direct manner, such as a self-help book, this approach to health anxiety can be helpful.

What is health anxiety?

There is no particular disease that people with health anxiety worry about. While some may worry about cancer, others worry about getting multiple sclerosis or heart disease or even mental illness. Some worry that they have the disease right now, while others worry about developing the disease in the future. Some may not worry about their own health as much as that a loved one may develop an illness. For instance, a parent who has noticed that their child has a sore head and neck may become worried that their child has meningitis, or a husband who has noticed that his wife has developed a new mole on her hand may begin to worry that his wife has skin cancer. Although the information contained in this chapter is directed at worries you may have about your own health, most of the exercises could also be used if you are anxious about the health of someone close to you.

When is health anxiety a problem?

Some amount of anxiety about one's health can be helpful as it tends to motivate us to do something such as taking medication and seeking medical attention when it's needed. At what point does health anxiety become a problem?

Health anxiety can be described as a problem when it:

- is excessive;

- is out of proportion to the realistic likelihood of having a serious medical problem;

- is persistent despite receiving negative results on medical tests and reassurance from medical professionals;

- leads you to check your body for symptoms, seek frequent reassurance about your health from medical professionals, family and friends, or avoid health-related information, doctor's appointments, or other people who are ill;

- has persisted for six months or more;

- has caused you significant distress or adversely affected day-to-day life.

Laura's story

Laura is a 38-year-old teacher who is married and has one daughter, aged 4. She began worrying about her health after she read a news story reporting that delaying childbirth until after 30 was associated with increased risk for developing breast cancer. Since then, she has become preoccupied with the idea that she will develop breast cancer. She also fears developing other types of cancer such as ovarian and skin cancer. When Laura notices a slight bump on her body, she will repeatedly check the bump to determine whether it has changed over the course of the day. She will often also ask her husband whether the bump looks 'normal' or like 'something serious'. Laura spends a significant amount of time on the internet each day (ranging from twenty minutes to several hours) looking up information on the signs and symptoms of cancer. In addition to her regular check-ups, Laura has made several visits to her general practitioner requesting additional tests (e.g., mammogram, ultrasound). When tests have been conducted, Laura is not reassured by receiving negative test results or 'good news' that she's in good health. Instead, she tends to fear that the healthcare professional made a mistake in the testing. She then continues to be preoccupied with the thought that she has cancer that has been undiagnosed. When Laura experiences a worry episode, the quality of her work as a teacher decreases and her ability to complete day-to-day tasks at home such as cleaning and looking after her daughter suffers. Laura avoids social events for fear that someone will bring up the subject of cancer and that this will trigger another bout of anxiety for her. Laura believes that the more cancer diagnoses she hears about, the more likely she is to develop cancer. Although she has a caring and supportive husband, their relationship has become strained because of her frequent requests for reassurance.

To know whether your health anxiety is a problem, we recommend asking yourself the following questions:

1. Do you spend significant time worrying about your health?

2. When you notice a bodily change or sensation, do you automatically think that something is wrong with you?

3. Do you think that having an illness will be awful and result in significant disability or death?

4. Do you think you would be unable to cope with having an illness?

5. Do you have low confidence in doctors and other health professionals?

6. Do you find you are on guard and watching to see if there is anything wrong with your health?

7. Do you have images of yourself being ill or having a serious disease?

8. Do you visit your doctor more than most people to ask about symptoms even though he or she has reassured you that there isn't anything physically wrong with you?

9. Do you find yourself frequently talking to your family and friends about your physical concerns?

10. Do you spend significant time looking up information about illnesses or diseases on the internet or elsewhere?

11. Do you spend time checking and monitoring your body for physical symptoms of a disease?

12. Have you stopped doing things that you enjoy because of your worry about your health?

13. Has your worry affected your relationships with others (e.g. partner, children)?

14. Is your worry or checking interfering with your ability to focus or get other things done (at work, socially)?

If you answered 'yes' to six or more of the questions above, then you may be suffering from health anxiety and we suggest you continue to read this chapter.

Negative impacts of health anxiety

Health anxiety can affect a person's life. Below are areas that are commonly affected by health anxiety.

Relationships with family and friends

Time spent worrying about your health or time spent seeking help from health professionals may affect your relationships and ability to focus on family. Sometimes family and friends might join you in your worrying, which contributes to everyone feeling distressed. Or they might become frustrated with you if you continue to worry or seek reassurance despite receiving negative test results. You might even notice yourself becoming frustrated with them for not understanding what you are coping with or for not helping you work out what is wrong. Health anxiety might also cause you to avoid social occasions because you fear that you might catch a disease or that the topic of conversation might turn to illness. Often people with health anxiety feel distant or alienated from others. You may be avoiding relationships because of your health anxiety. But people may also be avoiding you because they don't want to hear about your health worries.

Work or studying

Many people with health anxiety find it difficult to stop thinking about their health and signs of potential illness. When this happens, you might find it difficult to focus and concentrate on tasks at work or college. You might also have difficulty completing household tasks. A considerable amount of your work or study time might also be taken up by medical appointments or searching the internet, which may cause you to fall behind.

Life enjoyment and satisfaction

You may become so focused on your health and seeking reassurance about your health that you stop doing things you enjoy or that give you a sense of accomplishment. Stopping such activities can lead one to feel depressed. If you have not stopped doing activities, you may find that you are not enjoying things as much as you normally would. It is hard to enjoy things and be present in your life when your health is always on your mind.

As you make your way through this chapter, you will be provided with self-assessment tools that will help you judge the severity of your health anxiety symptoms.

What if I have a medical condition?

At this point, you might be wondering, 'What if I really have a medical condition? Does this mean I still have health anxiety?' Health anxiety can exist in people who are 'healthy' and in people who have a diagnosed medical condition (e.g. high blood pressure, multiple sclerosis). An individual who has diabetes or cancer, for instance, can also experience severe health anxiety or health anxiety that is above and beyond what others with these conditions experience. Research shows that quality of life is lower in people who have a medical condition and also experience health anxiety compared with those who have a medical condition but do not have health anxiety.

People who experience health anxiety, whether they have a diagnosed medical condition or not, experience physical sensations. These sensations are not imaginary; they are real. What is different about people who have health anxiety compared with those who do not is how much they focus on these sensations, and how they interpret the sensations. The person who has health anxiety believes that the sensations are a sign of serious disease and illness. The individual who is not anxious about their health may not even notice or may not worry about it. At times, someone who does not have health anxiety may worry about a symptom, though it seems the person takes a more 'balanced' approach to the sensation, thinking it could be a sign of something serious or it could be nothing.

Once medical attention is sought, if reassurance is given, the person who does not have health anxiety no longer notices or focuses on the sensation.

Key message

Whether or not you have a medical condition does not determine if your health anxiety has become a problem. What is central to determining whether you have health anxiety is how you are *responding* to and coping with bodily changes or sensations. If you respond to physical sensations with excessive and persistent worry, attention and vigilance, checking, reassurance seeking, or avoidance, then health anxiety may be a problem for you.

How does health anxiety develop?

There is not one specific cause of health anxiety. Research and patients have instead indicated that various types of experience may contribute to its development.

- **Genetic vulnerability.** If one or both of our parents struggled with anxiety (even if it was not related to health), then our chances of developing anxiety about health and anxiety more generally will be greater.

- **Observing family members or others experience a serious illness.** Witnessing others experience illness when we are a child or adolescent can contribute to how we respond to bodily changes or sensations. For example, if we witnessed someone experiencing pain and suffering, we may view illness as something awful and to be avoided at all costs. If we witnessed someone with a progressive illness leading to death, we may think that medical treatments are of little to no help. If we observe a family member struggle with an inherited illness, then we might focus on the chances that we, too, will develop such an illness.

- **Having a parent who has health anxiety.** If you grow up observing others worry about their health or frequently checking for signs of illness, then you will be more likely to behave in a similar way when faced with health issues or unexplained bodily sensations.

- **Information through the media or internet.** The media and internet can be helpful resources and offer you wide access to information about your health. However, you should keep in mind that media outlets often want to grab your attention. In an effort to do so, health stories frequently focus on rare diseases and fatal conditions. They may also report on stories where doctors made mistakes and patients went undiagnosed. Attending to these types of stories, rather than stories about medical successes, might lead you to question your own medical care and to view rare health problems as common.

Understanding what keeps you anxious about your health

Before you begin focusing on how to go about changing your health anxiety symptoms, it is important to understand what keeps your health anxiety alive. We are therefore going to tell you what therapists understand about health anxiety. This understanding has come about through several years of research.

Research suggests that people with high health anxiety have developed problematic beliefs and thoughts about health and illness (Marcus, Gurley, Marchi and Bauer, 2007). These beliefs can be triggered by external events such as illness-related media reports, hearing about someone who has become ill, or by internal events such as bodily sensations or changes (e.g., headache, heart palpitations, diarrhoea, blurry vision). Once these beliefs are triggered, people misinterpret harmless bodily sensations and changes as a threat. This misinterpretation leads them to feel fearful and anxious. In an attempt to make these feelings go away, people try to reduce their anxiety by checking their body, checking the internet, seeking reassurance, or avoiding situations that provoke anxiety. Although these behaviours reduce anxiety in the moment, research suggests that they actually increase anxiety in the long run. There are a variety of reasons why these behaviours increase anxiety. One is that if people look for information that suggests they are in danger, they are more likely to find this information. Another reason is that if we act as if we are in danger, then we are more likely to feel like we are in danger.

Triggers

Both internal and external situations may trigger health anxiety. Internal triggers are sensations and symptoms in the body. This can include increases or decreases in heart rate, digestive discomfort, tingling or numbness in parts of the body, and ringing in the ears. We may notice unusual sensations such as developing a strange taste in the mouth or a twitch in a muscle. External events can also trigger episodes of health anxiety. External triggers may include but are not limited to: media reports of health scares, medical appointments, hearing about someone who has been diagnosed with an illness, or receiving inconclusive results on a medical test.

Problematic beliefs about health and illness

The internal and external events can trigger certain beliefs and assumptions about health and illness that have developed over time. In general, people with high health anxiety tend to overestimate the probability that they have a serious illness and underestimate their ability to cope with illness. Perceptions of illness as being awful and medical services as ineffective are also common. You will have a chance to learn more about common thinking patterns in health anxiety in the following section.

Focus on body sensations

Focusing attention on a symptom or sensation can amplify the experience of that sensation. The more we focus on our symptoms, the more we become aware of that symptom. The symptom will also seem more intense. As the intensity of the symptom appears to increase, so will our concern about the symptom, and in turn our focus on it!

Checking and reassurance seeking

When it comes to our health, we are all encouraged to check our bodies and seek medical advice. For example, we are encouraged to monitor moles on our skin and women are encouraged to conduct self-examinations on their breasts. We are also encouraged to go for regular tests, for example of our blood pressure or cholesterol levels, and conduct self-exams. For most people, checking or obtaining reassurance about their health will usually lead to feeling less anxious and they will be able to continue with their day. However, people with health anxiety continue to worry about their health and feel anxious. They therefore continue to engage in checking and reassurance seeking to reduce these anxious feelings. For individuals with high health anxiety, checking and reassurance seeking is repeated and frequent.

Some examples of checking and reassurance-seeking behaviours include:

- Checking your body for new moles, lumps or areas of discoloration.

- Poking or pinching areas of your body.

- Examining bodily secretions (e.g. saliva, urine, faeces) for signs of blood or changes in colour.

- Monitoring bodily processes (e.g. taking pulse, checking blood pressure).

- Asking friends, family members, or healthcare providers about symptoms.

- Researching symptoms on the internet or other resources.

- Requesting additional medical tests and second opinions.

Avoidance and safety behaviours

While checking and reassurance seeking are used to reduce anxiety that is already present, avoidance and safety behaviours are strategies people use to prevent anxiety from occurring in the first place. To avoid internal triggers, you may avoid things that lead to changes in your body. For instance, exercise, coffee and certain foods. To avoid external triggers, you may also avoid certain people, places and situations that remind you of illness, for example:

- medical appointments;

- television shows related to health and illness;

- writing a will;

- social events where illness might be discussed;

- hospitals;

- visiting a friend or relative who was recently ill;

- phoning for test results;

- surgery and other medical procedures.

'Safety behaviours' are a more subtle form of avoidance. When people use safety behaviours, they may find they are able to face the situations they are frightened of and would like to avoid, but only if they take certain precautions or have certain plans put into place. For example, if we are afraid of catching swine flu, we might not go to public places unless we have hand sanitizer. If we are afraid of cancer, we might not go to the hospital unless we have our mobile phone and can look up medical symptoms that we become frightened about.

Putting it all together

Checking, reassurance seeking, avoidance, and safety behaviours may reduce your anxiety in the short term. This is the main reason you have continued to use them – they provide some relief in the moment. But they prevent you from learning that you can survive without them and that you can face your fears.

The following flow chart illustrates how health anxiety is triggered and then maintained.

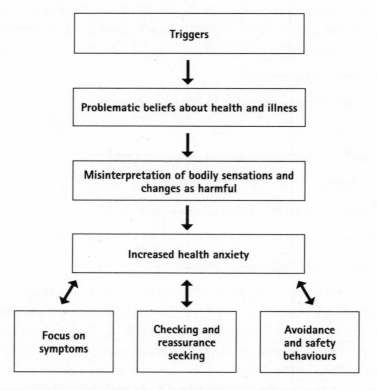

Figure 10.1: A cognitive behavioural model of health anxiety

To help you apply this approach to your own personal situation, look back at Laura's story on p. 289. Let's look at how her health anxiety symptoms fit into the framework above:

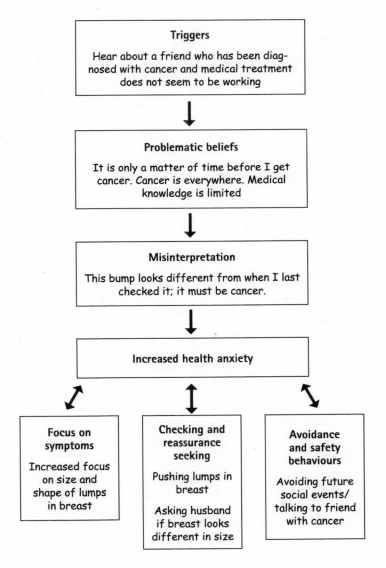

Figure 10.2: The Maintenance of Laura's health anxiety.

Now fill in the framework below based on *your own* experiences. It might help to think back to a time when your health anxiety was very bad or to a recent episode.

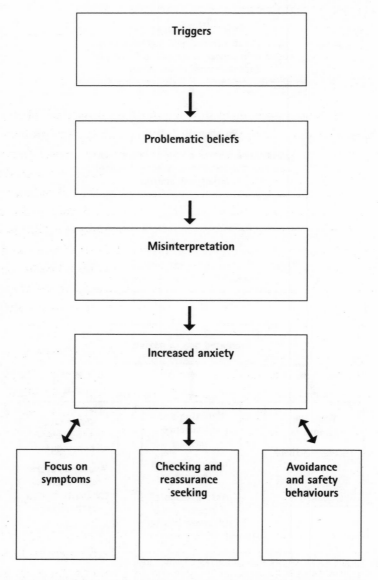

Figure 10.3: A blank diagram to help you work out what is maintaining your health anxiety.

Tips for supporters

If the person you are supporting is comfortable with doing so, you may find it helpful to review and discuss the form above.

Treatment overview

As we have seen, a number of things contribute to worries about our health. Some of our worry stems from thinking patterns and problematic beliefs that we may have developed about health and illness. Particular behaviours may also play a role in health anxiety, such as repeated and frequent checking and reassurance seeking as well as avoidance and safety behaviours. Such behaviours ensure that we continue to focus on physical symptoms, which in turn makes us think more about our health. Treatment involves gathering relevant evidence to (i) identify and (ii) challenge the thinking patterns and behaviours that keep health anxiety going. Treatment will help you find out that by changing the way you think and by changing your behaviour patterns, you can feel less anxious about your health.

CBT treatment for health anxiety typically consists of 12–20 sessions in total, with sessions being held once weekly. As described in Chapter 1, we recommend planning sessions with yourself as this will allow you to get the most out of the programme. People's individual experiences with health anxiety are varied, so this structure can be modified to best fit your own situation.

How to approach this self–help programme

This chapter covers several different skills and techniques all focused on overcoming your health anxiety. The skills and techniques build upon each other, which means you will get the most out of the programme if you read through and practise the skills in the order that they're presented. Certain aspects of health anxiety may be less troublesome for you, while others require more attention. If so, you may wish to spend more time on certain sections (e.g. confronting situations you currently avoid) over others (e.g. changing your anxious thoughts).

Are you ready to change your health anxiety?

Even though your health anxiety may be interfering with some aspects of your life and you'd prefer to live without it, sometimes this isn't enough for you to feel ready to take on a self-help programme and all of the effort that goes into it. Being ready to overcome your anxiety demands your attention, your desire and motivation, and a generous amount of your time. To know whether you're ready to take these steps, ask yourself: what are the *costs* and *benefits* of overcoming my health anxiety?

Some potential costs to consider may be the time you will have to devote to the self-help programme, such as completing forms, self-reflecting, and practising exercises. You may find some of these tasks tedious. Overcoming your health anxiety may involve tasks that are frightening, even if only temporarily. Taking part in this programme may also lead you to do things that you don't want to do or don't enjoy doing (e.g. going to visit relatives in hospital). Getting over your anxiety may mean that you receive less support or attention from your family or friends.

But there are benefits of taking part in this self-help programme. By engaging in treatment, you may be finally able to do things that are important to you. You may be able to live a life that is consistent with your personal values. You may become comfortable taking part in activities that you now avoid. You may feel happier and more calm or relaxed. Your self-esteem may be enriched. You may spend less time worrying or checking your body, which may lead you to be more effective at work, school or home. You may be able to focus on things that are important to you, *other than* your anxiety, which up until now you haven't been able to focus on. Ultimately, you may be less worried and anxious about your health.

Make a list of the benefits and costs of changing your health anxiety using the worksheet below:

Worksheet 10.1: Cost-benefit analysis of changing your health anxiety

Costs	Benefits

Do the potential benefits of participating in treatment outweigh the costs? If so, this may be a good time for you to begin the journey of changing your health anxiety.

Tip for supporters

Talk to the person you are supporting about the costs and benefits of treatment for health anxiety. Do you think this is a good time for the person to begin this journey? Are there any factors that may interfere with treatment at this time?

What do you hope to achieve through this self-help programme?

A useful strategy for keeping on track with a self-help programme is to set goals. This will help you to identify what treatment strategies will be most appropriate for you and can serve as a marker of how you are progressing. The key to goal-setting is identifying goals that follow the SMART acronym as described in Part 1, pp. 24–5.

An example of a SMART goal is: *'In 8 weeks' time, I would like to be able to spend several hours visiting my grandmother at her long-term care facility without needing to leave early or wear latex gloves.'* Before moving on to the next section, take an opportunity to record *your own* goals for treatment by following the SMART acronym.

Tip for supporters

Talk to the person you are supporting about their goal. Do you have any suggestions? Does the goal seem Specific, Measurable, Achievable, Relevant and Time limited?

Treatment – Stage 1: Psychoeducation

Why do bodily sensations occur when we're not actually ill?

As a person with health anxiety, you probably experience bodily sensations that cause you to worry. You may have been told that these sensations are not real, that they're 'all in your head'. What you have been told is incorrect. All of us experience bodily sensations daily and occasionally wonder what they might mean and why they're happening.

While the sensations are real, people who are health anxious tend to *misinterpret* these sensations as a sign of a looming health problem. The human body produces all sorts of sensations and symptoms and can even be rather noisy at times! In fact, even when our bodies are operating as they should be, we can have unwanted bodily sensations. Why does this happen? There are many reasons and sources of these symptoms:

Changes in diet, activity level, and sleeping habits. When our usual daily routine is disrupted, whether this is from eating at different hours, being more or less active, or waking up earlier than usual, this can trigger a number of bodily changes. For example, if your schedule gets overloaded and you don't get the chance to eat lunch at the usual time, your blood sugar might drop temporarily. This can lead you to feel faint, to sweat and have an increased heart rate. If you didn't get the typical 6–8 hours of sleep last night, your body might feel achy, shaky, and you may develop a headache or dry eyes later in the day. When you stand up quickly after sitting at your computer desk for a while, you might feel dizzy and unsteady. If there's been a considerable change in temperature outside (or in!), your body might go from normal to shivering and numbness if it's cold or feeling thirsty and lightheaded if it's hot. Alcohol or drugs can have an effect on your mental and physical functioning and bodily symptoms – while you're using them and the day after. These are just a few examples of the way changes in routine can lead to harmless but ordinary bodily sensations.

Prolonged inactivity. When your body has been inactive for several months or only a few days (depending on your usual activity level), you may experience a change in your cardiovascular fitness, the strength of your muscles, and how fatigued you feel when you're on the go. Inactivity is associated with shortness of breath, a rapid heartbeat, various pains and muscle aches, and feelings of low energy. Inactivity, even over the course of a day, can result in pain in one's neck or back and other areas of the body, especially if you are sitting at a computer desk and don't take periodic breaks to move around. If you've been inactive for a period of time and then begin to resume an active lifestyle, this can also produce short-term changes in bodily sensations as you build your strength and your cardiovascular health.

Minor ailments. Minor ailments or conditions can be the source of a number of bodily sensations. Minor ailments may include having a headache, allergies, a head cold or cough, a skin irritation, menstrual cramps, or heartburn. These temporary ailments are unpleasant and can lead you to feel head pain, a sore throat, itching, aching, difficulty breathing, chest pain, lower back pain, and all sorts of other symptoms. Although these ailments and their accompanying sensations are uncomfortable, they are *harmless*. They don't usually have long-term negative effects and are not life-threatening.

Fear and anxiety. We can also experience unwanted bodily sensations caused by anxiety and fear. More information about this can be found in Part 1.

Key message

There are many causes for bodily sensations. The bodily noise and sensations you experience are real. People with health anxiety quite often misinterpret such sensations as being a sign of a disease or illness. They also tend to focus their attention on their bodies and continuously monitor and check their body for signs and symptoms.

Tip for supporters

Have you noticed the person you are supporting become concerned with physical symptoms that could be attributed to any of the above factors? If so, it would be helpful to gently share this with them.

Treatment – Stage 2: Identifying and re-evaluating unhelpful thoughts

---

Laura learning about her bodily sensations

A critical component of Laura's education on health anxiety was learning about how her tendency to monitor and check her breasts resulted in increased rather than decreased worry about them. She also learned that constantly prodding for lumps could lead to swelling in her breasts. The swelling itself was alarming and caused her anxiety to worsen. Laura also learned that she noticed more of her bodily sensations during stressful periods of teaching and marking. She realized that her body's stress reaction probably caused many of the symptoms that caught her attention.

Sometimes it might seem that situations happen and then you feel anxious. However, it is important to keep in mind that *it is not the situation you are in that determines how you feel, but the thoughts and interpretations you have about that situation.* Imagine that you are meeting a friend for lunch at noon. It is 12.20 and your friend has not arrived. If you begin to think, 'My friend stood me up!' how might you feel? Perhaps angry. On the other hand, what if you think, 'This is not at all like my friend to be late; what if he/she was in an accident?' you will probably feel anxious. Finally, what if you think, 'He/she probably got stuck in traffic and will be here soon.' If this is your thought, it is likely that you will feel calm. You may also feel annoyed and impatient, but you would not feel angry or hurt. Part 1 has more information on this important idea.

In sum, this means that your perceptions of situations influence how you feel. Anxiety often occurs when we *perceive* that a *threat* is present. For example, if you are camping in the woods and you hear branches cracking, you may feel anxious as there may be a predator close by. Experiencing anxiety in a situation such as this is useful because it prepares you to either deal with the threat directly or to escape the situation.

In terms of health anxiety, people perceive there to be a greater amount of threat than there actually is. This does not mean that you should never feel concerned about your health. Rather, it is the tendency to interpret your symptoms and situations in a persistently catastrophic manner that brings about intense negative feelings and additional physical sensations.

People with health anxiety report experiencing common types of thinking patterns described in Part 1 in relation to health and illness. Some of the most common patterns include:

Common thinking patterns in health anxiety

- **Black and white thinking:** You look at things in black and white categories, rather than seeing the shades of grey. For example, you are either *completely healthy*, or *seriously ill*.

- **Gloom and doom predictions:** You make extremely negative predictions about your health. For example, *'My mother died of cancer. It is only a matter of time before I get cancer, too.'*

- **Negative interpretations:** You interpret unpleasant or unusual bodily sensations as a sign of serious illness. For example, *'This pain in my head is a sign that I have a brain tumour.'*

- **Intolerance of uncertainty:** You do not feel comfortable unless you have a complete explanation for the cause and nature of your bodily sensations.

- **Assumptions about:**

    ○ Likelihood of illness: You overestimate the probability of catastrophic outcomes and assume that an unlikely event is much more likely to occur than it is. For example, you may believe that serious illnesses are easy to catch and are present everywhere.

- ○ **Severity:** You overestimate the 'awfulness' of illness and death. For example, *'The process of dying would be unbearable, lonely, and painful.'*

- **Disqualifying evidence:** You focus only on certain pieces of information or facts that support your view, but ignore facts that are just as relevant if they do not support it.

- **Unrealistic expectations:** You hold extremely high expectations of health professionals. You expect that they should be able to understand your bodily sensations and give you a definitive explanation or cause for everything that you think might be wrong with you.

- **Anxiety about anxiety:** You might fear that health anxiety or emotional discomfort will lead you to 'go crazy' or 'lose control', or that there may be other harmful medical or physical consequences.

- **Distrust in medical services**: You believe that if you become seriously ill, medical professionals will be of little, if any, help and may end up harming rather than helping you.

List adapted from J.S. Abramovitz and A.E. Braddock, *Psychological Treatment of Health Anxiety and Hypochondriasis: A Biopsychosocial Approach* (2008). Boston: Hogrefe & Huber.

Challenging thoughts

Next you are going to learn how to address your anxious thoughts by challenging them directly. This means that you will start to look at the accuracy of your thoughts by questioning and evaluating them as described in Part 1. You can think of this process as similar to being a lawyer. Your thoughts are being put on trial and you are gathering all of the evidence to see whether they hold up or not. When you are starting out, it is best to evaluate your thoughts by writing them down and we suggest using a thought record to help with this process (see page 313).

The thought record will guide you through the evaluation process on paper and make things clearer and more helpful for you. Below you will find instructions on how to complete a thought record. Laura used the thought record to identify and challenge the anxious thoughts she had about developing cancer. A blank sheet is provided on p. 313 for you to examine your own thoughts.

The first step in completing a thought record is to identify a time when you notice that you're feeling worried about your health.

Column 1: Trigger

List the situation, physical sensation/symptom, or other trigger that is linked to feeling anxious.

Column 2: Anxious thoughts

List anxious thoughts that occur in response to the trigger in this column. Use the list of common thought patterns to help you identify your thoughts. Often these thoughts will be automatic or almost unconscious. It will take practice to identify your anxious thoughts. Try to come up with specific thoughts. Thoughts like 'something bad will happen' are too vague.

Column 3: Anxiety (0–100)

In this column, rate your anxiety on a 0–100 point scale: 0 = no anxiety at all; 100 = as anxious as you can imagine being.

Column 4: Evidence for the thought

List evidence that you feel supports your anxious thought.

Column 5: Evidence against the thought

List evidence that does not support your anxious thought. The evidence that you record should be information that others would probably agree with. It should not be how you feel, but instead, something that you could prove. Be objective in identifying potential evidence. Go through the following list of questions to help you generate evidence:

- Have I had any experiences that show that this thought is not completely true all the time?

- If a friend had this thought, what would I tell them?

- If a friend knew I was thinking this thought, what would they say to me? What evidence would they point out to me that would suggest that my thoughts are not 100 per cent true?

- Have I been in this type of situation before? When I felt this way in the past what did I think about that helped me feel less anxious? What have I learned from previous experiences that could help me now?

- Is there any information that contradicts my thoughts that I might be discounting as not important?

Column 6: New balanced thought

Review both the evidence for and against your original thought. Generate a new, more balanced thought that is based on this evidence. Remember that the goal is to develop a thought that is more realistic rather than to develop a thought that is 100 per cent positive.

Table 10.1: Laura's thought record

Day and date: Monday 9 July

Trigger	Anxious thought	Anxiety (0–100)	Evidence for the thought	Evidence against the thought	New balanced thought
Noticed a pain in my lower stomach	This pain must be an early sign of ovarian cancer	70	I've read that pain can be a sign of cancer	I've had pain in my stomach before and it didn't turn out to be cancer I ate some spicy food earlier, which sometimes causes me pain/discomfort There are other symptoms that people have when they have cancer, and I have none of these symptoms	Although pain is one sign of cancer, it's more likely that the pain I'm currently having is a result of the food I just ate and will therefore eventually pass in time. I have a habit of thinking the worst. Just because I think the worst doesn't make it likely

Worksheet 10.2: Thought record

Over the next week, fill in the thought record when you notice that your health anxiety has been triggered. If you have not had any significant episodes of health anxiety this week, think back to a recent time when you were experiencing health anxiety. Can you identify some thoughts that came up for you then? Work through the thought record using this past situation and the thoughts you had while it was happening.

Trigger	Anxious thought	Anxiety (0–100)	Evidence for the thought	Evidence against the thought	New balanced thought

Key message

Your perceptions and beliefs play a large role in how you feel. When you perceive a threat (real or imagined), it makes sense that you feel anxious. By changing your perceptions and thoughts, you can start to change how you feel. Keep in mind that this process can be difficult when you first start out. However, take heart in knowing that the more you practise the better you will become at identifying and challenging your anxious thoughts.

Tip for supporters

It may be helpful to work through the thought record above with the person you are supporting. When someone is anxious about their health it can be challenging to come up with evidence against a belief; talking through this with someone one can help.

Treatment – Stage 3. Testing beliefs through behavioural experiments

As previously described in Chapter 5, behavioural experiments are a powerful way of helping people who have anxiety. This holds true of health anxiety as well. We can use behavioural experiments to collect information to test whether our beliefs are true or whether an alternative belief may be more accurate. People with anxiety sometimes feel reluctant to carry out behavioural experiments, but when you can overcome this reluctance, you can benefit tremendously from the experience.

Sometimes people don't know how to set up the experiment. This section of the chapter is designed to give you an idea of how to take this step.

There is no one perfect experiment. The more experiments you can come up with and test the better. Sometimes you may believe it is enough to just think about the experiment and that it is not necessary to actually do it. In our experience, thinking about the experiment is not nearly as effective as performing the experiment (you could actually test this out if you like).

'If – then' statements

A helpful way to identify a behavioural experiment is to think of if – then statements that you say to yourself – or that you may be thinking without even realizing that you're saying these things to yourself – and then design a situation that allows you to test out the statement. In designing the experiment, be as specific as possible.

Let us give you an example of what we mean. Nigel felt that he absolutely could not visit a hospital. When asked how he would feel if he *did* visit a hospital, his prediction was that *'If I visit a hospital,* **then** *I will be overwhelmed with anxiety and won't be able to think about anything other than having multiple sclerosis.'* He was then asked to be more specific about his prediction. He was asked to rate how overwhelmed he'd feel if he were to visit a hospital for an hour. Nigel predicted that his anxiety would be 10 on a 1–10 scale (with higher ratings indicating extreme anxiety). Working with his therapist, Nigel then devised an experiment to test out his beliefs. The aim was that he would go to a local hospital and sit in the waiting room and rate his level of anxiety every ten minutes over the course of an hour, and then once an hour for the remainder of the day. Nigel felt he could not possibly do this; it was too overwhelming as a first step. He suggested that he would first drive up to the hospital and sit in his car across the street and rate his level of anxiety. The next day Nigel carried out the experiment. He parked across the street from the hospital and noted that he actually felt very little anxiety. He then decided to cross the street and sit on a bench outside the hospital. Again, he reported that his anxiety was very low and did not go above 2. Nigel then entered the building and sat in the waiting room for an hour. Again, his anxiety did not go above 2. Throughout the day, Nigel reported that when he rated his anxiety on an hourly basis it also did not rise above 2. Following the experiment, he revised his belief stating that *'Being in a hospital will not necessarily be unbearable and overwhelming and result in feeling more anxious about my health.'* Notice that when he revised his belief, he did not state it in an overly positive way; rather he chose to say it in a way that he felt was realistic for him.

But sometimes behavioural experiments don't always result in dramatic immediate changes like this. Sometimes predictions do come true – at least initially – and this provides important information as well. Helen, who feared having thyroid cancer, identified that she felt she had to read health-related articles on the internet at least once a day for at least half an hour (this was a minimum amount for her as her preference was to read articles first thing in the morning, over the lunch break and then before bed). When asked what she feared would happen if she did not read these articles, she said that she feared she would miss some important information about how to prevent, detect or treat cancer. Her therapist noted that this type of statement was difficult to disprove so he asked her to rate how she would feel if she did not engage in the behaviour. Her prediction was that her anxiety on the 1 to 10 scale would be 10. Her therapist then asked her to devise an experiment to test her prediction. She decided to start by not searching the internet in the morning. When she did this, she reported that in fact her anxiety was 10 in the morning when she did not engage in the behaviour. The next step was to ask her to note what her level of anxiety was when she *did* search the internet. Then Helen noticed that her anxiety was '15' on a 1 to 10 scale. What was interesting was contrasting how she felt when she searched the internet with how she felt when she did not search the internet. Her level of anxiety was *lower* when she didn't engage in this behaviour. Next, Helen talked with her therapist about different strategies she could employ when not searching the internet for health-related information. Specifically, she experimented with how she felt when she used various coping statements and identified that she in fact felt the best when she did not search the internet in the morning and instead identified and challenged negative thoughts she had about illness as described above. In this case, her rating of anxiety was a 4 on the 1 to 10 anxiety scale.

The form below will help you to set up your own experiments. We've completed this form with the first example in mind. There is then a blank form that you can use for your own experiments. We know that carrying out these experiments will be difficult to start with. After all, if the experiments were easy, you would have done them by now! You may find it helpful to do the experiment gradually. If you are afraid of thinking about or talking about a certain disease, you could start small and work your way up and see what happens when you progressively expose yourself to your fear.

Table 10.2: Nigel's behavioural experiment

Behaviour	Avoid hospitals
'If–then' belief	If I go near a hospital, then I will be overwhelmed with health anxiety
Specific 'if–then' belief	If I go into the hospital lobby, then my anxiety rating will be 10 on a 1–10 scale
Experiment	I will park across the street from the hospital, and then rate my anxiety
Result	When I parked across the hospital, I actually did not feel anxious. I rated my anxiety at 0. I then walked to the outside of the hospital, and my anxiety was at 2. I then sat inside the hospital lobby and my anxiety was still at 2. I did not experience any physical symptoms of anxiety
Revised belief	My anxiety will not necessarily be that high if I go near a hospital

Worksheet 10.3: Behavioural experiment worksheet

Behaviour	
'If–then belief'	
Specific 'if-then' belief	
Experiment	
Result	
Revised belief	

Other experiments

Beyond setting up your own experiments, there are some experiments that we find beneficial for those who worry about their health to try out. Each experiment only takes a short period of time, but can help you to gain a better understanding of your health anxiety. Again, we strongly urge you to actually do these experiments rather than merely read about them. This makes for much more effective learning.

1. Rub or touch a certain part of your body that you are anxious about to make sure your health is not in danger (e.g. lump in your breast), every hour for six hours; lightly pinch and rub the skin. How does it feel? Do you notice any changes in your skin? Most

find that repeatedly rubbing one's body will produce redness and uncomfortable sensations.

2. If you are focusing on a certain body part because you're concerned about an illness (e.g. your stomach because you are worried you have a stomach ulcer), spend a few minutes each hour for at least six hours concentrating on the bottom of your feet and how they feel. What do you notice at the end of the day? How do your feet feel? Unusual? Most will notice that by focusing their attention on a body part, they become aware of uncomfortable sensations that were not previously noticed.

3. Spend an hour reading about a disease you do not fear. How does it make you feel? Does it increase or decrease your anxiety? Most will find that this will make them feel anxious.

4. On different days of the week, spend varying amounts of time looking up information on the disease you fear. How do you feel the more time you spend seeking information? Most find that this will make them feel more anxious.

5. If you tend to be someone who checks a body part, notice how you feel if you limit your checking to once a day compared with checking every hour or every half hour. Most find that the more they check, the more anxious rather than less anxious they feel. They'll also notice the more they check, the more they think about physical sensations.

6. In your next conversation with family or friends, spend the entire time talking about your physical symptoms. Notice the response of the person you're talking to. Most will find that the response is negative.

7. Write down all of the symptoms that you are concerned about. Ask those you have a close relationship with whether they have had the same symptoms in the past and what they think the symptoms might mean. You could also do a survey of strangers.

8. Spend fifteen minutes coming up with an alternative and unworrying explanation for physical sensations that are of concern to you.

How does this make you feel? Does this reduce your anxiety or increase it?

9. Write down the following statement: '*I will develop cancer this year.*' How do you feel? Do you feel this increases your chances of developing cancer? Many people who have health anxiety believe that if they think a thought it will happen. As noted in Chapter 11, this is called thought–action fusion. Now write down this statement: '*I will win 100 million dollars this year.*' Does thinking this thought make it likely? What conclusion can you draw from this experiment?

10. Ask people who have the disease you are frightened about how they cope with the disease? How awful is life for them? What you'll notice is that the vast majority of people who have a disease are able to manage and cope with having a disease and can even generate positive aspects to having had an illness.

Tip for supporters

A great way to offer support is to do the above experiments with the person you are supporting. The person who is health anxious often benefits from learning how others respond to these same experiments.

Treatment – Stage 4: Reducing checking and reassurance seeking

People who are health anxious will often check their bodies and seek reassurance from their doctors, those around them, and even from the internet. Why do we do this? Often, we do this to ease our worrying, to help us to feel more in control and certain about being healthy, and to reassure ourselves that our health is not in danger. We may also do this to help ourselves prevent a disease from developing in the future. Checking and seeking reassurance gives us short-term relief from our anxiety.

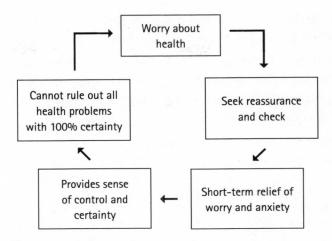

Figure 10.2: The vicious cycle of health anxiety

Even though your anxiety is relieved for a little while when you seek reassurance or check our bodies for signs of illness, if you suffer from health anxiety, your worry and anxiety eventually comes back. This is because you can never have a 100 per cent guarantee that your health is perfect. None of us, even the healthiest people we know, can ever confirm 100 per cent whether an ailment is lingering or whether we will become ill *some day*, in the future. While this uncertainty is likely to fuel your health anxiety, a goal of CBT is to *learn to tolerate this uncertainty*. Excessively checking your body or asking a family member for reassurance stops you from building up this tolerance and accepting that your health is uncertain. We also know from recent research that far from helping to reassure us in the long term, constant checking actually causes us to doubt our memory (see p. 379, Chapter 11 on OCD).

Laura's checking and reassurance seeking

Laura checks her body for bumps or moles every day for signs of breast or skin cancer. Whenever she notices a new bump, she monitors it all day to see whether or not it changes. She relies on her husband by asking him whether or not any marks or bumps seem 'abnormal'. Laura has made frequent visits to her doctor and has requested additional testing because she is worried that a diagnosis of cancer has been missed. Despite receiving reassurance from her husband and doctor, Laura continues to feel uneasy about her health and is certain that she will get cancer some day, if she doesn't already have it.

Tip for supporters

You may find it helpful to talk to the person you are supporting about how you fit into the above cycle. Do they come to you for reassurance? Do you notice that this results in only temporary relief? How do you feel when they talk to you about their health concerns? To help the person you are supporting reduce their reassurance seeking, it is important that you talk to them about this cycle. You should also discuss alternatives to offering reassurance. If they ask for reassurance about their health, then you should gently remind them about this cycle and encourage them to use other strategies to manage their health anxiety, such as examining the evidence for and against their concerns. If they are open to this, you could help review this evidence with them.

Step 1: What are my checking and reassurance-seeking behaviours?

The first step towards changing your checking and reassurance-seeking behaviours is to identify which behaviours feed your individual health anxiety cycle. Some of the behaviours may be apparent to you (e.g. searching for information on the internet), whereas others may be more subtle – you may have never considered talking about your body symptoms with your family as a way of seeking reassurance. Below is a list of common ways that people with health anxiety check or seek reassurance. In what ways do you check or seek reassurance?

Worksheet 10.4: Checking and reassurance-seeking behaviour checklist

✓ or X	
	Checking your body processes (e.g. taking pulse, checking blood pressure)
	Checking your body for changes (e.g. new moles, lumps, areas of discoloration)
	Poking, pinching, rubbing areas of your body to check for changes
	Researching your symptoms on the internet, in medical textbooks, in magazine articles, newspapers, or other media
	Posting your symptoms on internet sites to ask others for opinions about what they might mean
	Talking to family members or friends to get them to tell you everything is OK or to ask about your symptoms
	Thinking about going to your doctor
	Visiting your doctor to check whether you are ill
	Requesting medical testing and second opinions from other doctors
	Other forms of checking or reassurance-seeking behaviour [write these here]:

You may have checked off only one of the items in the above checklist or perhaps you checked off a few and even added a behaviour that wasn't on the list. If you checked off more than one, which behaviour takes up most of your time? Is there any behaviour that you do every day? Which behaviour do you think may be causing you the most distress? Answering these questions will help to narrow your focus to only one or two behaviours that you can work on in the next step.

Step 2: What are the benefits and downsides of my behaviour?

A strategy for reducing the amount of checking and reassurance seeking you do is to estimate how helpful these behaviours are, and then come up with and test out a new behaviour. To evaluate how helpful these behaviours are, we'd like you to identify the benefits and downsides of the checking or reassurance-seeking behaviour you currently do. You can use the table on p. 326 to record your answers to the following questions:

1. What do I hope to achieve when I check or seek reassurance?

2. Are there any *benefits* to carrying out this behaviour as often as I currently am?

3. Are there any *downsides* to carrying out this behaviour as often as I currently am?

4. Does this behaviour really achieve my goal?

In reviewing your answers to these questions, how helpful do you feel it is to continue carrying out this behaviour? Does the frequency with which you do it make sense? Do the downsides of this behaviour outweigh the advantages?

One thing to keep in mind in going through this process is that it is not always necessary to eliminate the unhelpful behaviour. When we think back to the more helpful nature of having concerns about your health, we know that checking and seeking help from a doctor is necessary and good for you at times. The goal of this section is to help you recognize when your behaviour is excessive and determine when you need to either reduce, delay, or eliminate checking or reassurance-seeking behaviour.

Reducing or delaying a behaviour. You may realize that you need to reduce, or delay a behaviour, if the behaviour is consistent with advice from your doctor but you are doing it excessively, too frequently, or in the absence of any significant bodily symptoms.

Stopping a behaviour: You may realize that it would be better to stop a behaviour entirely if it is at odds with the advice of a doctor. For instance, most doctors would recommend that you limit your use of the internet to self-diagnose your symptoms, including visiting chat rooms to ask other people what your symptoms might mean. This is because it is unlikely you will receive valid information. You can ask your doctor what the appropriate guidelines are for self-examinations and check-ups for a person your age.

Worksheet 10.5: Cost–benefit analysis of behaviour

	Benefits	**Downsides**
Behaviour:		
Alternative behaviour:		

Tip for supporters

Discuss the above form with the person you are supporting. It can be difficult for someone who is health anxious to think of alternative behaviours and so having your support will help.

Step 3: What can I do instead?

Whether you decide to reduce, delay or stop your checking or reassurance-seeking behaviour, the next step is to come up with a new or alternative behaviour. For some behaviours that you do, it may be relatively straightforward to stop them and replace them with more helpful behaviours – for example, if you have a tendency to research 'causes of stomach pain' on the internet to find out whether you are likely to have stomach cancer, a new behaviour might be to postpone any further researching on the internet. This alternative behaviour would give you the chance to see whether the stomach pain continues or goes away on its own. You might then set a goal of 'I'll wait one week and see if my stomach pain gets worse before I contact my doctor'.

You may need to stop or reduce some checking or reassurance-seeking behaviours more gradually. For these behaviours, you'll need to set up and plan specific steps for working towards a new, more helpful behaviour. First, you need to identify what you want the new behaviour to be and then identify steps for working towards it. Let's say that you poke your stomach ten times per hour in fear of having a tumour.

Your new behaviour goal may be to check only once a week. It would be an extreme shift to try to achieve this new behaviour straight away so instead you might take these smaller steps to meet this goal:

GOAL: Check stomach once per week

1. Check stomach eight times a day
2. Check stomach four times a day
3. Check stomach once a day
4. Check stomach every other day
5. Check stomach twice a week
6. Check stomach once a week

By breaking down a more challenging goal into something you can gradually change day by day, week by week, your new behaviour becomes more manageable! When you develop your own goals, focus on how you can reduce the *amount of time* you engage in the behaviour and/or the *frequency* of the behaviour. Below, set up your own steps for developing a new behaviour.

GOAL:

1.

2.

3.

4.

5.

6.

After you have worked towards replacing an older behaviour with new, more functional health behaviour, it can be useful to reflect on what you learned. What did you learn about yourself? What advantages were there to trying the new behaviour?

If you were not able to achieve your new behavioural goal, you may need to go back and re-evaluate the benefits and downsides to your old and new behaviours.

1. What are the advantages of trying this new behaviour?

2. How will this change your life?

3. You can also consider breaking down your new behaviour into even more manageable steps.

You can also try a behavioural experiment to reduce checking, in exactly the same way as is described for reduction of checking in obsessive compulsive disorder (see Chapter 11, p. 379).

> **Key message**
>
> Checking and reassurance seeking provide short-term relief. The more we check and seek reassurance, the less we learn to tolerate uncertainty about our health. You can reduce or eliminate your checking and reassurance seeking by estimating how useful your behaviours are and setting a new behavioural goal.

Treatment – Stage 5: Reducing avoidance and safety behaviours

As you might recall from earlier in this chapter, when you feel anxious or expect to feel anxious, you are likely to do one of two things to reduce your anxiety. You may engage in *avoidance behaviours*, where you stay away from certain situations, activities, things, people or places that trigger your health anxiety. Avoidance is a natural reaction to things that are uncomfortable, painful, sad, or anxiety provoking. You may also do what we call *safety behaviours*. These refer to anything you may do as a precaution so that you do not avoid a situation or activity outright.

Avoidance (or escape) brings about a feeling of relief. If you engage in avoidance enough times, it becomes a habit to cope with intense anxiety. Even though you experience relief of your anxiety by avoiding certain situations, you still have health anxiety. This is because avoiding only brings about *short-term relief*. The anxiety soon returns and may be worse the next time you are faced with your health-anxiety triggers. Moreover, by avoiding, you never give yourself the chance to gain evidence against your health-anxious beliefs. To see long-term effects and triumph over your anxiety, you need to confront the things that make you anxious!

Take a moment to review the section on avoidance and safety behaviours earlier in this chapter (p. 297). Below is a description of the avoidance and safety behaviours that were relevant for Laura.

Laura's avoidance and safety behaviours

Laura identified that she uses avoidance quite often to cope with her health anxiety. She often avoids talking to friends or acquaintances who have had cancer. She recently stopped talking to a childhood friend when she found out that her friend had been diagnosed with lung cancer. She avoids visiting the hospital and reading about certain aspects of getting cancer – such as what the treatment would be like and about recovery rates. In terms of safety behaviours, she ensures she only eats foods that aren't thought, rightly or wrongly, to be linked to cancer and does not go a day without taking antioxidant vitamins.

Using the worksheet provided below, identify the avoidance and safety behaviours you have noticed in your own life.

Worksheet 10.6: Identifying avoidance and safety behaviours

My avoidance behaviours	My safety behaviours
1.	1.
2.	2.
3.	3.
4.	4.
5.	5.

Key message

People use avoidance and safety behaviours as a way to cope with health anxiety. However, these behaviours provide only short-term relief, and, in fact, are part of the cycle that keeps health anxiety going. To overcome health anxiety, you need to confront the things that make you anxious without your security blankets!

How do I stop avoiding and using safety behaviours?

To stop avoiding and to start living your life, you can use a method called **graded exposure**. Graded exposure involves repeatedly exposing yourself to anxiety-provoking situations or activities in a structured and gradual way (see Part 1). In other words, graded exposure means facing your fears. While Stage 4 of the self-help programme in this chapter focused on replacing or stopping behaviours that you do to ease your anxiety (checking and reassurance seeking), graded exposure is about purposefully doing the things that you have been avoiding because of your health anxiety. You may have been avoiding or using safety behaviours for a while and it might be hard to imagine suddenly confronting all of your fears – the anxiety would be too much! The benefit of graded exposure is that you begin by first tackling the situations or activities that provoke the *least* amount of anxiety before *gradually* working your way up to more challenging activities.

Why does graded exposure work?

You will be teaching your body and mind a new response. By repeatedly confronting the situations you are afraid of, bodily sensations that make you worried, and anxious thoughts, you will discover that the anxiety you experience does not remain at a high level for ever. Right now, it is likely that you escape the situation you are afraid of when you become anxious or that you use a safety behaviour to stay in it (e.g. take a pill to calm you, ask a friend for reassurance). Until now, you have not given yourself the opportunity to learn that your anxiety *will* decline naturally over time. In fact, your feelings of anxiety will actually decrease after you enter a situation again and again for an extended period of time. This is called habituation – your body and mind adapt to the situation or sensation. Each time you come in contact with things you're afraid of, you are retraining your mind and body to respond in a 'non-anxious' way.

You will be learning that what you fear is not as dangerous as you think. While we can't guarantee that what you fear about a situation or bodily sensation will *never* happen, graded exposure teaches you that the risk involved in such situations is probably lower than you believe. When we're anxious, we tend to overestimate how likely and how intolerable a situation is. By staying in a situation long enough for your anxiety to subside, you will learn that: even though the anxiety is at first uncomfortable, what you're afraid of is not very likely; and despite the discomfort of anxiety, you *are* able to cope.

You will be increasing your confidence and courage. Every time you successfully confront your health-anxiety fears, you are boosting your self-confidence. After you succeed the first time you might think: 'I didn't think I could do it! Maybe I can do it again.' This success leads to further successes – you might start approaching other activities or situations you've been avoiding because the more you overcome, the more motivation you gain to continue conquering your fears!

Key message

Graded exposure involves exposing yourself to those things that trigger your health anxiety. Confronting your fears gradually will teach your body and mind that what you avoid is not dangerous and that the anxiety does naturally subside if you stay in the situation for a prolonged period.

What kinds of exposure work for health anxiety?

There are three kinds of exposure that can be used by people with health anxiety.

1. **Situational exposure**: The most common form of exposure for health anxiety is situational exposure. Situational exposure is used to confront situations, activities, information or disease-related objects that make you feel anxious about your health. These may include hospitals, GPs' surgeries, reading about a health problem, talking to an ill person, using a public lavatory, and so on. The situational exposures that you engage in will be specific to your own fears. The goal of situational exposure is to put your beliefs and assumptions about the situations to the test – does what you fear actually happen? Does the anxiety last for ever? Through situational exposure you'll learn that you can tolerate not being absolutely certain about whether an illness or some other feared outcome will occur. The key to choosing a situational exposure is that it needs to target what it is you're afraid of. For example, if you are afraid that your anxiety will become unbearable if you visit a hospital, the goal is to visit a hospital repeatedly and for a prolonged period of time. By doing so, you will find out that you can tolerate the anxiety that comes up.

2. **Imaginal exposure**: Sometimes entering a situation or doing something that triggers your health anxiety is too much to start off. In other cases, you may have certain thoughts or images (e.g. of you or a loved one dying) that cause you extreme anxiety. For these fears, it can be useful to begin exposure by *imagining* your fears. The goal of imaginal exposure is to help you confront mental images or thoughts that are anxiety provoking over and over again so that they no longer trigger an anxiety response. To confront thoughts or images, you can write out a script about an anxiety-inducing event or situation or even use a recording device to articulate your thoughts verbally.

3. **Interoceptive exposure (exposure to bodily sensations you fear)**: People with health anxiety are often afraid of bodily sensations.

If you fear developing lung cancer, you might be afraid of having shortness of breath. If you are afraid that you might develop heart disease or have a heart attack, a rapid heartbeat can often bring on anxiety. Interoceptive exposure involves intentionally bringing on the bodily sensations that you fear. For example, if you are afraid of a rapid heartbeat, you would practise running in one spot; if nausea scares you, you could spin in a chair. By bringing on these sensations in a systematic and prolonged manner without attempting to minimize them, you will learn that what you're afraid of is either unlikely to occur or is manageable and temporary. You will also learn that the intense fear eventually lowers even when experiencing extreme bodily sensations.

Generating an exposure hierarchy

The first step in starting exposure is to generate a list of items for your exposure hierarchy. You may want to refer to the avoidance and safety behaviour list that was provided earlier in the chapter for ideas (p. 233). On your exposure hierarchy, you will want to include a range of activities, situations, persons, places, as well as any bodily sensations that you avoid experiencing or try to minimize in your life due to health anxiety. Using the table on p. 337, you can insert the items according to how much anxiety they provoke. 'Easy' implies that it provokes the least anxiety, 'Medium' provokes moderate anxiety, and 'Hard' provokes the most anxiety. To help distinguish the amount of anxiety the item causes you, you can use an anxiety rating scale of 0 to 100, where 0 is equal to no anxiety and 100 is equal to maximum anxiety. Assign an anxiety rating to each of the items on your exposure hierarchy. Below is Laura's exposure hierarchy followed by the blank hierarchy for you to fill out.

Table 10.3: Laura's exposure hierarchy

Feared activities, situations, persons, places, sensations	Anxiety rating (0–100)
EASY (provokes least anxiety: 0–35)	
1. Watching a movie/TV show where the main character has cancer	30
2. Eating food linked to the development of cancer once per week	35
3. Reading the obituaries	35
MEDIUM (provokes moderate anxiety: 35–70)	**Anxiety rating (0–100)**
1. Going for coffee with a close friend whose mother died of breast cancer	60
2. Reading the statistics on the likelihood of getting breast cancer	50
3. Attending a fundraiser for breast cancer	70
HARD (provokes the most anxiety: 70–100)	**Anxiety rating (0–100)**
1. Visiting the cancer ward at a hospital	100
2. The image/thought of being diagnosed with ovarian or breast cancer	90
3. The image/thought that I will die of cancer	100

Worksheet 10.7: My exposure hierarchy

Feared activities, situations, persons, places, sensations	
EASY (provokes least anxiety: 0–35)	**Anxiety rating (0–100)**
1.	
2.	
3.	
MEDIUM (provokes moderate anxiety: 35–70)	**Anxiety rating (0–100)**
1.	
2.	
3.	
HARD (provokes the most anxiety: 70–100)	**Anxiety rating (0–100)**
1.	
2.	
3.	

Once you have generated a list of items on your exposure hierarchy, you will need to come up with a concrete plan of how to go about exposing yourself to these activities, situations, persons, places or sensations. A lot of the items on your hierarchy are probably lofty goals and need to be broken down into smaller steps so that they are more manageable to begin with. To ensure that your exposure is gradual and does not overwhelm you, first choose something from your 'Easy' category. That way you can work your way up to the harder (most anxiety-provoking) situations when you have become more confident and comfortable. It also helps to keep in mind that a good first exposure is one that can be easily arranged.

Concrete steps to take while planning your first exposure

1. Identify exactly how you're going to arrange the exposure.
    *   What steps are involved? Identify the situation or setting, the time of day, and how exactly you will go about confronting your fear.

2. Before you begin, practise thought-challenging strategies.
    *   Prepare your mind with an 'alternative thought' that you can have in place of the anxious thoughts you expect to have when in the actual situation.

3. Set a specific goal.
    *   The goal of the exposure should be realistic but challenging, and should focus on specific actions, not feelings (e.g. I am going to stay in the hospital for 30 minutes vs. I will not get anxious while at the hospital).
    *   The goal should be measurable (e.g. someone should be able to watch you and tell you whether you met your goal).
    *   The outcome of the goal should be completely under your control.
    *   Ask yourself: what is it that you want to learn through this exposure?

4. Begin the exposure.
    *   It's now time to do the actual exposure. Expect to feel some

anxiety the first few times – if you didn't become anxious you wouldn't need to do this!

- During the exposure, pay attention to how anxious or uncomfortable you feel.
- Keep track of your anxiety on the 0–100 anxiety rating scale to notice how your anxiety fluctuates over time.
- Your level of anxiety may not decrease during first exposure, but with more practice, the less anxious you will feel.
- Your anxiety ratings will usually come down each time you repeat the exposure.

5. Afterwards, review your goal.
   - Review the anxious thoughts you had before and during; compare them to what actually happened.
   - While you may have expected something terrible to happen, pay attention to what really happened – was it nearly as bad as you expected? Did something good come out of the exposure?

6. Continue with the same exposure again a few more times.
   - This will help to have an effect on your anxiety in that situation, and it will eventually lower with each practice.

7. Move on to the next item.
   - When an item on your exposure hierarchy no longer makes you especially anxious, it's time to try something more challenging on your list.
   - You may move to something else in the 'Easy' category, or try an item in the 'Moderate' category.

Key message

Exposures are **planned** and **predictable** (you know what to expect). Exposure works best when practices are carried out frequently (e.g. practise four or five times per week rather than once per week). Exposure is most effective when practices are prolonged.

Tip for supporters

Encourage the person you are supporting to do all items on the hierarchy frequently.

Eliminating safety behaviours

You learned earlier that safety behaviours are things that people with health anxiety do to help them feel safer or to cope in situations that provoke anxiety. The issue with safety behaviours is that they give you a false sense of security – they make you tell yourself that the situation or place is safer *because* you did something or made sure certain conditions were in place. For example, you may believe that you won't catch the swine flu virus when you go out in public because you took all of your vitamins and brought medication with you, you used hand sanitizer and will wear a face mask, and you won't use the public washroom while you're there. These 'precautions' actually make your anxiety stronger because you are reinforcing the idea that the hospital is dangerous. By going out in public *without* carrying out your safety behaviours, you will learn that being out in public isn't a threat for catching the swine flu virus.

When practising exposures, gradually reduce the safety behaviours you carry out. You may be able to give them up all at once. If you find this too unmanageable, however, to start off you can work on the safety behaviours one at a time. You should also keep in mind that checking and reassurance seeking also qualify as safety behaviours since you may use them to manage your anxiety. During exposure, we recommend that you work to reduce this behaviour.

Tip for supporters

If you are assisting in an exposure practice, it may help if you try doing the task first. This will give the person you're supporting confidence that they can do the task too. When exercises go as planned, be sure to offer encouragement by saying, 'You're doing great! See how your anxiety goes down on its own?' It is best to avoid providing reassurance, even if you are asked, 'Are you sure this is safe?' By promising that everything will be all right, you are only strengthening the reassurance-seeking behaviour of the person you are supporting. Instead, help him or her sit with the uncertainty.

Finding balance: when to seek medical attention

At the start of this programme, we discussed how both excessive concern and also lack of concern about one's health can be problematic. Although you have been learning how to decrease your focus and worry about bodily sensations, we do not want you to ignore symptoms that require medical attention. You might be wondering then, how do I know when to act on my concern and seek medical attention?

Unfortunately, there is no simple answer to this question. However, health-anxiety experts have suggested the following as some basic guidelines:

- Healthy-anxiety clinicians and researchers at the University of Manitoba, Canada have suggested that for symptoms such as pain or colds, it is helpful to try the 'wait two weeks' approach. Most symptoms will disappear without medical assistance over this period of time.

- If these types of symptoms persist for longer than two weeks, then you should see your doctor.

For people with a medical diagnosis or who are taking particular medications, then there may be specific indicators of when to seek medical attention. If this applies to you, then we would recommend speaking with your doctor about developing your own guidelines for when to delay seeking medical attention and when you should act on your concerns immediately.

Given that research and current opinions within the medical community can change from time to time, we would also recommend that you speak with your doctor regarding how often various tests (e.g. mammogram) should be performed.

Nearing the end

Now that you've reached the end of this self-help programme, where is your anxiety at now? This is a good time to reflect on all the progress you've made.

How much has your anxiety decreased during the course of this programme?

- Have you met the goals you set for yourself at the beginning of this programme?

- Have you noticed any changes in your mood?

- Have you noticed any changes in your ability to function at work, school or at home?

- Have you noticed any change in your relationships?

- Have you noticed any change in your ability to enjoy life and to participate in hobbies and other fun activities?

- Have you noticed changes in the behaviours you perform to reduce health anxiety?

> **Tip for supporters**
>
> Discuss the progress you have observed in the person you are support-
> ing. Sometimes we tend to overlook small changes. Even small changes
> can make a difference and so should be acknowledged.

Are there any areas in which your anxiety is still causing you difficulty?

- If you answered yes to this question, it would be helpful to go back through the programme and practise the strategies further. For example, if you find that you still struggle with being in certain situations, you may need to spend more time with exposure practice. Perhaps you can enlist a supportive friend or loved one to help you arrange the more difficult exposures. Remember that the cognitive skills (the expertise critical for learning) that you learned earlier in the programme should be used in conjunction with exposure – keep challenging those anxious thoughts!

- If you're still experiencing significant symptoms after giving this self-help programme a true effort, seeking support from a therapist or psychologist should be strongly considered. Speak with your family doctor about making such arrangements or receiving a referral in your community.

Preventing a relapse

In ending this self-help programme, the practice doesn't stop here. Living a life without health anxiety means that you need to continue practising the strategies you've learned until they become habits. This takes time and dedication, but it will be worth replacing your anxious reactions with healthier and more helpful responses. Your anxiety will no longer be in control of your life – you will be!

Integrating exposure into daily life

To ensure you maintain the progress you've made, we recommend that you make exposure practice a daily habit. To keep your motivation going, think of exposure in terms of rewards: what reward does it bring to keep up with exposure even beyond this self-help programme? Remember: short-term distress for long-term gain!

Motivation to continue with exposure can also come from listing all that you've achieved or been able to do since starting this self-help programme. When you see on paper how far you've come and what you've gained, this can give you further motivation to continue confronting your fears.

Preparing for setbacks

Even if you're now experiencing minimal health anxiety, you may experience the odd flare-up in the future. For example, your health anxiety may be triggered during times of high stress or if someone close to you becomes ill. When this happens, you need to remind yourself that such flare-ups are *common, temporary, and short-term*. This is not a full return of your health anxiety. Such flare-ups actually serve as a prompt to practise the skills you've learned to manage your health anxiety and take back control.

Preparing for high–risk situations

To help avoid setbacks, identify your high-risk situations. What situations can still trigger distress and health concerns? What situations have in the past? It may not be a situation, as such, but a bodily sensation or an object, or a particular person. When you anticipate encountering such high-risk situations, you can plan ahead and have various coping strategies ready to put into practice. You can:

- Have an alternative thought in place of your anxious thoughts.

- Remind yourself of your new behavioural goals so that you do not seek reassurance or check your body.

- Remind yourself that staying in a situation will have better effects on your long-term health anxiety than escaping or avoiding it will.

- Ask yourself, what other strategies have worked in the past?

Tip for supporters

One way to help the person you are supporting stay on track is by helping them create a contingency plan. What do you think might be high-risk situations for the person you're supporting? Which strategies do you think seem to help the person you have been supporting deal with their health anxiety best?

By making a list of the exercises or coping strategies that you've found effective, you can quickly refer to them when confronted with a high-risk situation. More information about how to maintain your progress can be found in Chapter 14.

11 Obsessive compulsive disorder

Roz Shafran and Adam S. Radomsky

Overview

On p. 10 of Part 1, you read a brief description of obsessive compulsive disorder (OCD); the flow chart on pp. 14–15 helped you see whether it might be relevant to you. If you think you might have OCD or you know that you definitely have this problem, then working your way through this chapter should help you to better understand why you have OCD, what might be keeping it going, and how you can recover. Change is not easy but it *is* possible and the changes and strategies we will set out in this chapter have been shown to work; many people with OCD who have this kind of cognitive behavioural therapy are able to recover fully and lead happy lives.

What is obsessive compulsive disorder?

Many people with obsessive compulsive problems suffer in silence and it takes an average of seven years before they seek help. Many, possibly including you, will read books about OCD, gather information on the internet and try to help themselves without going to their GP. If that sounds like you, then we hope the self-help programme set out in this chapter will help but we would also like you to know that you are not alone. Many people have these type of problems and, most importantly, with the right type of help you can completely recover. The type of problems people with OCD have is varied – many have the classic 'washing' and 'checking' forms, but it can take other forms as well. It is impossible to cover all of the forms of OCD in a single chapter but we will introduce you to the idea of obsessions and compulsions, the treatment that has been shown to work, and recommendations for further reading.

Obsessions

Most of us have thoughts that come into our heads which we think are strange and unpleasant. For some people, though, these thoughts completely take over and cause great distress. At this point we talk about people having 'obsessions'. Obsessions are thoughts that come into our heads and will not go away, even though we don't want them there and find them unacceptable or even repulsive. It's not just thoughts – obsessions can also take the form of *images* – pictures in your mind, or *impulses* – a strong urge to do something, usually something horrible. If we have obsessions we might feel tortured and terrified by our thoughts, images or impulses. Often they are about our very worst fears, and are completely at odds with our values and our views of how we should be as a person. As a result, obsessions tend to be around three main themes, which are all completely unacceptable to the person having them. These are aggressive, sexual or blasphemous thoughts. Let's look at Mo, Etay and Fiona's stories below.

Mo had aggressive obsessions, and had lots of images of himself causing harm to other people – including old people, children or relatives. He hated himself for having these thoughts, and was desperately worried by them. He was particularly frightened that he might go mad and strangle his elderly mother, who lived with him and his family.

Etay was a happily married man, but he kept having images of himself having sex with inappropriate partners, including elderly people, his mother-in-law and children. These thoughts were absolutely horrible for him.

Fiona was a quiet and gentle person who was raised as a Catholic. For the past ten years she had been unable to pray in church

> because whenever she said a prayer, she would have the thought 'you're a fake; you don't mean it; you don't believe in God'. She could not abide having such thoughts in such a holy place, and had to stop going to church or meeting any of her church friends.

Obsessions can also take many different and more complex forms. Some people may fear taking on the characteristics of others, for example becoming stupid, homeless or ugly. Others may have a preoccupation with whether they have done the right thing, for example the 'wrongness' of stealing paper towels. Some need to make sure that everything is done with symmetry, order and exactness. Others may be worried about becoming contaminated through contact with repulsive or germ-laden situations like dog mess; some people may feel contaminated without even having physical contact, for example by a person who has betrayed or humiliated them. No two people are exactly alike, but there are general ideas that help us to understand the nature of all obsessions and how they should be treated. We will describe these throughout this chapter.

Compulsions

It's not just the obsessions themselves that cause the distress; there is another part to the story. The thoughts are usually so unacceptable, and you are likely to feel so bad that you feel an overwhelming need to do something to try to make things 'all right'. We call what you need to do 'compulsions' or 'neutralizing'. Compulsions typically have three purposes: firstly to reduce the chance that the things you are thinking about will happen, secondly to calm your anxiety down, and thirdly to make sure that if something bad does happen you have at least done everything in your power to prevent it. Compulsions are often repetitive and tend to be done in a very particular way (e.g. always doing things in threes, twos or nines, or repeating particular phrases to yourself), and they can take over your life. They are often unconnected in any real way to the feared event that you are trying to prevent – for instance, someone may need to make sure the hangers in the wardrobe all face the same way, in order to prevent their wife having an accident.

The most common compulsions are:

- repeated checking, or washing and cleaning things;

- doing things in the 'right' order and the 'right' way;

- hoarding objects;

- carrying out elaborate rituals that involve tapping, touching or staring;

- seeking reassurance and asking the same question over and over again, for example: Did I lock the door? Is Joe OK? OCD has often been called the 'doubters' disease' for this reason;

- repeating phrases in your head or not physically moving while you're having a 'bad' thought.

Sofia's story

Sofia is a 25-year-old architect who lives with her partner. She is terrified of germs and becoming seriously ill and she worries a lot that she will get a serious illness such as HIV from accidentally sitting on a dirty syringe or stepping on one in the street. She is always on the lookout for used needles and avoids walking through the rough areas of town where she might come across them. She refuses to take the London Underground to work, but instead takes the bus and walks, even though it adds an extra twenty minutes on her journey. She is very close to her grandmother but worries that she will accidentally cause her harm, e.g. by giving her food poisoning if she bakes a cake. She repeatedly checks what she has put into any food she is cooking and doesn't trust her own memory. She has avoided seeing her grandmother recently as she worries that she could be unwell and might pass that on to her, which could prove fatal. She washes her hands a lot, and showers in hot water for a long time as she feels she needs to scrub all over at night to get rid of the germs that she has accumulated during the day. She is managing to go to work, do her job and keep her relationship with her partner going, but feels very tired and stressed all the time because she's so worried. She realizes that her worries about germs are excessive, but she cannot stop having them.

Step 1: Understanding what keeps your OCD going

In Part 1, we talked about how cognitive behavioural therapy focuses on what is keeping the problem going. We can help give you a head-start on trying to understand what keeps your problem going by telling you about the understanding that therapists have that is supported by research. The understanding about what keeps OCD going in general is that everyone has odd thoughts and images from time to time. However, if you have OCD you almost certainly see these thoughts as being *personally significant* so, unsurprisingly, they are upsetting and frightening to you. The meaning you place on the thoughts leads you to feel the need to try to do something to stop them, or the anxiety that they make you feel, or to prevent harm. Some of what you do to stop the thoughts, reduce anxiety or prevent harm is likely to be backfiring and may actually be keeping the problem going. For example, if you are repeatedly checking the stove to stop your worry, reduce anxiety and prevent a fire, then you will be experiencing more doubt and worry than if you only check once (see p. 379).

The importance of the personal significance people with OCD place on their thoughts is illustrated by Aaron.

Aaron, 21, had thoughts about raping children. He was repelled by such thoughts as he had younger sisters and he thought that it meant he was a wicked, evil person who was not safe to be around children. He tried to block out these thoughts. He started staying away from his sisters and even felt unable to go to work. Staying away from work in fact meant he had more time to focus on his thoughts. Even pictures of children would trigger the thoughts. He had so many of them he could only conclude that he was indeed a wicked person who subconsciously wanted to do these dreadful things. Aaron had OCD.

Ben, 21, had the occasional thought about raping children. He didn't much like having these thoughts, but he didn't really pay too much attention to them – he knew they were just random thoughts that popped into his mind and he was busy trying to find a job. When he had the thoughts, he just distracted himself – he knew he was a good person who would never harm children and he didn't react at all when he had the thoughts – he didn't feel the need. The thoughts faded of their own accord.

The two examples above show how it is not *having the thoughts* about raping children that made Aaron have OCD since Ben also had them – it was *the interpretation of the thoughts* and *the associated behaviour* that meant that Aaron had OCD while Ben did not.

Below are some typical examples of the personal significance/misinterpretations people place on thoughts/images:

1. Having an image of harming your child means that you are a dangerous person.
2. Having a thought about a sexually inappropriate repugnant act means that you are going crazy (mad).
3. Having an impulse to blurt out a swear word in church means that you are bad and evil.

Why does the personal significance you place on your thoughts make a difference?

The way we interpret our thoughts can make a huge difference to how we feel and how we react or respond to them. If we interpret unpleasant or disturbing thoughts as being true or meaning something, unsurprisingly, we will feel highly anxious, probably guilty and want to act to reduce our anxiety or prevent harm. For example, if we interpret having a fleeting thought of pushing someone in front of a train while we're standing on the platform as meaning that we are a potential murderer, firstly, it's not hard to imagine that we would feel terrible, frightened and repelled and, secondly, as we would naturally want to stop feeling that way, we'll want to stop these thoughts, or if we can't do that, to cancel (or 'neutralize') them

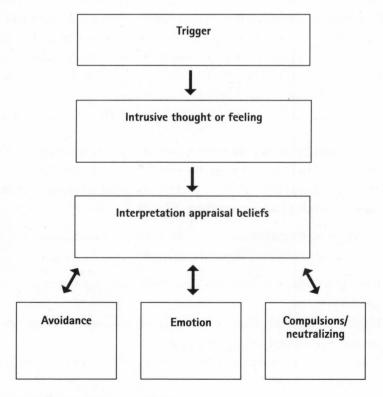

Figure 11.1: The maintenance of OCD

in some way. Responding to intrusive thoughts by avoiding situations, carrying out compulsions or other behaviours, such as 'rewinding' thoughts to 'cancel' them out, is what is likely to be interfering with your life and stopping you from enjoying it to the full; it is also likely to make your thoughts very important to you so you become trapped in a vicious cycle (as described earlier). This is shown in the diagram opposite.

The CBT approach to OCD can be applied to all forms of OCD. To help you to apply it to your own personal situation, let's look back at Sofia's story on pp. 349–50. Let's look at how her OCD symptoms fit into the framework above:

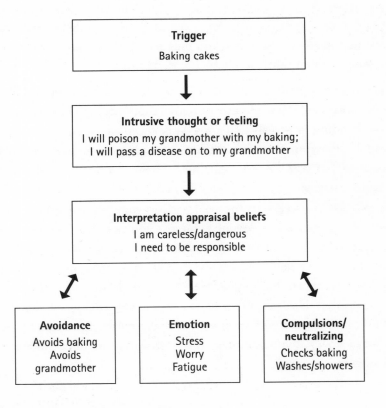

Figure 11.2: The maintenance of Sophia's OCD

If Sofia *knew* that instead of being careless, she was in fact extra careful, that instead of dangerous, she was actually a very safe person to be around, that instead of having a weak memory, she only *believed* herself to have a weak memory, and that instead of needing to be more responsible, she realized that she is already too responsible, then she would be able to recover from her OCD.

Helping you change

What needs to happen for you to change

If you have OCD, you are likely to believe that there is something significant – and possibly sinister – about your completely natural but unwanted intrusive thoughts. You may fear that the thoughts mean you are going mad, or that you are bad or dangerous.

The starting point to overcoming your OCD is understanding that the significance you place on your intrusive thoughts is the problem. Sadly, understanding is not all that's needed! What you need is some strong evidence that your own thoughts do not mean you are mad, bad or dangerous so that you can stop reacting to them and hence break the cycle. Unfortunately, simply telling you this will not be enough – you need to find out for yourself and the next section suggests ways that you can gather the personally relevant evidence you need to discover this for yourself. When we say 'personally relevant evidence' we mean that you are unlikely to be able to change the obsessions and compulsions unless you have demonstrated to yourself, in your own life and with your own problems, that there is another way of seeing the situation. You will need to find evidence that will convince you that your thoughts and behaviour do not mean what you fear they do, and that they are not significant, and not sinister.

Key message

The main way to help you change is to gather personally relevant information to help you re-examine the meaning of your intrusive thoughts and come to the conclusion that your thoughts do not have any significant meaning.

Tip for supporters

Help the person you are supporting think of times when they obtained personally relevant information about something that led them to view a person or situation differently, e.g. when they thought a friend ignored them but later found out the friend had his/her headphones on and so didn't hear when their name was called.

Treatment overview

Figure 11.1 illustrated that behaviour such as avoidance and compulsions can help reinforce the problem. It follows that by reducing the compulsions, this will also have a beneficial effect on reducing the intrusive thoughts you have and may help you test beliefs that help you change your interpretation of their meaning.

As we have seen, a number of factors contribute to keeping you thinking that intrusive thoughts are significant. Some of these relate to thinking style and cognitive biases (see p. 38); some of them relate to the emotional distress that the thoughts cause you; others relate to the role of avoidance and compulsive behaviour such as repeated checking and washing. Treatment involves gathering personally relevant evidence to (i) identify and (ii) change the thinking styles and behaviours that are keeping everything going. It also involves showing you how to cope with emotional distress, even if it is just learning how to accept that it is there. In essence, treatment involves you finding out for yourself that if you change the way that you think and behave *nothing bad will happen*, and you will be free to live your life as you would like.

Key message

Research suggests that it is the interpretation of your intrusive thoughts, images or impulses as personally significant that causes the obsessions. The compulsions follow from the obsessions. If you can change the significance you give to your intrusive thoughts, the obsessions (and the compulsive behaviour that follows) will be eliminated. Changing some of your compulsive behaviour will also help change the significance of the intrusive thoughts and change a vicious cycle into a virtuous one.

As described in Part 1, CBT involves 'sessions' that have a structure and are ideally held twice weekly at the beginning for the first month or so, followed by once a week with 12–20 sessions in total. We hope you will have planned 'sessions' with yourself or with a supporter so that you can get the most out of this programme. OCD varies, so this structure may sometimes need to be modified to fit the problem and your own situation. If you have a supporter helping you with this book, then it is best to discuss together how to change the structure, if necessary, to suit your personal needs.

How to approach this self-help programme

In Part 1, we discussed the structure and style of CBT so we won't repeat it here. We suggest you (and your supporter if you have one) follow this style and structure when using this self-help programme. First, start with setting a flexible agenda at the beginning of each session. It is a good idea to use the assessment measures in the OCD Inventory in the Appendices regularly throughout your self-help programme to see the progress you are making. You will need at least 12 'sessions' as you work through the self-help programme set out in this chapter, and you should start to see improvements by at least session 6. If you can't see any improvement at all, you may want to consider going to your doctor for some further help.

What is unique about this treatment compared with CBT for other anxiety disorders?

What is unique about the treatment for OCD is that it aims to change the meaning you place on your intrusive thoughts. The approach is based entirely on gathering useful and significant information about your thoughts and images that is personally relevant, and that leads to different reactions to those thoughts and images. As you'll read throughout this chapter, the information of most value will be that you get from doing the experiments, rather than simply reading about them. The main goal is to test out new ways of thinking about your intrusive thoughts, leading to changes in how you view and react in the real world. This CBT-based approach can be challenging, but it can also be fun! We encourage you to be creative in your approach – and to know that there is another way of understanding your difficulties that can be dramatically different than how you've been experiencing the problem up until now.

Step One: Starting treatment

Self-assessment

As you begin this self-help programme, it's a good idea to try to work out how severe your OCD is at the moment, as this will help you to understand it and, importantly, to measure your progress as you start to make changes. There are some self-report measures that are freely available for this purpose, which you can obtain from the internet. One of these is the Obsessive Compulsive Disorder Inventory – Revised, which is included in the Appendices (p. 484).

What is keeping your OCD going?

Working out the range of your thoughts and behaviours that are keeping your OCD going is important to help you to start to overcome it. It can be hard to work out exactly what is keeping it going, so it is a good idea to set some time aside and find a quiet place to sit down and do this. As well as measuring the severity of your OCD, scales can help you to work out the different interpretations you are placing on your intrusive thoughts. The Personal Significance Scale in the Appendices (pp. 489–91) can help you do this. The scale can be used at the beginning and end of treatment, and also every week to help focus treatment. It is important to do this because the focus of this treatment is on changing the personal significance you give your intrusive thoughts and you want to be able to monitor your progress.

After you have filled in the Personal Significance Scale, you should be able to answer the important question: *How am I interpreting my intrusive thoughts?* You can answer this question broadly by considering if you are interpreting the thoughts as meaning you are mad, bad, or dangerous, or you can be more specific in your response.

Having answered this question, ask yourself the following questions (these relate to the boxes in Figure 11.1 on p. 352). First, think back to a time when your OCD was very bad, or to a recent episode.

1. What triggers my OCD? What thoughts/images do I have that worry me?

2. Based on the personal significance scale and my own thinking, how am I interpreting my thoughts and/or images? What significance am I placing on them?

3. After I come up with these interpretations, how do I feel?

4. What am I avoiding doing because of how I'm interpreting my thoughts and/or images?

5. What do I do in response to my interpretations? How does how I

react (what I avoid or do in response) to my interpretations help to keep my OCD going? *Clue: the answer may be that you do not get a chance to disconfirm your fears, that you never discover your anxiety will not make you crazy, or it may be that you are creating doubt because you are repeatedly checking.*

6. What beliefs or biases might I have that are contributing to my OCD? *Beliefs broadly fall into six different areas:*

    Having an inflated sense of responsibility (believing that you need to take on more responsibility than you actually do to prevent harm).

    Overestimating threat (believing that threat and/or danger are more common than they actually are).

    Being perfectionist (believing that you need to think or do something perfectly in order to properly complete a task).

    Being intolerant of uncertainty (believing that unless you are completely certain, bad things can happen) – see page 199.

    Giving too much importance to your thoughts (believing that your thoughts are much more important than they actually are).

    Desiring full control over your thoughts (believing that your thoughts must be controlled to prevent harm).

When you ask yourself these questions, use the diagram in Figure 11.1 and fill in the boxes to get a picture of what is keeping the problem going. If you find this difficult, re-read Sofia's story (see pp. 349–50) and compare it to how she's filled in the diagram. You may find the interpretation/appraisal/belief section to be the most difficult, but remember that the common themes in OCD are beliefs that one might be mad, bad or dangerous.

Maintenance of OCD

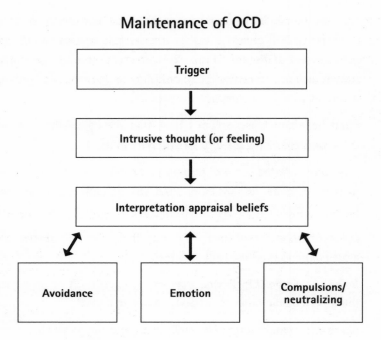

Figure 11.3: Maintenance of your OCD

Once you've filled the boxes in, how do you feel seeing your problems written down in a diagram like this? Some people can feel overwhelmed; others can feel that it provides a first step in beginning to understand where to make changes. Perhaps you feel both of these. Ideally, one thing is clear – change *is* possible. You have taken the first, and perhaps most important, step to successfully overcoming OCD and arrived at an understanding of what is keeping your problem going.

Step Two: Treatment

Effective treatment comes in two stages. You have already started the first stage, which involves understanding what is keeping your problem going. The rest of the first stage involves keeping track of the factors you identified and finding out some facts ('psychoeducation'). This corresponds to the first two steps of treatment described in

Chapter 5, pp. 54–60. The second stage is about gathering personally relevant 'evidence' by carrying out behavioural experiments (Steps 3, 4 and 5 described in Chapter 5, pp. 62–81) to help change the personal significance that you are currently placing on your unwanted intrusive thoughts.

Stage 1: Recording and fact finding

Keeping a 'real-time' record

You should now be starting to gain an understanding of how the different parts of your problem are connected and keeping it going. Well done! It's a great start but it can be relatively easy to do this in the comfort of your front room when you're feeling calm and objective. In reality, in times of stress and worry, the situation may be quite different. It is therefore important to understand what happens in 'real time', in real situations, as and when they are actually happening.

Sofia used Table 11.1 (see p. 352) to understand what was keeping her problem going. She found that she was doing a lot of things because of her fears (that she could be responsible for harming someone vulnerable like her grandmother) and she also realized that she had a range of fears and beliefs related to harming others that kept her OCD going. She also came to understand that stress and tiredness were important factors. For her homework before her next session, Sofia designed a record that kept track of both her thoughts and her behaviours, and also her stress levels in general. Table 11.1 is the completed record. She used one for each day. Importantly, she was **not** monitoring the personal significance of her beliefs at this stage, in other words how much she believes her thoughts or what she believes her thoughts mean. The aim of the 'real-time' record is just to get some information about how OCD manifests itself in your daily life. For that reason, you don't need to rate your thoughts or the strength of your emotions at this point (although you can if you'd like to). At this point the main purpose of this record sheet is to understand how OCD operates in your everyday life and to make sure that the diagram has captured the most important parts. A blank sheet is given on p. 364 for you to fill in to help you work out what is keeping your problem going.

Table 11.1: Sophia's thought and behaviour record

Day and date: Tuesday 20 May

Situation	Thought	Emotion	Behaviour	Consequence
Baking a cake	People can get salmonella from raw eggs. I need to make sure the cake is baked properly otherwise it could be fatal for Grandma	Anxiety	Overcooked cake and still didn't give it to Grandma	Sadness that I let Grandma down but I couldn't cope with the worry that would have come from giving her the cake
Walking along the street	Was that a needle? Did I touch it?	Panic	Went back to check if it was a needle more carefully. It wasn't	Relief but also embarrassed at being so weird
Taking a shower	The water needs to be hot to kill all germs	Anxiety – the water isn't really hot enough	Turned heat of the shower up	Unable to relax and enjoy the shower

Talking to my grand-mother	I haven't seen her in a while and would like to drop by but I don't want to kill her by giving her my germs	Fear, guilt and sadness	Made up an excuse about work and stayed home	I let Grandma down again and am starting to get angry at my own crazy thoughts and how they're ruining my life!
On way to work by bus	It's nice to be above ground on a rainy day, and not on the tube	Relief, although rushed when leaving home	Avoiding the tube	If I avoid the tube, I will be safer but my life is restricted

Homework: Copy the blank form into a notebook or photocopy this blank form to complete your own record for two to three days until your next session.

Worksheet 11.1: Blank thought and behaviour record

Day and date:

Situation	Thought	Emotion	Behaviour	Consequence

Once you have completed your record for 2–3 days, go back to the boxes you filled in on p. 364 and see if you now have a better understanding of what is keeping your problem going. Is there anything you left out when you were filling it in initially that you've included in your record? Was there any misinformation or misunderstanding about something important? If so, feel free to go back and change your diagram.

Key message

Your diagram will change as you work your way through this self-help programme and learn more about what is keeping your OCD going. Keep looking back at the diagram to work out what needs to change so you can recover from your OCD.

Tip for supporters

This is a hard exercise. Do it yourself to help understand and trouble-shoot any problems.

Psychoeducation

It is important to understand the difference between 'normal' and 'abnormal obsessions'. Hard though it can be for people with OCD to believe, we know that *almost everyone has unwanted intrusive thoughts*. Even 'normal' people who are not at all troubled by OCD can have very strange thoughts coming into their heads! What is more, the content of these thoughts is almost identical to the thoughts that people with OCD have. What is different in people with OCD and without OCD is not the **content** of the intrusive thought, but the *frequency of the thoughts*, the *distress they cause*, and *their persistence*. This is so important that we're going to write it here again – it's not a misprint!

Key message

What is different in people with OCD and without OCD is not the **content** of the intrusive thoughts or images, but **their frequency**, the **distress they cause**, and **their persistence**.

Don't believe us? That's OK! You're a scientist (as least as far as trying to overcome your OCD is concerned) and so you will need personally relevant information about it in order to believe it.

Stage 2. Starting to make changes

So now you *know* that everyone has these unwanted intrusive thoughts. Right? Well, you may have read it, but do you really **know** it? Does your head know it but your heart not? Do you respond to the information with a 'yes, but . . .'? What you will need in order to believe it is information that is personally relevant and meaningful to you. Everyone knows that smoking is bad for you but for some people it is only when they get ill that they really believe it. Similarly we all know we should exercise, but it is only when one reaps the personal benefits of doing exercise that it becomes a real change in lifestyle. We can tell you that everyone has unwanted intrusive thoughts, but there is nothing like finding it out for yourself.

Key message

You need personally relevant information in order to change your beliefs about the significance of your intrusive thoughts and the role that behaviour may play in keeping those beliefs going.

Conducting surveys

How can you find out for yourself? If you have a supporter, you can ask him/her about the more unusual thoughts and images they may have experienced about harming people, bad things happening, losing control, swearing in a holy place, being immoral *or whatever is most relevant to you*. It may be that you prefer to do a survey. Surveys are particularly important in the treatment of OCD. You could conduct a survey amongst your friends in which you list a range of intrusive thoughts and ask them if they have ever experienced them. If you prefer, you could say that you are doing research as part of a project. Alternatively, you might want to use a social networking website to help do the survey and to emphasize the survey's serious purpose.

Sofia's survey

Sofia was surprised to find out that everyone had thoughts that they might accidentally poison someone and she realized that she wasn't mad for thinking such thoughts and that she wasn't a bad person. However, she wanted to do her own survey to see if people she knew and respected, and thought were good, kind, responsible people also had such thoughts. She decided to ask her sister to help her in the survey. Her sister was a teacher and Sofia said that she had to do this survey as part of a work project. She asked her sister to help by asking some of her colleagues about their thoughts and images. Her sister agreed, and four colleagues and her sister returned the form. One person said that they never had any of the thoughts, but the other four all said that they had thoughts about accidentally harming people; for the teachers it was more commonly children than elderly people they were afraid of harming. Sofia ended her survey with an open-ended question: what do you do when you have the thoughts? Of the four colleagues who had them, three said that they busied themselves by doing something else, and the fourth said 'nothing; they go away'. This information was vitally important in helping Sofia to understand that it was her *reaction* to the intrusive thoughts – her interpretation of them as being personally significant and the way that she behaved as a result – which explained why she was having so many of them, and why they persisted. This was a real change from her previous assumption that having the thoughts meant she was a bad person.

Analysing the fate of past obsessions – using the past as a behavioural experiment

You may have found that your OCD has changed over time, and that you had thoughts and symptoms in the past which don't seem to trouble you so much now. Understanding your past obsessions – what provoked them and what led to their decline – can be of considerable importance. Can you think of a past obsession that has gone away? Can you see the connection between the personal importance you attached to the intrusive thought you had and the fate of the thoughts? Asking yourself the questions below may help. Sofia's answers are shown below to illustrate how this exercise helped her:

Table 11.2: Analysing the fate of past obsessions

1. Have any of your obsessions become less frequent/intense or even completely gone? Which ones?

   Sofia: Yes, when I was a little girl I used to worry that if I didn't do a bedtime ritual then my parents would die.

   When?

   Sofia: I had it for years, but I grew out of it I guess when I was about 12 or 13.

2. Explain why they decreased.

    Sofia: Well, I wanted to go for sleepovers with friends and I couldn't do the rituals there and I got back and my parents were OK so I knew I didn't really have to do them. They faded over time.

3. What do you conclude from their disappearance?

    That they will gradually disappear and I don't need to do the rituals I am doing.

4. Why did they weaken/go and others persist?

    I guess I found out I didn't need to do those rituals to keep my parents safe.

5. Were any of your past obsessions followed by unacceptable, catastrophic behaviour?

    Sofia: No, nothing bad ever happened to my parents. They are still around nagging me!

6. What can you conclude from this?

    Sofia: That I guess if I change how I respond to my obsessions, the problem may go away.

Tip for supporters

Help conduct the survey by asking *your* friends/family to take part as well as the friends and family of the person you are supporting. Help the person you are supporting to discuss what happened to their past obsessions and, at the end, help them to see what the discussion tells them about what their problem may be – are they a bad person or are they placing too much significance on what are normal intrusive thoughts and images?

Carrying out behavioural experiments

'Anxiety makes me mad /lose control'

In common with other anxiety disorders, you may well fear that you will lose control and go crazy when you have your intrusive thoughts if you do not engage in your compulsions; you may also be afraid that you will carry out some horrible act. As a result, you probably generally try to have complete control over your thoughts and behaviour every day, to guard against any slip-up. If this sounds familiar, it is important to ask yourself if you have ever carried out any of the horrible acts that you have imagined happening? Undoubtedly the answer will be 'no'. In all our years of treating patients with OCD, we have never known anyone act on their obsessions. If you have 'evidence' from newspaper articles of it happening, you should know that it is likely that the person did not have OCD. People with OCD are in fact the least likely of anyone to act on their thoughts.

You have this information but now you need it so that it is personally relevant to you. That is where *behavioural experiments* come in. If you are worried that anxiety will make you go mad and lose control, the best thing to do is to do an experiment whereby you try to go mad and lose control! What would going mad look like? Screaming? Shouting? Collapsing? Firstly, predict how likely it is that you would go mad and lose control if your anxiety reached 90 per cent. Now let's try it. Try to make yourself very anxious (not pleasant, but essential). This part should be straightforward: you could think of something happening to your loved ones or you could recall a past experience when you became very anxious. Now, when your anxiety is REALLY high (90%), what happens? Do you scream? Do you shout? Collapse? No? What can you conclude from this? Now re-rate how likely you now think you are to go mad if your anxiety reaches this point again. You can use the behavioural experiment sheet, Worksheet 5.2 on page 65 and in the appendices. A blank sheet is given below.

Worksheet 11.2: Behavioural experiment sheet

1) Thought/Belief to be tested and strength of conviction (0–100%):
2) Ideas for experiment to test the thought/belief. Circle the best one:
3) Specific predictions about what will happen and how you will record the outcome:
4) Anticipated problems and potential solutions:
5) Describe the experiment you carried out:
6) Describe what happened:
7) Re-rate your conviction in the original thought/belief (0–100%):
8) Revised thought/belief/behaviour that can be tested:

You can repeat this experiment as homework before your next session so that you gather a large amount of evidence that the likelihood of your going mad when you're feeling very anxious reflects the reality – zero.

The other chapters on specific anxieties also address the fear of control, so it may be worth also reading the relevant sections.

If we were betting folk, we would bet that although you read the paragraph above you have very little intention of actually carrying the experiment out. Sound about right? If so, we're not surprised. We're asking you to take a risk – the very great risk of going mad and losing control. We know this is a risk for you but we also know that it is one worth taking. With all behavioural experiments you need courage to try things a different way so that you can gather the information you need to make real changes in your life. We would like to encourage you to have such courage – we know what dramatic changes are possible if you can do some of the experiments. We also know that if you do not take some of these 'chances' and don't take risks, the unfortunate reality is that your OCD will persist. To encourage you to take the risk and to carry out the experiment, remember that courage is the *overcoming* of fear and not the *absence* of fear. Also keep in the front of your mind that nobody has ever gone mad or crazy or lost control from feeling anxious. We hope you can try all of the experiments we describe in this self-help programme and make progress in overcoming your OCD; it's difficult but worth it.

'Having the thoughts means that I will carry them out'

A young mother had terrible fears that she would harm her young daughter. She could not let herself bath her in case she pushed her under the water, and she could not go into her bedroom at night in case she smothered her with a pillow. She could not be alone in the house with her daughter, and her husband or mother had to be with her all the time. She was asked to carry out an experiment that involved taking a risk – the risk that she could bath her baby on her own (with her therapist in the room next door). With a great deal of anxiety, and a great deal of persuading, she carried out the experiment and realized that she could be in the bathroom with her daughter, and that *nothing bad happened*. Afterwards it was much easier for her to believe that she would NOT act on her thoughts, and she started to be able to do much more with her daughter – but she needed the experience of it to be sure. This was very, very difficult for her to do – but she managed and we hope that you can, too.

Key message

Experiment with taking risks (with support if possible). See what happens. Use the behavioural experiment sheet on p. 450 to help you.

Tip for supporters

Help make sure the risks are manageable and neither too demanding for the person to complete nor so easy that they don't provide useful information. You can take the risk as well and do the experiments together.

Controlling your thoughts

Your thoughts are so unacceptable to you that you are probably trying to suppress them but it is likely that your attempts to control your thoughts are backfiring. Here's another (much easier) experiment: try not to think about a white bear. What comes into your mind? A white bear? What does this show you? It is a universal finding that when you try not to think about something, it pops into your mind. For some people, it might be that the very attempt to suppress the thought is causing the thoughts to 'rebound' and you have more of them. What is certainly true for almost everyone is that we do not have perfect control over our thoughts – and you are not an exception to the rule. Your attempts to suppress your thoughts are either (i) going to make you feel bad that you can't control them and you are likely to have more of these thoughts when your mood is low or (ii) may actually be causing you to have more of them. Don't believe us? Put it to the test. Think of a troubling thought that you usually try to suppress and try *not* suppressing it for one hour. What happens? Do you have it more frequently or less frequently than when you try to suppress it? What happens to your mood? You should find that you have the thought less frequently and that your mood improves.

Attention to threat

Sofia spent a very great deal of time scanning the ground for used needles – that is, she was paying a great deal of attention to the threat that there might be needles there. She explained this by saying that she has to be on guard all the time, because if she was not then she could accidentally step on a needle.

You may find that you are constantly scanning the world around you in a similar way to Sofia. It is very common for people with OCD to spend a lot of time scanning their thoughts. So the next experiment is to try *not* to do this and see what happens.

Experiment

Step One: Make a prediction – what will happen if you refrain from scanning your thoughts or the environment?

Step Two: Stop scanning for danger the next time you are out for a walk. If it would help, you can tell yourself that you are 'off-duty' for this period and you can try to notice something else instead (e.g. billboard advertisements).

Step Three: What happens? Did your prediction come true?

You can also do another experiment in which you make a deliberate effort to pay a lot of attention to threat and notice *all* your thoughts and *all* possible sources of danger in the environment.

Sofia found that when she was paying a large amount of attention to potential threats she was more preoccupied with needles and HIV, and felt more anxious and more contaminated than when she was 'off-duty'. Importantly, she also found out that she did not step on any used needles when she was not scanning for them, and that she worried less and felt happier. She came to the conclusion that she need not pay so much attention to where she was walking, and that paying all this attention might give an explanation for why she had been having so many intrusive thoughts and images.

Key message

The more you look for danger, the more you will find it! Try it out and see for yourself by conducting a behavioural experiment in which you contrast paying a lot of attention to threat with not paying very much attention. Record the results in the behavioural experiments record sheet on p. 450.

Biases

In Part 1, we described a range of thinking errors and biases such as catastrophizing. There are lots of cognitive biases in OCD that can be tested using behavioural experiments:

- Do you increase your estimates of the chance of harm when you are anxious (although the actual chance of harm does not change, of course)?

- Do you feel you are being more responsible when you are anxious?

- Do you feel more responsible as a result of checking, although the goal of checking is to reduce responsibility for harm?

- Do you feel that when you are responsible, the chance of harm is higher than for others?

If you said 'yes' to any of the questions above, then you have biases in your thinking. Spend some time stepping back and testing such biases by carrying out experiments in which you increase or decrease your anxiety and then see the effects on how you estimate the chance of harm. It is also useful to do the same kind of experiment in which you increase/decrease responsibility by handing over responsibility to someone else and seeing the effect. Try doing this as homework before your next session and see what conclusions you draw.

Thought–action fusion

Identifying your thinking biases is important and stepping back and noticing when they are happening can help change them. In OCD, one common thinking bias is called 'thought–action fusion'. A key aspect of this is the belief that thinking about harm coming to someone else makes it more likely to happen. People with this kind of belief unsurprisingly feel responsible for potential harm being caused to others. If you find yourself often thinking this way, then the following experiment may be helpful, although you might find it difficult. If you have a supporter, encourage them to do it as well!

Test your beliefs about thought–action fusion

Write down the following sentence in your notebook:

I hope _____ (someone you like) has a minor car accident in the next twenty-four hours.

How do you feel? Guilty? Anxious? People with and without OCD tend to feel highly anxious when doing this experiment. Many people feel it is immoral to wish harm on others even if it is part of a self-help programme. They may also feel concerned that someone will find their piece of paper and think badly of them when they read what they've written. Do you fear 'bad karma'? Are you afraid about the accident happening and how you would feel if it really does happen?

All of these concerns are understandable, of course, but if you truly believe that your thoughts can cause harm to others, there is only one way to change this belief – try it and see what happens.

Tip for supporters

Be willing to offer your name for the person to write the sentence about.

We'll assume you have done the above exercise and nothing bad has happened to the person you liked. This isn't just wishful thinking; this is based on years of doing such experiments. If you have managed to do this and you are reading this next part twenty-four hours later then congratulations! Did writing the sentence down make it come true? What conclusion can you draw from this experiment? Can you now re-write the sentence replacing 'minor' with 'serious'? Can you now change it from someone you 'like' to someone you 'love'. What happens?

Of course, there is always a chance that something bad may happen to someone we care about, but if it does it would be a coincidence. Thinking through the way that bad thoughts could cause harm (there is no logical mechanism) can encourage you to see that the main effect of this experiment will be on your feelings and fear of harm rather than actually causing harm. If you have a supporter, discussing the unfairness of your way of thinking (i.e. that you focus on the negative) can be helpful. You are unlikely to think the power of your thoughts can cause you to win the lottery – why does it work only for bad events? If you do not have a supporter, then do your best to think these issues through alone – writing them down in your notebook may help you to understand your thinking better and help you to realize that thoughts are just thoughts.

Responsibility for harm

People with OCD often think their thoughts mean that they are responsible for harm or its prevention. Sofia felt responsible for potentially harming her grandmother. Responsibility is an important feature in OCD, particularly in checking behaviour. One way in which it can be tackled is (i) to assess how responsible you would be if a feared event occurred, (ii) to brainstorm all the other people who might also be responsible and allocate percentage responsibility to them in a pie-chart and (iii) to reassess your responsibility level.

For example, Sofia said that she would feel 100 per cent responsible if she baked a cake that gave her grandmother food poisoning. After some consideration, she thought that other people might have some responsibility too – the farmers whose eggs were sent to the manufacturers were considered to have 20 per cent responsibility, the supermarkets that stocked the eggs were given 30 per cent responsibility and her grandmother was given 10 per cent responsibility for not noticing that the cake was not baked all the way through. This left Sofia with 40 per cent responsibility rather than her original 100 per cent.

Key message

Use this percentage method to help you re-examine your beliefs about responsibility for harm.

Tip for supporters

Help the person see who else might be responsible for harm.

Checking causes doubting

There is a great deal of research showing that the more you check, the less sure you become. This sounds bizarre because people normally check because they want to be sure about something. A number of separate experiments conducted across the world show that when you check a stove repeatedly, you are likely to have dramatically less confidence in your memory (as well as a less detailed, less vivid memory) than if you check just once or twice. This has even been demonstrated in studies of mental checking, where participants were asked to check situations over and over again in their minds. A separate large amount of research shows that people with OCD have excellent memories, even though you may doubt this applies to you. Like the other experiments discussed here, reading about it probably isn't nearly enough. If you have recurring doubts about your ability to trust your memory in your life, try the experiment below.

Choose a situation in which you find yourself repeating or re-checking something. On one day, check it a lot. Do it for a set period of time (e.g. 20–30 minutes), or until you start to feel frustrated with the amount of checking you're doing. Twenty minutes or so later, jot down how clear your memory is for the checking you completed earlier, perhaps on a scale of 0 to 100. Another day, check the same thing just once. Later on, write down information about the clarity of your memory as you did on the day when you checked a lot. Did you notice any difference between the two occasions? Sofia carried out this experiment focusing on her repeated checking for syringes while walking in the street and found that when she checked a lot, she began to question whether or not she had actually seen any on the street. She felt that she hadn't seen them, but she also didn't really trust this feeling and couldn't say for sure that she hadn't. However, when Sofia checked just once for syringes during her walk, she was markedly more confident in her memory and *knew* that there had been no needles on the street. Sofia came to the realization that checking actually causes doubt.

> **Key message**
>
> The more you check, the more you will doubt. Try it out and see for yourself by comparing your memory confidence when you check something just once compared to when you check something multiple times. Use the behavioural experiments record sheet to help (p. 450)

> **Tip for supporters**
>
> You can do this experiment easily together by checking just once if you have switched your phone on to 'silent' mode and by checking it multiple times.

Avoidance

Behavioural experiments can be used to establish the helpful or unhelpful effects of avoidance. Typically, avoidance helps us in the short term by providing relief from our anxiety but it can also play an important role in keeping the problem going as we don't discover that what we fear does not in fact occur. Sofia conducted an experiment in which she gave a cake to her grandmother that had been cooked according to the instructions on the packet rather than burned to ensure all traces of salmonella had been eradicated. She predicted she would worry about it for at least forty-eight hours after her grandmother had eaten the cake. She shared some cake with her grandmother so that she would see if she also got symptoms of salmonella. She discovered three important things from this experiment. First, her grandmother did not contract salmonella (nor did she). Secondly, she worried about it considerably less than she predicted she would and was able to throw herself into a project at work rather than finding that she couldn't concentrate because she was so preoccupied by her grandmother. Thirdly, she could make a really great cake!

Can you think of any experiments you could do to help you work out the role of avoidance in your OCD and to see how reducing your avoidance could change some of your beliefs (as well as giving you more freedom)?

Key message

Avoidance interferes with your life; experiment with what happens when you avoid certain situations, objects or people, and what happens when you don't.

Tip for supporters

Ensure that any experiments carried out are neither too demanding nor too easy.

Hiding your difficulties

People with OCD take an average of seven years to seek treatment. If you have never sought treatment, part of the reason may be a fear of having to reveal the content of your thoughts to someone. Many people with OCD are ashamed of their thoughts and worry what others would think of them if they knew the content of their thoughts. Knowing that everyone has these thoughts is particularly important information and it is also important to realize that keeping your thoughts a secret prevents you from ever learning that your fears are not likely to be realistic. Keeping your thoughts a secret will also stop you from finding out that other people do not place the same significance on your thoughts as you do. Keeping these thoughts to yourself is in fact likely to contribute to your believing that your thoughts ('obsessions') reveal your very worst qualities. An important step in overcoming OCD can involve sharing your thoughts with a trusted friend, relative or your therapist in a planned way, or anyone who is sympathetic to the problem. It takes courage and we know it is not easy but it is worthwhile. When Sofia finally told her partner the full details of her obsessions, he was far more supportive than she predicted and said he had experienced occasional thoughts of that nature also. He asked what he could do to support her when she was trying to overcome her anxiety. He also said she had been so distant and preoccupied at times that he had worried she might be having an affair. Sofia was shocked by this and they agreed to be more open with each other in future.

Key message

Concealing the nature of your thoughts may be part of the problem. Try telling your therapist, a trusted friend or family member about your thoughts and images and see what happens.

Tip for supporters

If the person you are supporting does not want to tell you their thoughts, that's OK. Be encouraging and patient.

Re-thinking the significance you give your intrusive thoughts

It is likely that you have some evidence that supports your original interpretation of your intrusive thoughts and is the reason why you decided they were significant in the first place. What are they? Can you write them down in your notebook? Many people feel that their thoughts and images are so strong and persistent that they think they might really want them and that they might go crazy. Understanding how your responses to your intrusive thoughts might actually be contributing to their persistence might help you re-think the view that you must really want them. After you have written down the list of evidence that led you to interpret your intrusive thoughts in this way, can you step back and re-examine it? Is the evidence really that strong? Is the evidence based on facts or feelings? Can you think of it a different way? For example, Peter had OCD centred around the fear that he would go mad and commit a terrorist atrocity. He provided evidence that people who committed major acts of terrorism must have been preoccupied with such thoughts beforehand and that they were clearly mad. He discussed the difference between the terrorists' thoughts and his own thoughts with his therapist and found it very helpful. It became clear to him that the terrorists' thoughts were welcome and consistent with their religious values, whereas his own thoughts were unwanted and unacceptable to him.

What information do you need to help you re-think what a intrusive thought may mean? How can you get it? What might get in your way? How can you overcome those obstacles? Set yourself the task of gathering any information required to help you re-think the personal significance you place on your intrusive thoughts.

Key message

Step back and re-examine the evidence you have that influences the significance you place on your intrusive thoughts. Can you think of the evidence in a different way now?

Tip for supporters

Help the person you are supporting see the difference between their old way of thinking and their new way of thinking (i.e. that their thoughts are not personally significant).

Boring, basic but important!

Regular eating and sleeping is vital to good mental health in general and that includes those with OCD. Thinking rationally and helping your heart and head act consistently with each other depends on a reasonable amount of sleep and a nutritious diet. Low mood worsens OCD and having OCD puts you in a bad mood so it is important that you have some activities in your daily life which give you pleasure and that you make sure you eat and sleep properly.

Nearing the end

By now you will have gathered some reasonable evidence about the nature of your OCD through the education, surveys, experiments and re-thinking the amount of significance you give your intrusive thoughts. You should understand that it was your interpretation of your thoughts and your response to them that made them personally significant and meant that your OCD persisted. Sometimes though you may reach a stage where you're not quite sure what to think. On the one hand, there is increasing evidence that the significance you've given your thoughts is the problem and that they may not be so meaningful while, on the other hand, it's likely you have been thinking this way for many years and changing can be difficult. In such circumstances, we suggest you act as if you believe your thoughts are not personally significant. You can do this as an experiment to test a specific belief, but you can also do it simply to have the experience of acting and behaving according to a new belief system. You may find that acting in such a way provides further evidence that changing one's way of thinking and behaviour really helps in your recovery from OCD.

Preventing a relapse

We hope you have made good progress using this chapter. You can measure the progress you have made by using the scales that you used at the start so you can see the difference. The scales are in the appendices. Alternatively, you can try more detailed self-help books listed in the recommended reading. It is important to maintain the gains you've made using the advice on preventing relapse covered in Chapter 14 of this book (p. 416).

If you feel you have not benefited from working through this chapter, then contact your GP and try to get further support, or refer yourself to a local service (if you are in the UK you can find the details of such services on the NHS Choices website – www.nhs.uk).

In Sofia's case, she was planning to start a family within the next few years so her relapse prevention plan included a section on how she would deal with fears of contamination when she was pregnant, giving birth and having a newborn baby at home. Her plan was successful and she managed times of anxiety well by re-reading her notes from these sessions and other relevant chapters of this book.

Key messages

- Everyone has unwanted intrusive thoughts, impulses or images.

- It is the *personal significance* you place on the thoughts, impulses or images you have that is central to the problem.

- Some of your behaviours (in other words, your compulsions or avoidance) because of the personal significance you place on your thoughts, images or impulses are likely to be backfiring and helping to keep your problem going.

- Change and full recovery from OCD *is* possible. If you have used this self-help programme and recovered, we would love to know. Please contact www.ocd-uk.org to tell us.

12 Post-traumatic stress disorder

Jennifer Wild and Anke Ehlers

Anyone who has ever suffered a traumatic event, such as a car crash, a brutal act of violence, the sudden loss of a loved one or a natural disaster like severe flooding, knows the suffering that occurs in the immediate aftermath of trauma. Unwanted distressing memories typically replay over and over in our minds. We may feel jumpy and on edge, tearful and frightened. We may try hard to avoid thinking about what happened, avoid places and people who remind us of the event and withdraw from friends. Usually these symptoms calm down over a period of weeks, but for a number of people they continue. They may even become more frequent. When the symptoms last for more than a month, they may indicate post-traumatic stress disorder (PTSD). When they last for three months or longer, they may indicate chronic PTSD, which means that our symptoms of PTSD have persisted and caused problems in our lives for a long time. National guidelines for the treatment of PTSD in the UK and the USA recommend that PTSD is treated with psychological therapy. The therapy that has the most evidence of helping people to recover from PTSD is cognitive behavioural therapy (CBT), specifically trauma-focused CBT, delivered by a therapist. Whilst several self-help books are available for PTSD, the evidence suggests that PTSD is best treated with the help of a therapist. This is because some of the factors that keep PTSD in place, such as a terrifying memory for the trauma and extreme avoidance of trauma reminders, are often very painful or scary to fully confront alone. For example, it can be difficult to update our memory for the trauma with the same level of detail that we can achieve with the help of an experienced therapist. In the future, it may be possible to overcome PTSD with self-help tools, such as books, or with a combination of self-help materials and seeing a therapist, since scientific research is continually advancing and improving self-help treatments. However, currently the evidence suggests that trauma-focused therapy with a therapist is the most effective way to overcome chronic PTSD. This chapter shows you how to determine whether or not you are suffering from PTSD and what to expect in your CBT treatment for PTSD.

What is PTSD?

Post-traumatic stress disorder is a severe stress reaction that occurs in some people after unexpected horrific events, such as a car crash, major disaster, the sudden loss of a loved one, or a brutal physical or sexual attack. The memory of the traumatic event is usually unbearable and leads to a number of symptoms as people try to push the memory out of their mind and avoid reminders that trigger its recall. Symptoms of PTSD fall into three categories: re-experiencing, avoidance and arousal.

Re-experiencing feels as though the memory for the trauma is in over-drive. Typical examples include recurrent, intrusive memories of the trauma, flashbacks and nightmares. Examples of avoidance symptoms include making great efforts to avoid reminders of what happened, avoiding talking about what happened and trying hard to avoid feelings linked to the trauma. The arousal symptoms include difficulties sleeping, poor concentration, and feeling overly alert, watchful, jumpy and on guard, for example. Whilst some of these symptoms are perfectly usual in the month after a traumatic event, when they persist for more than a month and interfere with how someone functions in their day-to-day life, they usually indicate PTSD.

Bill

Bill was with a group of friends celebrating his birthday at a nightclub. A fight broke out and Bill ended up being stabbed. He was rushed to hospital. The surgeons repaired the cut to his kidney from the stabbing and he survived. Memories of the stabbing repeatedly popped into Bill's mind when there were reminders, such as seeing groups of lads wearing hoods over their heads, seeing a kitchen knife and hearing dance music. Bill felt scared and made a lot of effort to avoid reminders. This meant he started to avoid going out. He slept with the light on since he found that darkness was a reminder. This interrupted his sleep, leading to tiredness and concentration problems. When Bill did go out, he was hyper-alert for possible signs of danger, which kept him continually on edge, tense and jumpy. After a year of these feelings, Bill went to his GP, who diagnosed him with PTSD.

Janet

Janet was driving to work early one morning in the winter on country roads that were icy. She was driving cautiously. However, out of nowhere, another car spun out of control coming around a bend and ploughed into the driver's side of her car. As the car hit her, she thought she would die. But Janet survived without injuries. After the accident, she felt jumpy and on edge, particularly when there were unexpected, sudden movements that occurred on her right-hand side, such as when cyclists suddenly approached her from the right. When Janet was in similar situations to the accident, such as driving or sitting in a car as a passenger, distressing memories of the accident would pop into her mind and she often felt as though it were happening all over again. Consequently, she started to avoid driving because she thought this would help to avoid reminders of what happened. But even television programmes, especially ones that showed car crashes, also brought back the memories and Janet found it hard to sleep at night. She developed concentration problems and generally felt on edge. The symptoms seemed to get worse over time and, within a couple of months, Janet was diagnosed with PTSD.

How do I know if I have PTSD?

PTSD develops after a traumatic event. The first step is to determine whether or not you have suffered a traumatic event. A number of unpleasant events are typically considered traumatic, such as rape, a brutal attack such as a stabbing, a medical emergency, a natural disaster such as severe flooding or an earthquake, a fire or explosion, or a terrorist attack. The traumatic event may be an event we experience or one that we witness or hear about happening to someone else. Traumatic events are also linked to extreme feelings, such as terror, loss, helplessness and horror. However, in some cases, people describe that they felt numb or shocked during the event itself, and that their strong feelings only started afterwards when they came to realize what had happened or could have happened to them.

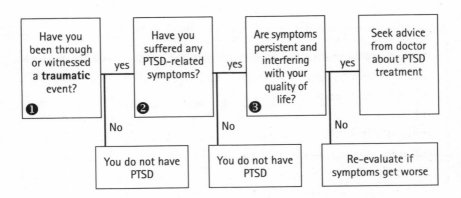

Figure 12.1: The PTSD pathway

Step 1: Have you been through or witnessed a traumatic event? ☑

Examples of traumatic events include a rape, physical attack, robbery, road traffic accident, terrorist attack, natural disaster such as flooding, earthquake, tsunami, medical emergencies, combat trauma or torture. Have you suffered or witnessed any of these or another traumatic event?

Step 2: Symptoms

Are you suffering from any of the following? ☑

- Repeated unwanted and distressing memories of the trauma

- Flashbacks

- Nightmares

- Feeling scared or upset in response to reminders

- Physical reactions, like having a racing heart or feeling sweaty, when you're reminded of what happened

- Making great efforts to avoid thinking or talking about what happened

- Avoiding people or places that remind you of what happened

- Feeling less interested in activities you used to enjoy

- Feeling emotionally flat as though you no longer have strong feelings about anything

- Feeling as though you will no longer achieve plans for your future

- Trouble sleeping

- Trouble concentrating

- Feeling overly alert

- Feeling on edge and jumpy

Step 3

Have these symptoms lasted for more than a month? ☑

Are they interfering with your life, such as your ability to take care of yourself, look after your family, work and socialize? ☑

If the answer to these three questions is yes, then you may be suffering from PTSD and it would be worthwhile visiting your GP and seeking a referral for trauma-focused CBT. More details on how to do this are described at the end of this chapter (p. 399).

How common is PTSD?

PTSD affects about twice as many women as men. Over the course of their lifetimes, 8 per cent of women and 5 per cent of men will suffer from PTSD. At any one time, 1.6 per cent of the population is suffering from PTSD. Given that the population of the UK is roughly 62 million people, that means at any one time in the UK, almost 1 million people are suffering from PTSD.

Why does PTSD develop in some people and not others?

Some people recover after a traumatic event while others go on to develop symptoms of PTSD. This has led scientists to study why PTSD develops in some people and not others. A team at the University of Oxford studied people who already had PTSD and discovered the key factors that kept them from recovering. They grouped these factors into three categories, which form a PTSD Cycle and relate to: the **memory** for the trauma, **thoughts** about the trauma and its consequences, and **behaviours** after the trauma. The PTSD Cycle helps to explain why PTSD persists once it is established. The team has also assessed trauma survivors soon after their trauma and again six or twelve months later. They discovered that some of the factors that keep PTSD going also explain why PTSD develops in the first place.

Risk factors

Memory: Traumatic events are unexpected and overwhelming. This means that it is hard for us to fully take in everything that happens at the time. We may end up with a memory of the event that is confusing and misses important information that would make remembering the event less threatening now. For example, during trauma most people have moments where they believe that they are going to die, and when they later remember these moments they do not update them with the information that they actually survived the trauma. Many survivors of violence blame themselves for not fighting back more, and they do not update their memories with information for why this was not possible at the time, such as that the perpetrator had a knife or they were already injured. A memory that is not updated stops at the worst moments and therefore keeps the sense of threat from the trauma alive.

Unhelpful thoughts: Trauma can have a profound effect on how we think about ourselves or the world. Some ways of thinking make us feel threatened much beyond the trauma, in the here and now. Some people believe that the trauma revealed something bad about themselves that they find hard to live with. They may blame themselves for what happened or believe that the trauma showed that they were inadequate, unable to cope with life, a bad person or similar. Others believe that the trauma showed that the world is much more dangerous than they thought, for example, that another trauma is going to happen soon or that they cannot trust anyone. Sometimes the unhelpful thoughts are about consequences of the trauma rather than the trauma itself, such as 'My flashbacks mean I am going mad' or 'My scars look revolting to other people'.

Behaviours: Avoidance and excessive precautions are understandable reactions after trauma. If we believe that another disaster is going to strike, it is sensible to take precautions. However, some people restrict their lives unnecessarily because the trauma memory gives them the impression that they are in great danger of another trauma. This keeps their PTSD going because they don't have the opportunity to find out that the world is not more dangerous than before the trauma; that is, they cannot update their memories and cannot correct their unhelpful thoughts.

Dwelling about the trauma is another risk factor for PTSD. If people spend a lot of time focusing on why it happened or dwell for long periods about the consequences of what happened, this stops people from moving forward or thinking more proactively about how to resolve the effects of what happened. It is a behaviour that reinforces unhelpful thoughts, for example thoughts of self-blame or unfairness, and it can also trigger distressing memories of the event.

Suppressing thoughts and trying to avoid thinking about the trauma have also been linked to future PTSD. When people suppress memories of the trauma, this can backfire and can make it more likely for the memories to pop into their minds.

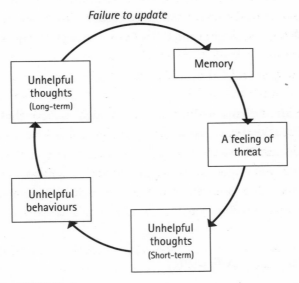

Figure 12.2: The PTSD Cycle

The PTSD Cycle

Applying the PTSD Cycle to Janet's symptoms explains what is keeping her PTSD going. Janet's intrusive memories were of the worst moment of the accident in which she saw the other car speeding towards her. Janet had not linked the worst moment to information that she had now: that she survived. Her memory of the accident always stopped at the worst moment, and this made her very anxious each time. Janet's **memory of the accident** is disorganized or not fully updated. It pops up frequently and when it does it triggers a **sense of threat** as it missed the information that the trauma is over and that Janet did not in fact die. The memory also gives rise to **unhelpful thoughts**, such as that driving is always dangerous. To help her to feel safe and to control her sense of threat, Janet understandably tried a lot of different strategies or **behaviours**, such as avoiding driving and thinking over and over about why the accident happened. The strategies stopped her from updating her memory and re-evaluating her thoughts of danger. Because her memory did not get updated, it continued to pop up unexpectedly and to cause her distress, so that there was a vicious cycle of memories, unhelpful thoughts and strategies to feel safe, which prevented her from updating her trauma memory.

Trauma-focused CBT

Trauma-focused cognitive behavioural therapy is a psychological treatment for PTSD that has the most evidence of efficacy. It is called trauma focused because it specifically involves talking and thinking about the trauma and what it means to you rather than avoiding it. The treatment has a number of effective components and your treatment for PTSD should include the following:

Main treatment components

Supportive relationship: Importantly, a trauma-focused CBT therapist will offer a supportive relationship whilst offering a structured therapy that is focused on the traumatic event and how you have coped with it since. Your CBT therapist will help you to think about the trauma differently by considering the most painful, worst moments you've been trying hard to avoid. This is necessary to update your trauma memory, which will help to reduce your intrusive memories, and reduce your sense of fear and threat.

Reclaiming your life: Early on in your treatment, your therapist will help you to establish plans to reclaim your life. That is, to plan activities that you have started to avoid or have neglected since the trauma but that you used to enjoy. These may involve simple pleasures, such as having a bubble bath or gardening or may involve more substantial activities, such as socializing with friends, going to the cinema or working out in the gym. Your therapist will work with you to establish your goals for re-establishing the activities you want to 'reclaim' in your life and will work with you at a pace that you're comfortable with in order to reach those goals.

Reliving or writing about the trauma: Reliving is a technique in which your therapist will encourage you to close your eyes and recall the traumatic event. Your therapist will ask you to 'relive' it. That is, to talk through your memory of the traumatic event in the first person present tense (e.g. I am driving on the motorway, I hear brakes screeching. . .). Talking through the traumatic memory step by step in this way helps to move the trauma memory on beyond the worst moments and to uncover information that your therapist may use to update the worst meanings of the trauma. Reliving also helps us to stop avoiding the trauma memory, which makes it less fearful, and reduces our sense of threat in the present. If Bill were to relive his stabbing in therapy, he would begin, saying, 'I am at a nightclub celebrating my birthday. My mates, Ron and Pete, are with me. We're drinking and joking about the loud music. I notice . . .' and he would go on to detail the rest of the traumatic event. Another way to work on the trauma is to write out, with the support of your therapist, what happened, what went through your mind and how you felt, moment by moment.

Talking about what the trauma means to you: One of the purposes of reliving or writing about the trauma is to take a closer look at the worst moments and what they mean to you because this will help you and your therapist understand and change how you are feeling now. Feelings of anxiety, guilt, anger, shame or loss are all common after trauma. Your therapist will provide a supportive space and encourage you to express your feelings, and will then help you identify the thoughts that are linked to these feelings and help to update them where possible.

For example, enduring **anxiety** after a frightening trauma is common because trauma shakes up our sense of safety in the world. A trauma can make us more aware of real danger. It can also lead us to *overestimate and exaggerate* danger. After her car crash, Janet *felt* that an accident was waiting to happen around every corner. In her mind it *seemed* likely that history would repeat itself and she felt afraid whenever she was in traffic. In therapy, she discovered that she was responding to her memory rather than to current danger, and that an accident was not more likely than it was before.

After a trauma, feelings of **guilt** or **shame** are also common. This happens when people blame themselves for things they did or did not do during the trauma. You may go over and over in your mind about how you think you should have done things differently or moments that you are ashamed about. Your therapist will help you consider these thoughts and talk about whether you are judging yourself unfairly. After being stabbed, Bill blamed himself for what happened and thought over and over again that he should have celebrated his birthday elsewhere. In therapy, he discovered that he judged his decision unfairly as he could not know at the time that he would end up being stabbed.

There can be a lot to feel **angry** about after a trauma, and some people feel unable to come to terms with the unfairness of the trauma. They may be angry with other people because they hurt them, abused them or disrupted their lives, or because they let them down during or after the trauma. Bill was angry with one of his friends who he believed should have helped him during the fight. In therapy, when he considered what happened in detail, he concluded that his friend had been unable to help him because he had also been injured.

Updating the memory and linked meanings: Trauma-focused CBT therapy will change the way you think about the memory of your trauma. This usually happens through 'reliving' the trauma and discovering information that you may not have had at the time. This includes carefully looking at what happened and by talking with your therapist about the worst moments of your trauma, the 'hot spots'. This may involve looking at what went through your mind at the time, what it means to you and what you know now. Your therapist may help you to think differently about the consequences of the trauma as well as particular moments of the actual trauma. You may be required to bring this new information into the trauma memory when you recall it.

Discriminating: Some trauma-focused CBT therapists will help you to discriminate between what happened in the past and what is going on in the present. This will help you deal with unwanted memories when they pop up. Your therapist will help you to find out what the triggers of your memories are and will help you see that these are actually quite different from the trauma. Triggers can be difficult to spot. They commonly have some features that are similar to things you perceived at the time of the trauma, such as a similar colour, shape, sound, taste, smell or movement. For example, Janet had intrusive memories of the car speeding towards her whenever sudden movements occurred on her right-hand side. Her therapist helped her to look at, rather than avoid, sudden movements and to describe how they were different to the car that crashed into her. Bill's main intrusive memory was seeing a hooded man lunging towards him. Hooded strangers usually triggered intrusive memories and fear. Bill's therapist deliberately took him to parts of the city where there were young men wearing hoods and deliberately had him look at them to describe the differences between what he saw today and what he had seen at the nightclub. As part of the discrimination training, your therapist may take you back to the site of the trauma and guide you to focus on what is different about the site now so that it is easier to see the trauma as an event in the past that is no longer happening today. This will help you take in that the trauma happened in the past, and is now over.

Dealing with avoidance and unnecessary precautions: Your therapist will help you to overcome your avoidance. This may involve listing the situations you are avoiding and planning steps to re-introduce those activities into your life again. For example, Janet had been avoiding driving, and her therapist helped her to plan specific dates and times to drive. Initially, the therapist took Janet driving. Bill had been avoiding going out at night and his therapist helped him to plan activities, such as going to a newsagent in the evening. He also gave up his unnecessary precaution of sleeping with the lights on. Overcoming avoidance and unnecessary precautions helps us to learn that our fears about danger are linked to the trauma, which is in the past, rather than being signs that something dangerous is about to happen now.

Dealing with other unhelpful ways of coping with the trauma: Dwelling on parts of the trauma or its after-effects is an understandable reaction but can also be a way of avoiding really thinking about the things that upset you most. It also keeps thoughts about self-blame and unfairness going and prevents people from moving on from the trauma. Your therapist will help you to overcome unhelpful dwelling on the trauma.

Trying to push memories and emotions away does not stop them coming back. It makes them come back more often because they do not get put away properly. You end up feeling even less in control. Your therapist will help you to deal with your memories differently.

Imagery: If your trauma involved the sudden loss of a loved one, your therapist will most likely at some point in your therapy encourage you to close your eyes, imagine your loved one and say things you may not have had a chance to express when they were alive. Your therapist may also use imagery if you have suffered a trauma that resulted in disfigurement. Your therapist may help you to develop an image of how you look based on fact rather than one based on how you feel, which has likely been distorted by your sense of fear.

Other problems that are common after trauma

PTSD is rarely the only problem that develops after a traumatic event. Feeling down and depressed is common in the aftermath of trauma.

The symptoms of PTSD are debilitating and can cause problems at work and in relationships, and significant sleep problems, which can lead to depression.

Feeling panicky or suffering panic attacks is also common in the aftermath of trauma. Additionally, people may turn to alcohol or drugs to try to cope with the distressing feelings and memories and can develop alcohol- or drug-use problems.

It is important to recognize your symptoms as early as possible and seek professional help. When PTSD is the primary problem, then once your treatment is under way your mood, panic, and sleep will improve and you will feel less inclined to turn to substances to help you cope. If possible, avoid alcohol and other substances. Recognize your desire to cope with alcohol or substances as a sign that you need help with your PTSD.

How long does treatment last for?

Trauma-focused CBT is a short-term therapy that lasts for about three months depending on your needs. Typically between eight and twelve sessions are offered; these may last sixty to ninety minutes each session. If you have had more than one trauma, treatment is likely to last longer so that the therapist can help you come to terms with everything that has happened to you.

What should I do if I think I have PTSD?

If you are in the UK, go to your GP and ask for a referral for trauma-focused psychological therapy. Depending on where you live, you may have access to the Improving Access to Psychological Therapies Programme (IAPT), which offers trauma-focused CBT for PTSD sufferers.

Other helpful resources are listed in the Appendices.

Key messages

- PTSD is an anxiety disorder that develops in some people after a traumatic event.

- A traumatic event is an extreme event, such as a rape, stabbing, road traffic accident, robbery, natural disaster or medical emergency.

- More women than men suffer from PTSD.

- Risk factors for PTSD are: a trauma memory that has not been updated; unhelpful thoughts about what the trauma means about you or the world; and unhelpful behaviours such as avoidance, dwelling on the trauma, or suppressing memories.

- PTSD can be treated.

- Trauma-focused CBT has the best evidence for helping people to recover.

- If you are receiving trauma-focused CBT, your therapy should include key interventions, such as reliving or writing about the trauma, spotting memory triggers and discrimination, reclaiming your life, updating your memory and how you think about the trauma and its consequences, and dealing with painful emotions.

- If you think you have PTSD, you should ask your GP for a referral for trauma-focused psychological treatment. Depending on where you live in the UK, you may be able to have treatment as part of the Improving Access to Psychological Therapies Programme (IAPT).

Part 3

Tackling other problems and maintaining progress

13 The importance of mood and relationships in anxiety

We hope that by the time you come to this section of the book you will have worked your way through the chapters that are relevant to your particular anxiety problem. It may be, however, that you still have some remaining difficulties, or that your progress in overcoming your anxiety has been hampered by problems such as low mood or problems in relationships.

Anxiety and low mood

If you suffer from an anxiety disorder then it is highly likely that you will also experience periods of low mood, or even depression. It may be that having the anxiety problem is making your mood low, or that having low mood is making the anxiety problem worse.

When we talk about low mood we mean a whole range of symptoms, including those listed below. These are not the only symptoms of low mood that can accompany anxiety, but they are some of the common ones. For a more complete description of symptoms of depression, see Table 13.1 on p. 406:

- You are likely to have a sense of feeling rather flat and lacking in motivation. It might seem as though normal activities are just too much.

- Feelings of hopelessness. You might find that you feel demoralized, and think there's no point trying, because nothing's going to work.

- You might find that you have very little energy, get tired easily, or suffer disruption to your sleeping pattern.

- You might find that you think about yourself in a negative way and feel worthless and useless.

Why do low mood and anxiety overlap so much?

If you have been feeling anxious for a while you can easily lose confidence in yourself. If your anxiety leads you to feel that you can't do the activities that you used to be able to do, or that life is generally more difficult, then you may well start to think, 'What's the matter with me? I'm so useless now; I can't do anything.' Thinking that you are useless or a failure can seriously affect your self-esteem, and lead to low mood or depression.

Furthermore, it is *tiring* being anxious all the time and being tired and worn down can drag your mood down, too. This means that you will have less energy to tackle your difficulties, and are therefore more likely to feel hopeless and demoralized.

Finally, we have seen that it is common for people to avoid certain situations when they feel anxious, resulting in an ever more narrow, restricted life. Not only does this affect your confidence, but you are probably not doing as many enjoyable activities as in the past. We know that when people do not have activities in their life that are enjoyable and rewarding for them, their mood suffers and they start to feel low.

Once your mood has started to get low, it can also make the anxiety itself worse. This happens for a number of reasons. Firstly, low mood can affect you so that you end up not eating or sleeping properly, and tiredness will also exacerbate your anxiety. Secondly, feeling 'flat' or 'sad' can make it harder to think rationally, and cause you to think negatively about yourself. This impacts on confidence and your beliefs about your ability to overcome your anxiety problems. Thirdly, low mood impedes memory and concentration so that it becomes harder to undertake everyday tasks, even if you want to do them, and harder to remember what you have managed to accomplish. Fourthly, low mood makes you less likely to enjoy social activities and events, so naturally you stay in more. Ultimately this will make going out again even more of a challenge.

In effect, the relationship between low mood and anxiety can act like another vicious cycle. Like other vicious cycles, the good news is that this can become a virtuous one, too!

Anxiety

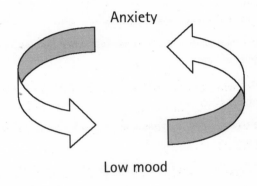

Low mood

Figure 13.1: The anxiety–low mood vicious cycle

If your low mood has become very bad, you should consider whether you may be depressed.

Table 13.1 below gives the symptoms of depression adapted from the *Diagnostic and Statistical Manual of Mental Disorders* (*DSM-IV*). As we said in Part 1, only a trained mental-health professional can diagnose you as having a particular mental-health disorder. However, the list of symptoms of depression in the table may help you assess yourself.

Table 13.1: Symptoms of depression (based on the *DSM-IV* criteria)

If you are depressed you will have either 1 or 2 (or both):

1. Your mood has been depressed most of the day, nearly every day, for example, feeling sad, empty.

2. You have noticed a marked diminished interest or pleasure in all, or almost all, activities most of the day, nearly every day.

If you are depressed you will also have at least three or four of the following:

3. You have lost a significant amount of weight (when not dieting), or you have gained a significant amount of weight.

4. You have had difficulty sleeping or have being sleeping a great deal more than usual nearly every night.

5. Other people have noticed that you have been agitated or slowed down nearly every day.

6. You have been tired and have had no energy nearly every day.

7. You feel worthless or guilty nearly every day.

8. You have noticed that you are having trouble concentrating, or that you are indecisive, nearly every day.

9. You think about death a lot, and may have suicidal thoughts, or suicidal plans.

10. Your symptoms make it difficult for you to function at work and at home, or in your social life or other important areas of life.

11. Your symptoms are not due to the physical effects of a substance such as a recreational drug, a medication, or a general medical condition such as an underactive thyroid.

What's the difference between low mood and depression?

Sometimes it can be hard to tell the difference between low mood and depression because they are so closely linked. The main differences between the two are:

- The depth and intensity of the mood disturbance in depression is much worse than in a passing, manageable low mood.

- Depression seems to go on without any let-up – people's mood is low and depressed pretty much all of the time.

- Both low mood and depression make it harder to tackle normal life, but in depression this is more than just a feeling that things are difficult. Depression has a significant effect on people's ability to function, so that even small things seem impossible to tackle.

Dealing with low mood and depression

If you think that you may be depressed, there are two main ways forward. The first is to try to tackle this using self-help methods. There are several good self-help books for depression, including *Overcoming Depression* by Paul Gilbert (see p. 439). The second is to talk to your GP and discuss whether antidepressant medication may be helpful, or whether a referral to a therapist might be best.

If your mood is not as bad as in a full depression, then the 'top tips' below may be sufficient to help you tackle it:

1. Try to make sure you have something pleasurable to look forward to each day. This may be small (for example, turning on an electric blanket at night, having a bubble bath, watching a good TV programme, or listening to music) but it has to be planned and present every day.

2. Use problem solving to tackle specific problems that are causing your low mood (see Chapter 8 on Generalized Anxiety Disorder and Worry).

3. Make sure you have a structure to your day, for instance, getting up at and going to bed at a reasonable time and eating properly.

4. Do not isolate yourself from your friends and family; try to go out and see if it is actually more pleasant than you predict.

5. If you feel that doing too much is contributing to your low mood,

then try to slow down for a couple of days as an experiment and see the consequences.

A final word about depression and low mood

Sometimes when your mood gets very low you can start to think that there really is no hope and no escape, and that you and other people might be better off if you were not around. If you recognize these thoughts, and fear that you are feeling suicidal, please get help straight away. You can make an appointment with your GP or physician. If it is out of hours, then your local Accident and Emergency Department (A&E) has people who can help. You don't have to live with these thoughts and feelings on your own. The right assistance for recovery is available. You can find a list of helpful resources in the appendices.

Anxiety and relationships

Another common aspect to anxiety is that it can affect your relationships with other people, particularly those who you are close to. Problems in relationships can increase our feelings of anxiety. As with so many other aspects of psychological problems, these difficulties can best be described as a vicious cycle, in this case between anxiety and relationship problems.

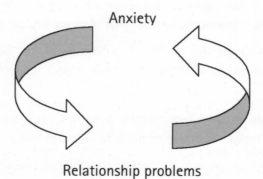

Figure 13.2: The anxiety–relationship problems vicious cycle

How are anxiety and relationship problems linked?

There are a number of ways in which this vicious cycle can work. Firstly, relationship problems can have a big effect on your anxiety. If you are having difficulties with your partner, or with a child or a parent, and are involved in arguments and tension, then you might well feel anxious. You might be going through a period of upheaval in your life – such as divorce, changing job, moving house, arguing with a family member or forming a new romantic relationship. You might have moved and be finding it hard to make friends and become anxious about whether people will like you. You might have lost someone close to you, and as well as feelings of grief and sorrow, worries about how you are going to cope without them may surface. All of these scenarios can provoke anxiety and anxious ways of thinking and behaving.

Secondly, anxiety itself can have a big impact on relationships. For instance, you might stop going out because you just get too anxious in crowds, or in open or unfamiliar places. This means that you are likely to avoid your friends, who can end up feeling rejected, and may even stop contacting you. You might find that you commit to social activities but make excuses at the last minute, which makes people close to you feel let down. It is common for people who suffer from anxiety to cancel holidays at the last minute, even expensive and well-planned ones, because at the final moment their anxiety about leaving home or getting on a plane is too great. Such behaviour will clearly have a significant impact on your partner. Another way in which anxiety can affect relationships is that you might spend a lot of time asking for reassurance from people close to you, or insisting that they take part in your anxious rituals (particularly true of OCD). Or your partner might feel that you have changed and be uncomfortable or frustrated with this new side of you. All of these eventualities can place a great strain on relationships.

If you have anxiety you might be worried about being rejected or abandoned by other people. You might find it harder to deal with conflict in your close relationships, even 'normal' levels of conflict that are part of the manageable interactions of everyday life. Sometimes, people with anxiety are so worried about how other people are behaving towards them that they forget to think about how they are behaving themselves. You might find that you are behaving in ways that make the relationship worse without even realizing it. For instance, you might get angry if you think someone is rejecting you – even if they're not – but because you are angry, they get angry with you, further straining the relationship.

Relationship problems can be present in all types of anxiety. Table 13.2 below shows some of the common issues in relationships that can arise with the different anxiety disorders.

Table 13.2: Anxiety and relationships

Anxiety disorder	Common relationship issues
Panic	Always needing your partner to accompany you to places where you fear having a panic attack, such as a supermarket
OCD	Relying on people too heavily for reassurance and help with checking Making life difficult by imposing rules of behaviour on them
GAD	Worrying about rejection, abandonment, hostility and conflict, and constantly seeking reassurance Withdrawing from friendships
PTSD	Becoming detached and withdrawn from loved ones Becoming suspicious and hostile to strangers
Social phobia	Avoiding social situations; feeling cut off from people Relying too heavily on a small number of people
Specific phobia	Interference with normal life, including relationships
Health anxiety	Relying on people too heavily for reassurance Alienating health professionals and those close to you

There are two particular aspects of relationship problems that we think are especially worth addressing:

Avoidance of relationships

We have spoken a great deal about avoidance and the role it plays in anxiety. Avoidance of relationships can increase your sense of isolation. We all need other people. We need people for love and affection, and to feel important and valuable. We also need other people to have fun with! When you avoid situations where you will come into contact with other people, you end up depriving yourself of some very important needs. Your friends will feel rejected if you avoid seeing them, particularly if they don't know the cause. When you avoid people because you are too anxious to go out, your relationships start to suffer, and you can end up feeling friendless and isolated. This is likely to make your mood lower, and as we have seen this can make your anxiety worse. The bottom line is that we need to find a way to keep relationships and friendships going even when you are most anxious.

Ask yourself: 'Is my anxiety making me avoid my friends and family? Am I feeling lonely and neglected because my friends and family have given up trying to contact me?' If the answer to these two questions is yes, then have another look at pp. 62–9 on behavioural experiments to deal with avoidance. Set up an experiment to help you to get back in touch with people and see what happens. Remind yourself that you need people. Even if the prospect of seeing them makes you feel anxious, it really is worthwhile.

'Compassion fatigue'

There is a typical pattern when we develop problems, whether these are financial, medical, social or anything else. When the problem first occurs, other people usually rally round to help – the crisis brings out the best in people, and they are likely to be kind and sympathetic. If the problem goes on for a long time, people can't keep the 'crisis' level of sympathy going.

They stop being so helpful and sympathetic, and at worst can even seem to be fed up with you, or blame you for how you feel. We sometimes call this change in how people respond 'compassion fatigue' – it's as if your friends and family just get worn out with being sympathetic, so you can end up feeling abandoned and rejected, often when you need help most.

If you have had an anxiety problem for a long time, you and your friends and family are likely to feel fed up. You will probably all feel demoralized and start thinking that you'll never get better. None of you may know what to do to make things better. People commonly treat those closest to them harshly, so you and your friends and family may be frustrated with each other, and blame each other when things don't go right. As the diagram of the vicious cycle on p. 408 illustrates, both the relationship and the anxiety can get worse.

It's important to understand why your friends and family can lose sympathy. It's common for those around us to become demoralized because their attempts to help us don't seem to have achieved much. Our loved ones can start to feel useless and powerless when their suggestions and support don't work. They can feel sad and rejected. If the anxiety has had a big impact on you, and on your joint lives, your partner might feel a strong sense of loss for how you used to be, or how things were between you. Even though it is you who has the anxiety problem, the impact on your close relationships, particularly with your partner, can be pretty serious, too.

What can I do about relationship problems?

One of the first steps to improving relationships is to become aware of whether the vicious cycle is affecting you, and in what way.

Ask yourself, 'Am I having problems with my friends or my family? Are these problems making my anxiety worse? Or is my anxiety making the problems in my relationships worse?'

Think about the important people in your life. How do you feel when you see them or think about them? Do you feel calmer and more secure?

Or do you feel more tense and wound up? Does being with them make your anxiety better or worse? Do you have the same arguments again and again, and repeat the same old lines without either of you listening? Are there issues that repeatedly come up that never seem to be resolved?

If the answer to these questions is that you feel worse around the important people in your life, then you have taken a brave step and you should acknowledge it. It is important to realize that neither of you is deliberately damaging your relationships. It is worth trying:

- Firstly, try to talk to them about what is going on. Getting problems out in the open can be an enormous relief to everyone. Make a deal that you will both try to talk without blaming the other person, and that you will both do your utmost to listen properly and try to understand the other person's point of view.

- Secondly, try to put nice words and behaviour back into your relationship. Make an agreement that you will both pay each other compliments, even on small daily tasks like cooking, doing the washing up, or on clothes and hair. Try doing something that you know the other person will like – bring them tea in bed, or mow the lawn. When relationships start out people do a lot of these kinds of behaviours, and then forget to do them as time goes by. Even small compliments can help to rekindle the good feelings between you.

- Thirdly, don't get cross and act rejected (even if you feel it) when your partner or close friend doesn't respond as you would like. Remember that it is difficult for them, too. You could try letting them know that you understand what it is like for them to live with someone suffering from anxiety.

- Fourthly, try to find a way in which you can be together sometimes where the anxiety problem doesn't intrude. If you used to like going out to clubs together but you can't face it now, then hire a karaoke machine and run your own disco at home for the two of you! If you liked going out for meals, then find a quiet pub where you can have a meal together in a corner where no one will intrude. Try to find a 'calm' space somewhere in your lives where you can be happy and relaxed together.

If you feel that you need more help than is contained in these simple suggestions, then there are a number of books listed in the Resources section at the end of this book that give you more detail about how to tackle relationship problems. Or you could try going to an organization that helps people with relationship problems, such as Relate – again details are given in the Resources section (see p. 446). You don't have to be married or heterosexual to go to Relate, and you can even go on your own if your partner won't come with you.

Key messages

- Anxiety problems are often related to problems with mood and relationships.

- If your mood is low, then try some of the steps above to see if you can make a difference. If your mood does not improve, then it might be worth going to see your GP to discuss what else you can try to give you the boost you need.

- Think about your relationships – are they contributing to your anxiety? Think of what steps you can take to make improvements.

Tips for supporters

- Help the person you are supporting to think about their mood and their relationships, and to notice how these are linked to their anxiety.

- Sometimes people might think that low mood and poor relationships are normal and they do not realize that these are problems that can be dealt with. Help them to make a realistic appraisal of the areas of difficulty and see if they would be helped by making positive changes.

- If they have problems in more than one area, help the person to decide which to tackle first, and encourage them to focus on one problem at a time – their anxiety, mood or relationships.

14 Relapse prevention: your 'blueprint' for survival

What is my 'message in a bottle'? It is that I don't need to suffer with anxiety any more and that I need to remember to use all the tools in my toolkit!

Murat, 21

Advantages of CBT

One of the big advantages of CBT is that the gains that you make in treatment can be maintained. In other words, once you finish CBT, you should have learned skills and techniques that will stand you in good stead for the rest of your life. This self-help book is designed to be read, used, followed and then re-read as necessary, with the exercises repeated as you come across stressful and anxious periods in your life. Anxious situations will inevitably occur, as they do for everyone. It is how you deal with them that matters.

Once you have used this book and made progress to prevent the anxiety recurring, we suggest you complete the relapse prevention worksheet, worksheet 14.1. It is best to do this after you've read Parts 1 and 2. We also recommend that you type this up (unless you have very neat hand-writing) as it's an important document that will summarize everything you've learned from reading this book and doing the exercises. It is important this document is easy to read when you come back to look at it in a few months, years or even decades. You can see how both Nicky and Stefan went about filling in this worksheet and there's a blank one for you to use at the end of the chapter and in the appendices.

Nicky's story

Remember that when Nicky went for help, she and her psychological wellbeing practitioner (PWP) – her supporter from the GP practice – realized that she had a number of different symptoms of anxiety. These were:

- Panic attacks – Nicky experienced very strong panic attacks when she thought that there was something different about her breathing, and she thought that she would suffocate and die.

- OCD – She was nervous about eating anything, and had started to check food carefully before she could eat anything at all.

- PTSD – She felt traumatized by the experience since she had genuinely thought that she might die. She had nightmares about it, and wouldn't go near anything that reminded her of it.

- Social phobia – Nicky thought that other people thought she was pathetic, and she had started to become anxious about being around other people, particularly her brothers, because of this.

With her psychological wellbeing practitioner, Nicky worked through the chapters in this book. She started with the Panic Disorder chapter, because this seemed to be the most problematic part of her anxiety. The PWP helped her to understand what was happening, and to do behavioural experiments to show her that she was not going to suffocate when her breathing changed. The PWP also helped her to pick out sections from the OCD chapter that would be helpful – in particular stopping checking her food. Nicky was able to work on her social anxiety by making herself think about other people, not herself, when she was in social situations. The PWP also helped her to see that the way that she had reacted was natural and understandable – the experience with the chicken bone had been very frightening – and that she was not a wimp. Realizing this made it easier for her to be around other people. Finally, by talking about what had happened in the course of therapy, and having a chance to adjust to it, Nicky's PTSD symptoms got a lot better, and she no longer woke in the night with nightmares about dying.

Nicky's relapse prevention worksheet

How did my anxiety start?

When I choked.

What made my anxiety persist? *Clue: refer to the diagram that you drew for the anxiety problem you've been experiencing. Think of the meaning you were placing on particular events, and what you were doing to try to improve the situation but which might have backfired, e.g. avoidance.*

Because . . . I started to feel so frightened if anything about my breathing wasn't right that I got anxious and hyperventilated – a self-fulfilling prophecy.

I avoided going out or eating very much, especially chicken, so I carried on thinking it would happen again if I did.

I thought that being in this situation was my fault for being pathetic and so I assumed everyone else thought that, too.

What have I learned in this self-help book that has been useful? *Clue: Put as much as you can here.*

Anxiety makes you breathe so fast that it feels like you can't get enough oxygen, and this can make you think you're dying, and then you panic.

Actually the physical response to breathing so fast is physically normal and it cannot lead to any serious physical problem.

My thoughts are not 'the truth' sometimes – I have to learn to stand back from them and make sure that they really fit the situation. I will try to remember to examine the evidence.

DO NOT AVOID THINGS – it just keeps the problems going and makes everything worse.

What situations might lead to a setback for me? *Clue: think about some of the triggers that led to the development of the problem in the first place, or other stressors in your life.*

I have realized that I am quick to imagine that other people think I'm stupid. Before this realization I hadn't appreciated that I tended to feel a bit inferior. I need to make sure that I stop trying to mind-read.

I'm mainly OK about eating, but I think I still worry if I'm somewhere strange and I'm given something to eat and don't know what's in it.

What will be the early warning signs of a setback for me? *Clue: Think back to a recent episode of anxiety – what signs were there that this episode might be about to happen? Catching your anxiety early is going to be helpful.*

The last time I had a problem was when I was invited to dinner and I didn't want to go – I started to have all the same fears that something would go wrong, I'd choke, I'd make a fool of myself etc. etc.

I think early warning signs would be my wanting to avoid foods, situations and people again, checking my food, or starting to worry about breathing.

What will I do about it? *Clue: have a realistic plan for how to tackle setbacks.*

Remind myself of what I've learned.

Anxiety can make my breathing go funny, but I understand that now. I know how to control my breathing if I need to do so.

Phone my Mum. She's been really good at following what I've been doing, and she's agreed that if I start 'having a worrying reaction' she'll make me go out, and encourage me to eat things.

How will I distinguish between having a setback and being back at square one? *Clue: if you have a difficult period, you don't want to catastrophize it and think you have learned nothing from going through this book. Distinguish between a lapse (or slip) and a full relapse.*

I don't think this is going to be a problem – I don't think that I could ever go back to square one now that I understand what happened. I feel pretty confident that taking the steps above make me a more confident and happier person.

How do I see myself in:

1 month:
I hope that I'll be back to doing most of what I could do last summer – I might still be a bit nervous though, but I think that's understandable.

6 months:
Good! I'll be back to normal. Actually I hope that my having worked so hard and so successfully to overcome my anxiety problems will have made me a nicer person – I'll be much more understanding if someone in my aerobics classes seems to be having trouble now.

1 year:
I would like to get involved in some work assisting people with anxiety problems. Perhaps I could learn to run classes for breathing and relaxation as well as doing aerobics.

5 years:
No idea. It's too far ahead; I don't have a clue what I'll be doing.

I'm pretty confident I won't be having major problems with anxiety, though.

Finally, what is my 'message in a bottle'? *Clue: If you could only remember three things you have learned from this book, what would they be?*

Don't panic!

It was understandable that I developed problems – I did nearly die after all.

When you get anxious you 'hyperventilate'. Rapid breathing is a normal part of anxiety and not a sign that you're about to die.

Avoiding and checking makes the problem worse, not better, even if it seems to help at the time.

This and the following relapse prevention worksheets adapted with permission from D. Geenberger and C. Padesky (1995) *Mind Over Mood*. New York: Guilford Press.

Stefan's story

Remember Stefan? He is a Czech builder who was working in England and sending money home, but when the economic situation became difficult, he started to develop troubling symptoms of generalized anxiety disorder (GAD). He started to worry all the time about what could go wrong. He was having difficulty sleeping, and was tense and irritable. He was low in spirit, and missed his wife and young children. After a while Stefan realized that something was wrong, and he started to talk a lot to his wife about his concerns. He also did a lot of research on the internet and with self-help books.

Stefan's relapse prevention worksheet

How did my anxiety start?

It started when the economic situation got worse, and everyone got nervous about spending money. I had one job that was cancelled because the customer couldn't afford it. And Magda was pregnant again, so I was really worried about money.

Why did my anxiety persist? *Clue: refer to the diagram that you drew for the anxiety problems you've been experiencing. Think of the meaning you were placing on particular events, and the types of behaviours that you were engaging in to improve the situation but which might have backfired, e.g. avoidance.*

I started to worry about everything – I thought I wouldn't get another job, and that the people I was working for hated what I was doing. I avoided asking them about friends of theirs I knew wanted me to do work on their house because I assumed they'd say they'd changed their minds. Then because I was avoiding I got more worried about the lack of work, and then more anxious – exactly the kind of vicious cycle that the book describes!

What have I learned in this self-help book that has been useful? *Clue: Put as much as you can here.*

I've learned to recognize that I tended to worry all the time and have learned the difference between 'real' and 'hypothetical' worries. As a result I've learned how to solve real problems in a more systematic way and when it is sensible to dismiss hypothetical worries. This has been really good, because I'm not spending the whole day winding myself up any more.

I thought the idea of 'behavioural experiments' was a bit strange at first, but when I do try to do them it helps me to find out whether what I am afraid of will come true.

Keeping track of my anxiety on a regular basis was really useful as I could easily gauge the level of my anxiety and how it was changing.

I like the idea of cognitive errors, too – it was really helpful to realise that I was just seeing the worst in everything and forgetting all the good I've done.

What situations might lead to a setback for me? *Clue: think about some of the triggers that led to the development of the problem in the first place, or other stressors in your life.*

The really big situation is if I can't get work – because then I would be really worried that I wouldn't be able to support Magda and the kids.

What will be the early warning signs of a setback for me? *Clue: Think back to a recent episode of anxiety – what signs were there that this episode might be about to happen? Catching your anxiety early is going to be helpful.*

Not sleeping is a sure sign, and also if I realize that I'm spending all day worrying and focussing on things I've done wrong.

What will I do about it? *Clue: have a realistic plan for how to tackle setbacks.*

I will, firstly, not think that I have to cope on my own, and remember that it was really helpful to talk to Magda. I think that she and I could make a list of things she can remind me of, like 1) remember the difference between real and hypothetical worries, 2) remember not to focus on small faults, and also to talk to other people when I'm worrying what they think, 3) try not to get too caught up in my thoughts. I could also make a list of all the kind words that people I've worked for have said, so at least I can think that if there is work going I'll stand a good chance of getting it.

How will I distinguish between a setback and being back to square one? *Clue: if you have a difficult period, you don't want to catastrophize it and think you have learned nothing from going through this book. Distinguish between a lapse (or slip) and a full relapse.*

When I was at my worst I wasn't sleeping or eating much, and I was really irritable and found it difficult not to snap at everyone. And I imagined terrible situations, like Magda and the kids wandering in the snow with no shoes. This is really different from when I have bad days now.

How do I see myself in:

1 month:
A lot better. It's true I'd rather be at home, but actually work is going well here, and people do like me. If I remember to put what I've learned into practice and not worry so much, then it's much easier to see a more positive view of the future.

6 months:
About the same.

1 year:
What I'd really like to be able to do is to find work at home – it's even possible that Magda could go back to teaching, even with the new baby, and I could look after the children. We'd have a bit less money, but at least we'd be together. She's said that she feels she'd like to be back in the world again. Or I could try again to get enough work at home. Even if that's not possible, then I am much more confident that I can keep work going here.

5 years:
I'm just keeping my fingers crossed but I am optimistic about my future now!

Finally, what is my 'message in a bottle'? *Clue: If you could only remember three things you have learned from this book, what would they be?*

Anxiety is understandable, and you can manage it if you take a step back, think about what is keeping the problem going and then make changes.

I have to take active steps to stop worrying, or else it just takes my life over.

Remember the behavioural experiments: Have the courage to check things out with people.

Now that you have had a chance to see Nicky and Stefan's relapse prevention worksheets, have a go at filling in the blank one below.

Worksheet 14.1: Relapse prevention worksheet

How did my anxiety start?

Why did my anxiety carry on? *Clue: refer to the diagram that you drew for the anxiety problem you've been experiencing . Think of the meaning you were placing on particular events, and what you were doing to try to improve the situation but which might have backfired e.g. avoidance.*

What have I learned in this self-help book that has been useful? *Clue: Put as much as you can here.*

What situations might lead to a setback for me? *Clue: think about some of the triggers that led to the development of the problem in the first place, or other stressors in your life.*

What will be the early warning signs of a setback for me? *Clue: Think back to a recent episode of anxiety – what signs were there that this episode might be about to happen? Catching your anxiety early is going to be helpful.*

What will I do about it? *Clue: have a realistic plan for how to tackle setbacks.*

How will I distinguish between having a setback and being back at square one? *Clue: if you have a difficult period, you don't want to catastrophize it and think you have learned nothing from going through this book. Distinguish between a lapse (or slip) and a full relapse.*

How do I see myself in:

1 month:

6 months:

1 year:

5 years:

Finally, what is my 'message in a bottle'? *Clue: If you could only remember three things you have learned from this book, what would they be?*

Key messages

- Developing a plan to prevent relapse will help you keep up the progress you have made in the tough times.

- Try not to lose your relapse prevention plan! It would be helpful if you can put it somewhere where you know you can find it if you need it again in the future.

Tip for supporters

It is worth helping the person you are supporting quite actively with this worksheet to ensure that it is as comprehensive as possible and therefore as useful as possible to look back upon when times are tough in the future.

Concluding comments

Overcoming anxiety problems is not easy. We hope that you have used the range of techniques described in this book and that doing so has helped you to overcome your anxiety. If you have not made improvements, or not as many as you would like, then don't despair. Self-help books such as this can help some people, but they're not for everyone. Some people need the extra help that working with a therapist can bring. Some people also benefit from medication for anxiety. Your GP will be able to discuss with you whether a referral to a therapist, or some kind of medication, would be the right way forward for you. We do hope that the book has helped you to make some improvements in your anxiety, so that you are able to live a happier and more fulfilling life. If this is the case, be sure to give yourself a pat on the back, and we hope you enjoy your new-found freedom.

Appendix 1 – References

J. S. Abramowitz and A. E. Braddock (2008). *Psychological treatment of health anxiety and hypochondriasis: A biopsychosocial approach.* Cambridge, MA: Hogrefe & Huber Publishers.

American Psychiatric Association (2000). *Diagnostic and statistical manual of mental disorders* (4th ed., text revision). Washington, DC: American Psychiatric Association.

American Psychiatric Association (2012). *DSM-5 Development.* Retrieved from www.dsm5.org.

American Psychiatric Association (APA) (2000). *Diagnostic and Statistical Manual of Mental Disorders,* 4th edition. Text revision. Arlington, VA: American Psychiatric Association.

D. Barlow, T. J. Farchione, C. P. Fairholme, K. Ellard, C. L. Boisseau, L. B. Allen and J. Ehrenreich-May (2011). *Unified protocol for transdiagnostic treatment of emotional disorders.* NY: Oxford University Press.

A. J. Barsky and D. K. Ahern (2004). Cognitive behavior therapy for hypochondriasis: A randomized controlled trial. *Journal of the American Medical Association, 291,* 1464–1470.

A. T. Beck (1976). *Cognitive Therapy and the Emotional Disorders.* New York: Penguin Books.

J. S. Beck and A. T. Beck (2011). *Cognitive Behavior Therapy, Second Edition. Basics and Beyond.* New York: Guilford Press.

G. Butler and A. Hackmann. (2004). Social Phobia. In J. Bennett-Levy, G. Butler, M. Fennell, A. Hackmann, M. Mueller and D. Westbrook (2004). *The Oxford Guide to Behavioural Experiments in Cognitive Therapy.* Oxford: Oxford University Press. pp 141–58.

Centre for Clinical Interventions (2008). Overcoming health anxiety. http://www.cci.health.wa.gov.au/resources/infopax.cfm?Info_ID=53

D. A. Clark and A. T. Beck (2010). *Cognitive Therapy of Anxiety Disorders: Science and Practice*. New York: Guilford Press.

D. M. Clark (1986). A cognitive approach to panic. *Behaviour Research and Therapy, 24*, 461–470.

D. M. Clark (1996). Panic disorder: from theory to therapy. In P. M. Salkovskis (ed.). *Frontiers of cognitive therapy* (pp. 318–44). New York: Guilford Press.

D. M. Clark (2006). *Cognitive Therapy for Panic Disorder*. American Psychological Association video. Available from www.apa.org/pubs/videos/4310781.aspx

D. M Clark and A. Wells (1995). A cognitive model of social phobia. In R. G. Heimberg, M. R. Liebowitz, D. Hope et al., eds.). *Social Phobia – Diagnosis, Assessment, and Treatment*, pp. 69–93. New York: Guilford.

D. M. Clark and P. M. Salkovskis (2009) *Panic Disorder Therapist Manual for IAPT High Intensity Therapists*. A treatment manual for the cognitive therapy that the panic disorder chapter (Chapter 7) is based on. This paper is downloadable from the IAPT section of the OxCADET website: http://oxcadet.psy.ox.ac.uk/

D. M. Clark, P. M. Salkovskis, A. Hackmann, H. Middleton, P. Anastasiades and M. G. Gelder (1994). A comparison of cognitive therapy, applied relaxation and imipramine in the treatment of panic disorder. *British Journal of Psychiatry, 164*, 759–69.

Department of Health, IAPT Data Handbook, 2010. www.iapt.nhs.uk/silo/files/iaptdata-handbook-appendicesv2.pdf (p.24). The IAPT Phobia Scales used in Chapter 6 is reproduced with kind permission from this publication.

M. J. Dugas, F. Gagnon, R. Ladouceur and M. H. Freeston (1998). Generalized anxiety disorder: a preliminary test of a conceptual model. *Behaviour, Research and Therapy* 25: 551–8.

P. Furer, J. R. Walker and M. B. Stein (2007). *Treating health anxiety and fear of death: A practitioner's guide*. New York, NY: Springer Science & Business Media; US.

D. Greenberger and C. Padesky (1995). *Mind Over Mood*. New York: Guilford Press.

A. Greeven, A. J. van Balkom, S. Visser, J. W. Merkelbach, Y. R. van Rood, R. van Dyck et al. (2007). Cognitive behavior therapy and paroxetine in the treatment of hypochondriasis: A randomized controlled trial. *The American Journal of Psychiatry*, 164(1), 91–99.

N. Grey, P. M. Salkovskis, A. Quigley, A. Ehlers and D. M. Clark (2008). Dissemination of cognitive therapy for panic disorder in primary care. *Behavioural and Cognitive Psychotherapy, 36,* 509–20.

H. D. Hadjistavropoulos, J. A. Janzen, M. D. Kehler, J. A. Leclerc, D. Sharpe and M. D. Bourgault-Fagnou (2011). Core cognitions related to health anxiety in self-reported medical and non-medical samples. *Journal of Behavioural Medicine, 32,* 150–161.

E. Hedman, G. Andersson, E. Andersson, B. Ljótsson, C. Rück, G. J. Asmundson and N. Lindefors (2011). Internet-based cognitive-behavioural therapy for severe health anxiety: Randomised controlled trial. *British Journal of Psychiatry*, 198, 230–236.

C. Hirsch and F. McManus (2007). Social phobia: Treatment. In Stan Lindsay and Graham E. Powell (eds.) (2007). *Handbook of Clinical Adult Psychology 3rd Edition*. London: Brunner-Routledge.

M. Kehler and H. D. Hadjistavropoulos (2009). Is health anxiety a significant problem for individuals with multiple sclerosis? *Journal of Behavioral Medicine, 32,* 150–161.

R. C. Kessler, W. T. Chiu, O. Demler, K. R. Merikangas and E. E. Walters (2005). Prevalence, severity, and comorbidity of 12-month DSM-IV disorders in the National Comorbidity Survey Replication. 'Archives of General Psychiatry,' 62, 617–27.

R. Klorman, J. Hastings, T. Weerts, B. Melamed and P. Lang (1974). Psychometric description of some specific fear questionnaires. *Behavior Therapy*, 5, 401. The Spider Phobia Questionnaire used in Chapter 6 is from this publication.

F. McManus and C. Hirsch (2007). Social phobia: Investigation. In Stan Lindsay and Graham E. Powell (eds.) (2007). *Handbook of Clinical Adult Psychology 3rd Edition*. London: Brunner-Routledge.

D. K. Marcus, J. R. Gurley, M. M. Marchi and C. Bauer (2007). Cognitive and perceptual variables in hypochondriasis and health anxiety: a systematic review. *Clinical Psychology Review*, 27, 127–139.

K. Meares and M. Freeston (2008). *Overcoming Worry: A Self-help Guide Using Cognitive Behavioral Techniques*. London: Robinson.

National Institute for Health and Clinical Excellence guidelines for PTSD: http://www.nice.org.uk/nicemedia/pdf/CG026publicinfo.pdf

S. Rachman (2012). Health anxiety disorders: a cognitive construal. *Journal of Behaviour Research and Therapy*, 50, 502–512.

P. M. Salkovskis (1996). *Frontiers of Cognitive Therapy*. New York: Guilford Press.

H. Seivewright, J. Green, P. Salkovskis, B. Barrett, U. Nur and P. Tyrer (2008). Cognitive-behavioural therapy for health anxiety in a genitourinary medicine clinic: Randomised controlled trial. *British Journal of Psychiatry*, 193(4), 332–337.

J. Siev and D. L. Chambless (2007). Specificity of treatment effects: cognitive therapy and relaxation for generalized anxiety and panic disorders. *Journal of Consulting and Clinical Psychology*, 75, 513–22.

A. Silver, D. Sanders, N. Morrison and C. Cowey (2004). Health anxiety. In J. Bennett-Levy, G. Butler, M. Fennell, A. Hackman, M. Mueller and D. Westbrook (eds.). *Oxford guide to behavioural experiments in cognitive therapy* (pp. 81–99). Oxford: Oxford University Press.

A. Wilkinson, K. Meares and M. H. Freeston (2011). *CBT for Worry and Generalised Anxiety Disorder*. London: Sage.

Appendix 2 – Further Reading

Anxiety – General

Helen Kennerley (1997). *Overcoming Anxiety: A self-help guide using Cognitive Behavioral Techniques*. London: Robinson.

From the *Overcoming* series, this is a popular and user-friendly self-help book written by a leading CBT expert in the UK.

Michelle Craske and David Barlow (2006). *Mastery of Your Anxiety and Worry: Workbook (Treatments That Work)*. Oxford: Oxford University Press.

A classic book that provides step-by-step help for overcoming anxiety and worry. It has an accompanying therapist's guide and is written by the leading clinical researchers in the US.

Ron Rapee, Ann Wignall, Sue Spence and Heidi Lyneham (2008). *Helping Your Anxious Child: A step-by-step guide for parents*, 2nd edition. Oakland, CA: New Harbinger Publications.

Cathy Creswell and Lucy Willetts (2007). *Overcoming Your Child's Fears and Worries: A guide for parents using Cognitive Behavioral Techniques*. London: Robinson.

The above two books are written by some of the leading clinical researchers in the field of CBT for childhood anxiety. They are highly accessible and practical, and are recommended for all parents whose children are suffering from anxiety.

Specific Phobias

Martin M. Antony, Michelle G. Craske and David H. Barlow (2006). *Mastering Your Fears and Phobias: Workbook: Client Workbook (Treatments That Work)* second edition. Oxford: Oxford University Press.

A self-help book which outlines a CBT treatment programme for those suffering from specific fears and phobias, including fear of blood, heights, driving, flying, water, and others.

Panic Disorder

Derrick Silove and Vijaya Manicavasagar (1998). *Overcoming Panic and Agoraphobia: A self-help guide using Cognitive Behavioral Techniques.* London: Robinson.

From the *Overcoming* series, this is a practical and easy-to-follow self-help book written by two leading CBT clinicians.

Vijaya Manicavasagar (2010). *Overcoming Panic and Agoraphobia: Talks with your therapist.* London: Robinson (audio).

An audiobook based on the self-help book *Overcoming Panic and Agoraphobia*, written by the same author.

Generalised Anxiety Disorder

Mark Freeston and Kevin Meares (2008). *Overcoming Worry: A self-help guide using Cognitive Behavioral Techniques.* London: Robinson.

From the *Overcoming* series, this book offers a step-by-step self-help programme written by the authors of the generalised anxiety disorder and worry chapter in this book.

Social Phobia

Gillian Butler (2008). *Overcoming Social Anxiety and Shyness: A self-help guide using Cognitive Behavioral Techniques*. London: Robinson.

From the *Overcoming* series, this is an easy-to-follow self-help guide written by one of the authors of the social phobia chapter in this book.

Gillian Butler (2007). *Overcoming Social Anxiety and Shyness Self-Help Course: A 3-part programme based on Cognitive Behavioural Techniques*. London: Robinson.

An extended, more interactive adaptation of Gillian Butler's original book *Overcoming Social Anxiety and Shyness*.

Gillian Butler and Tony Hope (2007). *Manage Your Mind: The mental fitness guide*. Oxford: Oxford University Press.

A practical and comprehensive self-help guide providing advice and information on building self-confidence, overcoming anxiety and depression, improving relationships, managing stress and improving decision-making. Written by one of authors of the social phobia chapter in this book.

Health Anxiety

David Veale and Rob Willson (2009). *Overcoming Health Anxiety: A self-help guide using Cognitive Behavioral Techniques*. London: Robinson.

From the *Overcoming* series, this is a practical self-help guide written by two leading experts in the UK.

Martin M. Antony and Peter J. Norton (2008). *The Anti-Anxiety Workbook*. New York: Guilford Press.

A practical self-help offering a toolkit of proven strategies based on CBT. Includes self-assessment worksheets and exercises.

Katherine M. B. Owens and Martin M. Antony (2011). *Overcoming Health Anxiety: Letting go of your fear of illness.* Oakland, CA: New Harbinger Publications.

Written by two psychologists who specialise in treating anxiety, this book offers readers effective CBT techniques for overcoming hypochondriasis and health-related fears.

Gordon J. G. Asmundson and Steven Taylor (2005). *It's Not All in Your Head: How worrying about your health could be making you sick – and what you can do about it.* New York: Guilford Press.

A straightforward and effective self-help programme for those suffering from health anxiety.

Steven Taylor and Gordon. J. G. Asmundson (2004). *Treating Health Anxiety: A cognitive-behavioural approach.* New York: Guilford Press.

A treatment manual for therapists and students.

Obsessive Compulsive Disorder

David Veale and Rob Willson (2005). *Overcoming Obsessive Compulsive Disorder: A self-help guide using Cognitive Behavioral Techniques.* London: Robinson.

From the *Overcoming* series, this is a user-friendly book, which provides lots of detail about overcoming OCD and further information on some of the methods described in this chapter.

David Veale and Rob Willson (eds.) (2011). *Taking Control of OCD: Inspirational stories of hope and recovery.* London: Robinson.

From the publishers of the *Overcoming* series, this is a collection of inspiring first-person accounts of living with and overcoming OCD. Includes an introductory chapter on OCD written by the authors of *Overcoming Obsessive Compulsive Disorder*.

Christine Purdon and David A. Clark (2005). *Overcoming Obsessive Thoughts*. Oakland, CA: New Harbinger Publications.

A well-written workbook that describes how CBT can help you overcome your obsessive thoughts. Many of the principles overlap with those set out in this book but describe the methods in more detail.

Stanley Rachman (2003). *The Treatment of Obsessions*. Oxford: Oxford University Press.

This treatment manual formed the basis of the therapy used in research trials and focuses on the treatment of obsessions rather than OCD. It provides a useful toolkit for therapists, which can be used by people with OCD as well.

Stanley Rachman and Padmal de Silva (2009). *Obsessive-Compulsive Disorder: The Facts*. Oxford: Oxford University Press.

This book provides an overview of the different symptoms of OCD and contains a large number of different case examples. It is great for people such as friends and family members who know little about OCD.

Paul M. Salkovskis, Victoria Bream Oldfield and Fiona Challacombe (2011). *Break Free from OCD: Overcoming Obsessive Compulsive Disorder with CBT*. London: Vermillion.

This self-help book is written by the leading UK experts in the field of OCD therapy and research. It is highly recommended.

Post-Traumatic Stress Disorder

Claudia Herbert and Ann Wetmore (1999). *Overcoming Traumatic Stress: A self-help guide using Cognitive Behavioral Techniques*. London: Robinson.

From the *Overcoming* series, this is a practical book, which provides information on traumatic stress, including post-traumatic stress disorder.

Relationships

Aaron T. Beck (1989). *Love is Never Enough: How couples can overcome misunderstandings, resolve conflicts, and solve relationship problems through cognitive therapy.* London: Penguin Books.

Based on cognitive therapy, this book offers concrete help and advice on relationship problems. It will help the reader to think clearly and straightforwardly, preventing misjudgement and miscommunication in relationships.

Norman Epstein and Don Baucom (2002). *Enhanced Cognitive-Behavioral Therapy for Couples: A contextual approach.* Washington, DC: American Psychological Association.

The classic guide to CBT for couples. Written for students and clinicians, it is also accessible for those with a personal interest in the topic. It provides plenty of clinical examples and is written by the leading clinical researchers in the field of Couples Therapy.

Sarah Litvinoff and Relate (2001). *Better Relationships: Practical ways to make your love last.* London: Vermilion Books.

This book sets out practical steps that couples can take to keep their love alive for the long term.

Michael Crowe (2012). *Overcoming Relationship Problems: A self-help guide using Cognitive Behavioral Techniques.* London: Robinson.

From the *Overcoming* series, this self-help guide is based on experience in self-help strategies developed at the Couples Clinic of the Maudsley Hospital in London. It uses a combination of CBT and systemic approaches derived from family therapy to provide an effective way to counter the difficulties that can arise in close relationships.

Depression

Paul Gilbert (2009). *Overcoming Depression: A self-help guide using Cognitive Behavioral Techniques,* third edition. London: Robinson.

From the *Overcoming* series, this bestselling book is divided into three parts. The first is about understanding depression, the second is about learning how to cope and the third concerns developing supportive relationships with ourselves. Reviews on Amazon from people who have used the book describe it as 'fantastic'.

Mark Gilson, Arthur Freeman, Jane Yates and Sharon Morgillo Freeman (2009). *Overcoming Depression: A cognitive therapy approach workbook (Treatments That Work).* Oxford: Oxford University Press.

From the *Treatments that work* series from the US, this book provides clear guidance on how to become less depressed, presented in a highly accessible and practical format. There is an accompanying clinician's guide and it will be of use for those with depression as well as their supporters.

Mark Williams, John Teasdale, Zindel Segal and Jon Kabat-Zinn (2007). *The Mindful Way Through Depression: Freeing yourself from chronic unhappiness.* New York: Guilford Press.

An award-winning book written by the leading clinical researchers in mindfulness in the UK, Canada and USA. Its four parts help the reader understand depression and the principles of mindfulness.

Appendix 3 – Other Useful Resources

Resources for emergencies

Useful phone numbers

Emergencies – 999

NHS Direct in England and Wales – 0845 4647

NHS Direct in Scotland – 08454 24 24 24

Non-emergency medical help – 111(calls are free but currently only available in some parts of the UK)

If a person's mental or emotional state quickly worsens, it can be treated as a mental-health emergency or mental-health crisis. In this situation, it is important to get help as soon as possible.

If you feel that you, or a person you are with, is in immediate danger call 999.

Urgent care centres provide a variety of services but vary in different areas. You may be able to attend such a centre rather than going to your local Accident & Emergency department, but it is best to phone ahead or call NHS Direct (or NHS 111) to find out what services are available. If no urgent care centre is available in your area, visit your local Accident & Emergency department.

If you do not live in the UK but feel you may be in danger of harming yourself, go to your local hospital or walk-in-clinic, which will be able to help.

Samaritans

www.samaritans.org

24-hour helplines:

UK – 08457 90 90 90

Republic of Ireland – 1850 60 90

Email support: jo@samaritans.org

Postal address: Chris, PO Box 9090, Stirling FK8 2SA

This charity aims to provide emotional support to people who are experiencing feelings of distress or despair, including those which may lead to suicide. Volunteers offer support by responding to phone calls twenty-four hours a day, as well as emails and letters during office hours. Alternatively, you can drop into a branch to have a face-to-face meeting.

Further resources for anxiety

Anxiety – general

British Association for Behavioural and Cognitive Psychotherapies (BABCP)

www.babcp.com

The BABCP can provide you with information on how to find an accredited CBT therapist in your area.

Anxiety UK

www.anxietyuk.org.uk

Helpline: 08444 775 774 (open Mon–Fri 9.30am–5.30pm)

Anxiety UK is a user-led charity run by sufferers and ex-sufferers and supported by a medical advisory panel. Their website provides information, support and other services, including moderated chat rooms and special events for people with anxiety. They also offer one-to-one therapy.

No Panic

www.nopanic.org.uk

Helpline: 0800 138 8889 (open 10am–10pm daily)

No Panic is a voluntary charity that helps people who suffer from panic attacks, phobias, obsessive compulsive disorders and other related anxiety disorders. It specialises in self-help through recovery groups and one-to-one mentoring over the telephone using CBT methods.

The Anxiety and Depression Association of America

www.adaa.org

This organization provides a range of information and resources for those suffering from anxiety and depression.

Specific Phobias

Anxiety UK – see above

The Centre for Anxiety Disorders and Trauma

http://psychology.iop.kcl.ac.uk/cadat/GPs/specific-phobia.aspx

The out-patient unit at this centre specialises in the treatment of anxiety disorders. Visit their website for helpful background information on the nature of phobias, self-help organisations and treatment for phobias in the UK.

Panic Disorder

NHS Choices

www.nhs.uk/Conditions/Panic-disorder/Pages/Introduction.aspx

The NHS Choices website carries information on panic disorder, including videos of people describing their experiences, and CBT therapists describing how treatment works.

No Panic – see above

Generalised Anxiety Disorder and Worry

The National Institute for Health and Clinical Excellence (NICE)

http://guidance.nice.org.uk/CG113/PublicInfo/pdf/English

NICE is the national body that advises healthcare professionals in the UK on treatments for physical and mental health problems. Visit their website for comprehensive information on generalized anxiety disorder and its treatment (see Guideline 113, Generalized Anxiety Disorder and Panic Disorder (with or without agoraphobia) in adults (2011)). The website link above leads to advice written for members of the public.

Anxiety Disorders Laboratory

http://psychology.concordia.ca/fac/dugas/downloads_en.html

People with generalized anxiety disorder and worry may find the website above helpful. It has a collection of worry-specific questionnaires, which you can download in order to assess how you relate to uncertainty (see the Intolerance of Uncertainty Scale), or to explore your worry rules (see the Why Worry II). Other measures look at cognitive avoidance and problem-solving skills. You can use these questionnaires to assess your progress as you work on your worry. There is also more information about GAD on this website.

Social Phobia

The Oxford Centre for Anxiety Disorders and Trauma

http://oxcadat.psy.ox.ac.uk

This research centre's website has helpful information on social anxiety.

Health Anxiety

The websites below all contain useful information for those suffering from health anxiety.

www.anxietyuk.org.uk/about-anxiety/anxiety-disorders/health-anxiety/

www.veale.co.uk/resources-support/public-information/health-anxiety/

www.cci.health.wa.gov.au/resources/infopax.cfm?Info_ID=53

Obsessive Compulsive Disorder

OCD-UK

www.ocduk.org

Helpline: 0845 120 3778 (open Mon–Fri 9am–5pm)

A national self-help charity for people with OCD. Their website has videos and other useful resources for those with OCD, their families and their therapists. The organisation also holds an annual conference in the UK for sufferers where you can hear and even ask questions of experts on OCD from around the world.

PTSD

The Centre for Anxiety Disorders and Trauma

http://psychology.iop.kcl.ac.uk/cadat/anxietydisorders/PTSD.aspx
Based at the Institute of Psychiatry, London, this research centre has a helpful website, which offers information about PTSD. The centre also accepts referrals – see their website for details.

The Oxford Centre for Anxiety Disorders and Trauma

www.kcl.ac.uk/cadet

This research centre's website has helpful information on PTSD.

Improving Access to Psychological Therapies (*IAPT*) programme

www.iapt.nhs.uk

This NHS-run programme has information on how to get help for anxiety disorders in many parts of England.

Relationship Problems

Relate

www.relate.org.uk

Tel: 0300 100 1234

Relate offers advice, relationship counselling, sex therapy, workshops, mediation, consultations and support. They do this via face-to-face meetings, by phone and by email. Their website has information on how to find your local Relate service.

Depression

Depression Alliance

www.depressionalliance.org

This UK charity provides information and support services to those suffering from depression.

Appendix 4 – Blank Worksheets

Form to help guide therapy sessions

Agenda (Plan for the session)
Review of Progress
Review of Homework
Moving forward (What is the next stage of my self-help programme?)
Homework (What will I do between sessions?)
Summarizing
Date of next session:

A standard record sheet

Situation	Thoughts	Feelings	Behaviour	Context/comments

Behavioural experiment sheet

1) Thought/Belief to be tested and strength of conviction (0–100%):

2) Ideas for experiment to test the thought/belief. Circle the best one:

3) Specific predictions about what will happen and how you will record the outcome:

4) Anticipated problems and potential solutions:

5) Describe the experiment you carried out:

6) Describe what happened:

7) Re-rate your conviction in the original thought/belief (0–100%):

8) Revised thought/belief/behaviour that can be tested:

Taking a new perspective

Situation	Feelings	Thoughts	Alternative view after working through questions above	Feelings now
Where I am, what I'm doing	E.g. frightened, scared etc. How bad is it (0–10)?	Exactly what is going through my mind?	What is a different way of thinking about the situation?	E.g. frightened, scared. Re-rate how bad it is (0–10).

Maintenance form used in phobia treatment

Week: 1–4

NAME: _____

IF YOU CONTINUE TO DO THE FOLLOWING EACH WEEK

1: _____

2: _____

3: _____

4: _____

THEN IN THE FUTURE YOU WILL BE ABLE TO:

1: _____

2: _____

3: _____

4: _____

Record the respective number in the columns below each time you have performed the practice task. Make any comments that you may have on the reverse side of the form. Do not skip the practice any week but keep practising regularly. This is particularly important during the first six months after the treatment. Then send your supporter the form in the way that you will hopefully have agreed upon.

My catastrophic belief before treatment was: _____

After treatment I believed: _____

Day	Week 1 Date Activity	Week 2 Date Activity	Week 3 Date Activity	Week 4 Date Activity
Monday				
Tuesday				
Wednesday				
Thursday				
Friday				
Saturday				
Sunday				

Send this form to [insert your supporter, if you have one]: _____

Address: _____

Phone number: _____   Email _____

Reproduced with kind permission from *Intensive One-Session Treatment of Specific Phobias*, T. Davis, T. Ollendick and L-G. Öst, New York, Springer, 2012 (Chapter 4).

Spider phobia questionnaire

The SPQ is a 31-item self-report instrument that measures fear of spiders. Scores can range from 0 – 31 with higher scores indicating greater fear. Answer True (T) or False (F) to the following questions. T= I point, F= 0 points.

1. I avoid going to parks or on camping trips because there may be spiders about.
O   True
O   False

2. I would feel some anxiety holding a toy spider in my hand.
O   True
O   False

3. If a picture of a spider crawling on a person appears on the screen during a film or on TV, I turn my head away.
O   True
O   False

4. I dislike looking at pictures of spiders in a magazine.
O   True
O   False

5. If there is a spider on the ceiling over my bed, I cannot go to sleep unless someone kills it for me.
O   True
O   False

6. I enjoy watching spiders build their webs.
O   True
O   False

7. I am terrified by the thought of touching a harmless spider.
O   True
O   False

8. If someone says that there are spiders anywhere about, I become alert and edgy.
O   True
O   False

9. I would not go down to the basement to get something if I thought there might be spiders down there.
O   True
O   False

10. I would feel uncomfortable if a spider crawled out of my shoe as I took it out of the wardrobe to put it on.
O   True
O   False

11. When I see a spider, I feel tense and restless.
O   True
O   False

12. I enjoy reading articles about spiders.
O   True
O   False

13. I feel sick when I see a spider.
O   True
O   False

14. Spiders are sometimes useful.
O   True
O   False

15. I shudder when I think of spiders.
O   True
O   False

16. I don't mind being near a harmless spider if there is someone there in whom I have confidence.
- ○   True
- ○   False

17. Some spiders are very attractive to look at.
- ○   True
- ○   False

18. I don't believe anyone could hold a spider without some fear.
- ○   True
- ○   False

19. The way spiders move is repulsive.
- ○   True
- ○   False

20. It wouldn't bother me to touch a dead spider with a long stick.
- ○   True
- ○   False

21. If I came upon a spider while cleaning the attic I would probably run.
- ○   True
- ○   False

22. I'm probably more afraid of spiders than of any other animal.
- ○   True
- ○   False

23. I would not want to travel to countries such as Mexico, Australia or countries in Central America because of the greater prevalence of tarantulas.
- ○   True
- ○   False

24. I am cautious when buying fruit because bananas may attract spiders.
- ○   True
- ○   False

25. I have no fear of non-poisonous spiders.
- ○ True
- ○ False

26. I wouldn't take a course in biology if I thought I might have to handle live spiders.
- ○ True
- ○ False

27. Spider webs are very artistic.
- ○ True
- ○ False

28. I think that I'm no more afraid of spiders than the average person.
- ○ True
- ○ False

29. I would prefer not to finish a story if something about spiders was introduced into the plot.
- ○ True
- ○ False

30. Not only am I afraid of spiders, but millipedes and caterpillars make me feel anxious.
- ○ True
- ○ False

31. Even if I was late for a very important appointment, the thought of spiders would stop me from taking a shortcut through an underpass.
- ○ True
- ○ False

Reproduced with kind permission from R. Klorman, J. Hastings, T. Weerts, B. Melamed, & P. Lang, (1974). Psychometric description of some specific fear questionnaires. *Behavior Therapy*, 5, 401–9

IAPT phobia scales

Choose a number from the scale below to show how much you would avoid each of the situations or objects listed below. Then write the number in the box opposite the situation.

0	1	2	3	4	5	6	7	8

| Would not avoid it | | Slightly avoid it | | Definitely avoid it | | Markedly avoid it | | Always avoid it |

Social situations due to a fear of being embarrassed or making a fool of myself ☐

Certain situations because of a fear of having a panic attack or other distressing symptoms (such as loss of bladder control, vomiting or dizziness) ☐

Certain situations because of a fear of particular objects or activities (such as animals, heights, seeing blood, being in confined spaces, driving or flying). ☐

Reproduced with kind permission from Department of Health, *IAPT Data Handbook, 2010*, www.iapt.nhs.uk/silo/files/iapt-data-handbook-appendices-v2.pdf (p.24).

Identifying what makes you anxious

Make a list of *all* the possible causes of this symptom. Put the *worst* explanation last on your list. It would also be worth asking your supporter and other people what explanations might occur to them if they had this symptom, and adding them to your list.

The *symptom* you worry about most:

The *possible cause* you fear the most:

Various possible causes of this symptom

1.

2.

3.

4.

5.

6.

7.

8.

9.

The cause I fear the most:

Prediction experiment outcomes and learning

Date and situation	Prediction What do I think will happen? What are my worst fears? How much do I believe this (0–100%)?	Experiment What can I do to put this to the test? What precautions do I need to drop?	Outcome What actually happened? Was the prediction correct?	Learning What have I learned? How likely is my worst fear to happen (0–100%)? Any 'yes, but's? How can I further test my worst fears?

Panic Diary

OVERALL ANXIETY		PANIC ATTACKS	S Y M P T O M S											
	DAY	DESCRIPTION OF SITUATION WHERE PANIC OCCURRED	Breathlessness	Palpitations/heart racing	Choking	Chest tight/uncomfortable	Sweating	Dizziness/unsteady/faint	Unreal/distant feeling	Nausea	Hot or cold flushes	Trembling/shaking	Numbness or tingling	Fear of dying/going mad/loss of control

FULL ATTACK	LIMITED ATTACK	RATING OF SEVERITY	PANIC FREQUENCY (per day)	LIMITED ATTACK FREQUENCY(per day)	Main bodily sensations / thoughts of disaster (rate belief 1–100%)	Negative Interpretation of the sensations/ thoughts of disaster rate belief 0-100%	Rational Response / answer to thoughts (re-rate belief 0-100%)

Safety-seeking behaviour questionnaire

When you are at your most anxious or panicky, how often do you do the following things?

Try to think about other things	Never	Sometimes	Often	Always
Hold on to or lean on to something	Always	Often	Sometimes	Never
Hold on to or lean on someone	Never	Sometimes	Often	Always
Sit down	Always	Often	Sometimes	Never
Keep still	Always	Often	Sometimes	Never
Move very slowly	Never	Sometimes	Often	Always
Look for an escape route	Never	Sometimes	Often	Always
Make yourself do more physical exercise	Always	Often	Sometimes	Never
Focus attention on your body	Always	Often	Sometimes	Never
Try to keep control of your mind	Never	Sometimes	Often	Always
Try to keep tight control over behaviour	Always	Often	Sometimes	Never
Talk more	Never	Sometimes	Often	Always
Take medication	Never	Sometimes	Often	Always
Ask people around for help	Never	Sometimes	Often	Always
Change your breathing	Always	Often	Sometimes	Never

Reproduced with permission from *Panic Disorder Therapist Manual for IAPT High Intensity Therapists*, Clark and Salkovskis, 2009.

Worry about worry

Consider each belief in the table below and ask yourself which of these beliefs applies to you?

Worrying excessively means that	How strongly do you believe this thought? Not At all true Totally True 0%-----------------------100%
I am out of control	........................%
I will be overwhelmed	........................%
I will go crazy	........................%
I will be unable to focus or work or perform	........................%
I will be condemned to a life of anxiety	........................%
I will become ill	........................%
I lack confidence	........................%
I am weak	........................%

Questions to help develop your worry diagram

1. Situation Date and time	
2. 'What if?'	
3. Worry	
4. Anxiety Feelings, bodily sensa- tions and actions	
5. Demoralization/ exhaustion What were your after- effects of worrying?	

How the intolerance of uncertainty influences our actions

The table below highlights the costs associated with how worriers manage uncertainty. Complete the questionnaire, and then choose one or two items and think about the gains or benefits you would get if you could tolerate the uncertainty and do things in a different way. Maybe completing this questionnaire will give you some ideas about what needs to change in your life.

Actions and costs	Rating
	Very unlike me Very like me
To what extent do you do the following ?	**Please circle**
Ask for reassurance on a decision you have made, and then feel stupid for having asked in the first place because you knew you were right.	1 2 3 4 5 6 7
Check e-mails, letters or cheques several times before sending them, and then get behind on other jobs.	1 2 3 4 5 6 7
Not allow your kids to do things for themselves in case they don't get it quite right. And then feel annoyed that you have to do everything yourself.	1 2 3 4 5 6 7
Want to know where everything is, and feel unsettled if things are out of place, even when you don't need to use them right now.	1 2 3 4 5 6 7
Need to have the plans for an evening clearly laid out beforehand and get upset when they don't go as planned, even though everyone is having fun.	1 2 3 4 5 6 7

Do things in the same routine and complicated way for fear of going off track and then complain how boring life is.	1 2 3 4 5 6 7
Avoid committing yourself to something just in case it might go wrong.	1 2 3 4 5 6 7
Find good but imaginary reasons for not doing things and then realize that you have missed out on something you would have enjoyed if you had taken the chance.	1 2 3 4 5 6 7
Avoid (or keep contact to a bare minimum with) people who may act unpredictably, thus missing out on other aspects of their company.	1 2 3 4 5 6 7
Get lots and lots of information to help you make a decision, and then be incapable of making sense of it all.	1 2 3 4 5 6 7

Rate your anxiety/discomfort

Anxiety/discomfort scale

None		Slight		Moderate		High		Extreme
1	2	3	4	5	6	7	8	9

Session No._____

Day or date _____Start time ___:___ Finish time ___:___

Place _____Worry _____

Anxiety/discomfort   Before _____   During (max) _____   After _____
(please use scale)

Did you use any avoidance strategies? No _____ A little _____ A lot _____

How did you avoid?_____

Understanding your social phobia

Aspect of the model	
Trigger situation	
Beliefs and assumptions	
Seeing danger	
Self–consciousness	
Safety behaviours	
Symptoms	

Social anxiety flow chart

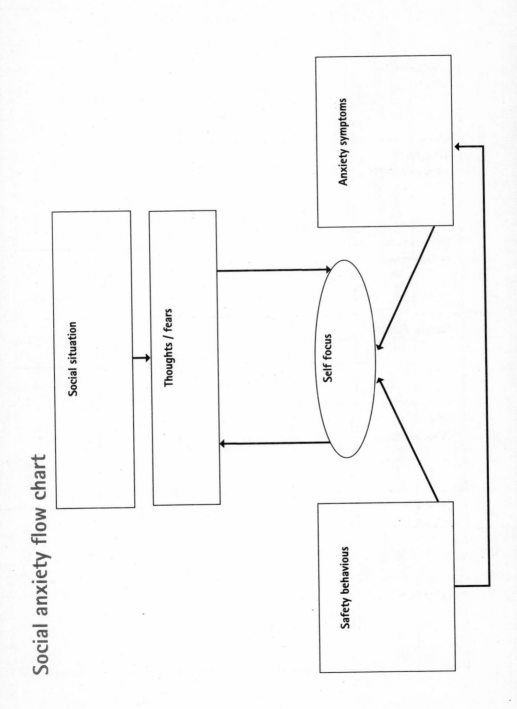

Social phobia thought record

Situation	Feeling (intensity %)	Thought (belief %)	Evidence for the thought	Evidence against the thought	Balanced view and/or action plan

Social Phobia Rating Scale (SPRS)

1.) How distressing/disabling has your social anxiety been in the past week?

not at all   *couldn't be worse*

0   1   2   3   4   5   6   7   8   9   10

2.) How much have you avoided social situations because of anxiety in the past week?

not at all   *half the time*   *all the time*

0%   10   20   30   40   50%   60   70'   80   90   100%

3.) How self-conscious have you felt in difficult social situations in the past week?

not at all   *couldn't be worse*

0   1   2   3   4   5   6   7   8   9   10

4.) People cope with their social anxiety in different ways – place a number from the scale below next to each item listed (and to any items you add) to show how often you do the following when you are socially anxious:

not at all   *half the time*   *all the time*

0%   10   20   30   40   50%   60   70   80   90   100%

---

say little_____control my thoughts_____hold my arms still_____
take slow breaths_____try to relax_____focus on my voice_____

grip objects tightly_____sit down_____avoid eye contact_____
move slowly_____cover my face_____speak quickly_____
use distraction_____wear certain clothes_____focus on my hands_____

Other coping methods not already listed

_____   _____   _____   _____

5.) Below are a number of thoughts that people have when they are socially anxious – indicate how much you believe each thought **when you are socially anxious** by placing a number next to each one from the scale below:

do not believe   *completely convinced*
the thought   *the thought is true*

0%   10   20   30   40   50%   60   70   80   90   100%

I look bad _____ they'll notice I'm anxious_____they don't like me_____
I'm boring_____I'll drop and spill things_____I'll look abnormal_____
I'm losing control_____everyone is looking at me_____they won't respect me_____
I'll look foolish_____I'll babble and talk funny_____I'll be unable to speak_____
I'm inadequate_____they think I'm stupid_____I'll look childish_____

Other thoughts not already listed

_____   _____   _____   _____

(Adapted from: Wells (1997) A *Cognitive Therapy of Anxiety Disorders.* Chichester: John Wiley)

Identify what is maintaining your health anxiety

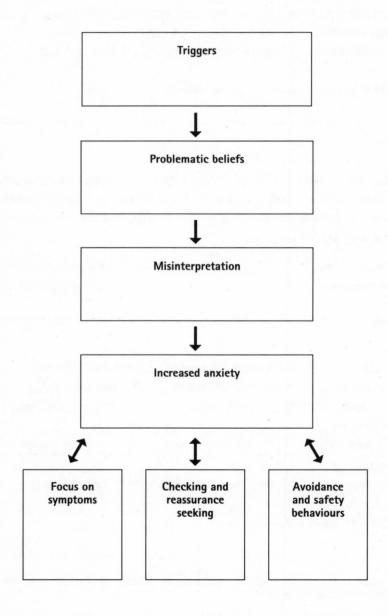

Cost–benefit analysis of changing your health anxiety

Costs	Benefits

Health anxiety thought record

Over the next week, fill in the thought record when you notice that your health anxiety has been triggered. If you have not had any significant episodes of health anxiety this week, think back to a recent time when you were experiencing health anxiety. Can you identify some thoughts that came up for you then? Work through the thought record using this past situation and the thoughts you had while it was happening.

Trigger	Anxious thought	Anxiety (0–100)	Evidence for the thought	Evidence against the thought	New balanced thought

Health anxiety behavioural experiment worksheet

Behaviour	
'If–then belief'	
Specific 'if–then' belief	
Experiment	
Result	
Revised belief	

Checking and reassurance-seeking behaviour checklist

✓ or X	
	Checking your body processes (e.g. taking pulse, checking blood pressure)
	Checking your body for changes (e.g. new moles, lumps, areas of discoloration)
	Poking, pinching, rubbing areas of your body to check for changes
	Researching your symptoms on the internet, in medical textbooks, in magazine articles, newspapers, or other media
	Posting your symptoms on internet sites to ask others for opinions about what they might mean
	Talking to family members or friends to get them to tell you everything is OK or to ask about your symptoms
	Thinking about going to your doctor
	Visiting your doctor to check whether you are ill
	Requesting medical testing and second opinions from other doctors
	Other forms of checking or reassurance-seeking behaviour [write these here]:

Identifying avoidance and safety behaviours

My avoidance behaviours	My safety behaviours
1.	1.
2.	2.
3.	3.
4.	4.
5.	5.

My exposure hierarchy

Feared activities, situations, persons, places, sensations	
EASY (provokes least anxiety: 0–35)	**Anxiety rating (0–100)**
1. 2. 3.	
MEDIUM (provokes moderate anxiety: 35–70)	**Anxiety rating (0–100)**
1. 2. 3.	
HARD (provokes the most anxiety: 70–100)	**Anxiety rating (0–100)**
1. 2. 3.	

OCD thought and behaviour record

Day and date:

Situation	Thought	Emotion	Behaviour	Consequence

OCI-R (Obsessive Compulsive Disorder Inventory-Revised)

The Obsessive Compulsive Disorder Inventory

The following statements refer to experiences that many people have in their everyday lives. Under the column labelled FREQUENCY, **circle** the number next to each statement that best describes how **frequently you have had the experience in the past month**. The numbers in this column refer to the following verbal labels:

0 = Never, 1 = Almost Never, 2 = Sometimes, 3 = Often, 4 = Almost Always

Then, in the column labelled DISTRESS, **circle** the number that best describes how much that experience has **distressed or bothered you during the past month**. The numbers in this column refer to the following verbal labels:

0 = Never, 1 = Almost Never, 2 = Sometimes, 3 = Often, 4 = Almost Always

	Frequency	Distress
1. Unpleasant thoughts come into my mind against my will and I cannot get rid of them.	0 1 2 3 4	0 1 2 3 4
2. I think contact with bodily secretions (perspiration, saliva, blood, urine, etc.) may contaminate my clothes or somehow harm me.	0 1 2 3 4	0 1 2 3 4
3. I ask people to repeat things to me several times, even though I understood them the first time.	0 1 2 3 4	0 1 2 3 4
4. I wash and clean obsessively.	0 1 2 3 4	0 1 2 3 4

5. I have to review mentally   0   1   2   3   4   0   1   2   3   4
past events, conversations
and actions to make sure that
I didn't do something wrong.

6. I have saved up so many   0   1   2   3   4   0   1   2   3   4
things that they get in the way.

7. I check things more often   0   1   2   3   4   0   1   2   3   4
than necessary.

8. I avoid using public toilets   0   1   2   3   4   0   1   2   3   4
because I am afraid of disease
or contamination.

9. I repeatedly check doors,   0   1   2   3   4   0   1   2   3   4
windows, drawers etc.

10. I repeatedly check gas and   0   1   2   3   4   0   1   2   3   4
water taps and light switches
after turning them off.

11. I collect things I don't   0   1   2   3   4   0   1   2   3   4
need.

12. I have thoughts of   0   1   2   3   4   0   1   2   3   4
having hurt someone without
knowing it.

13. I have thoughts that I   0   1   2   3   4   0   1   2   3   4
might want to harm myself
or others.

14. I get upset if objects are   0   1   2   3   4   0   1   2   3   4
not arranged properly.

15. I feel obliged to follow a   0   1   2   3   4   0   1   2   3   4
particular order in dressing,
undressing and washing myself.

16. I feel compelled to count   0   1   2   3   4   0   1   2   3   4
while I am doing things.

17. I am afraid of impulsively doing embarrassing or harmful things.

0 1 2 3 4   0 1 2 3 4

18. I need to pray to cancel bad thoughts or feelings.

0 1 2 3 4   0 1 2 3 4

19. I keep on checking forms or other things I have written.

0 1 2 3 4   0 1 2 3 4

20. I get upset at the sight of knives, scissors and other sharp objects in case I lose control with them.

0 1 2 3 4   0 1 2 3 4

21. I am excessively concerned about cleanliness.

0 1 2 3 4   0 1 2 3 4

22. I find it difficult to touch an object when I know it has been touched by strangers or certain people.

0 1 2 3 4   0 1 2 3 4

23. I need things to be arranged in a particular order.

0 1 2 3 4   0 1 2 3 4

24. I get behind in my work because I repeat things over and over again.

0 1 2 3 4   0 1 2 3 4

25. I feel I have to repeat certain numbers.

0 1 2 3 4   0 1 2 3 4

26. After doing something carefully, I still have the impression I have not finished it.

0 1 2 3 4   0 1 2 3 4

27. I find it difficult to touch garbage or dirty things.

0 1 2 3 4   0 1 2 3 4

28. I find it difficult to control my own thoughts.

0 1 2 3 4   0 1 2 3 4

29. I have to do things over and over again until it feels right.	0 1 2 3 4	0 1 2 3 4	
30. I am upset by unpleasant thoughts that come into my mind against my will.	0 1 2 3 4	0 1 2 3 4	
31. Before going to sleep I have to do certain things in a certain way.	0 1 2 3 4	0 1 2 3 4	
32. I go back to places to make sure that I have not harmed anyone.	0 1 2 3 4	0 1 2 3 4	
33. I frequently get nasty thoughts and have difficulty in getting rid of them.	0 1 2 3 4	0 1 2 3 4	
34. I avoid throwing things away because I am afraid I might need them later.	0 1 2 3 4	0 1 2 3 4	
35. I get upset if others change the way I have arranged my things.	0 1 2 3 4	0 1 2 3 4	
36. I feel that I must repeat certain words or phrases in my mind in order to wipe out bad thoughts, feelings or actions.	0 1 2 3 4	0 1 2 3 4	
37. After I have done things, I have persistent doubts about whether I really did them.	0 1 2 3 4	0 1 2 3 4	
38. I sometimes have to wash or clean myself simply because I feel contaminated.	0 1 2 3 4	0 1 2 3 4	
39. I feel that there are good and bad numbers.	0 1 2 3 4	0 1 2 3 4	

40. I repeatedly check anything which might cause a fire.   0 1 2 3 4 | 0 1 2 3 4

41. Even when I do something very carefully I feel that it is not quite right.   0 1 2 3 4 | 0 1 2 3 4

42. I wash my hands more often or longer than necessary.   0 1 2 3 4 | 0 1 2 3 4

W	C	D	O	Ob	H	N

Total [ ]

Scoring guide

The measure is made up of seven subscales: washing (W), checking (C), doubting (D), ordering (O), obsessing (Ob), hoarding (H) and mental neutralizing (N). Each of these is first scored separately, and then the final score is calculated by adding all of these subscales.

To determine your score for each of the subscales, add your scores for the questions listed below and place each total in the corresponding boxes.

Washing: Add your scores for questions 2, 4, 8, 21, 22, 27, 38 and 42

Checking: Questions 3, 7, 9, 10, 19, 24, 29, 32 and 40

Doubting: 26, 37 and 41

Ordering: 14, 15, 23, 31 and 35

Obsessing: 1, 12, 13, 17, 20, 28, 30 and 33

Hoarding: 6, 11 and 34

Mental neutralizing: 5, 16, 18, 25, 36 and 39

To determine your total score add up all of the subscale scores (or add all the items on the questionnaire).

Reproduced with kind permission of Edna Foa.

Personal significance scale (Form PSS)

Please read the following statements carefully and circle the number that best corresponds to the extent to which you agree with each statement regarding your intrusive thoughts and images.

Specific thoughts, images: _____

_____

_____

Please use the following scale:

0	1	2	3	4	5	6	7	8

Not at all   Somewhat   Totally/
definitely

1. Are these thoughts really personally significant for you?	0 1 2 3 4 5 6 7 8
2. Do these thoughts reveal something important about you?	0 1 2 3 4 5 6 7 8
3. Are these thoughts a sign that you are original?	0 1 2 3 4 5 6 7 8
4. Do these thoughts mean that you might lose control and do something awful?	0 1 2 3 4 5 6 7 8
5. Do these thoughts mean that you are an imaginative person?	0 1 2 3 4 5 6 7 8

6. Do these thoughts mean that you might go crazy one day?	0 1 2 3 4 5 6 7 8
7. Is it important for you to keep these thoughts secret from most or all of the people you know?	0 1 2 3 4 5 6 7 8
8. Do these thoughts mean that you are a sensitive person?	0 1 2 3 4 5 6 7 8
9. Do these thoughts mean that you are a dangerous person?	0 1 2 3 4 5 6 7 8
10. Do these thoughts mean that you are untrustworthy?	0 1 2 3 4 5 6 7 8
11. Would other people condemn or criticize you if they knew about your thoughts?	0 1 2 3 4 5 6 7 8
12. Do these thoughts mean that you are really a hypocrite?	0 1 2 3 4 5 6 7 8
13. Do these thoughts mean that you have an artistic talent?	0 1 2 3 4 5 6 7 8
14. Would other people think that you are crazy or mentally unstable if they knew about your thoughts?	0 1 2 3 4 5 6 7 8
15. Do these thoughts mean that one day you may actually carry out some actions related to the thoughts?	0 1 2 3 4 5 6 7 8
16. Do these thoughts mean that you enjoy the company of other people?	0 1 2 3 4 5 6 7 8
17. Do these thoughts mean that you are a bad, wicked person?	0 1 2 3 4 5 6 7 8
18. Do you feel responsible for these thoughts?	0 1 2 3 4 5 6 7 8

19. Is it important for you to cancel out or block the thoughts? | 0 1 2 3 4 5 6 7 8

20. Would other people think that you are a bad, wicked person if they knew about your thoughts? | 0 1 2 3 4 5 6 7 8

21. Do you think that you should avoid certain people or places because of these thoughts? | 0 1 2 3 4 5 6 7 8

22. Do these thoughts mean that you are weird? | 0 1 2 3 4 5 6 7 8

23. Should you fight against and resist these thoughts? | 0 1 2 3 4 5 6 7 8

24. Do these thoughts have any other significance for you? Details: _____

_____

25. What caused your thoughts to occur when they started? _____

_____

26. Why do these thoughts keep coming back? _____

_____

Relapse prevention worksheet

How did my anxiety start?

Why did my anxiety carry on? *Clue: refer to the diagram that you drew for the anxiety problem you've been experiencing . Think of the meaning you were placing on particular events, and what you were doing to try to improve the situation but which might have backfired e.g. avoidance.*

What have I learned in this self-help book that has been useful? *Clue: Put as much as you can here.*

What situations might lead to a setback for me? *Clue: think about some of the triggers that led to the development of the problem in the first place, or other stressors in your life.*

What will be the early warning signs of a setback for me? *Clue: Think back to a recent episode of anxiety – what signs were there that this episode might be about to happen? Catching your anxiety early is going to be helpful.*

What will I do about it? *Clue: have a realistic plan for how to tackle setbacks.*

How will I distinguish between having a setback and being back at square one? *Clue: if you have a difficult period, you don't want to cata-strophize it and think you have learned nothing from going through this book. Distinguish between a lapse (or slip) and a full relapse.*

How do I see myself in:

1 month:

6 months:

1 year:

5 years:

Finally, what is my 'message in a bottle'? *Clue: If you could only remem-ber three things you have learned from this book, what would they be?*

Index